Communication as Comfort

D0026748

This exceptional work explores the complexities of communication at one of the most critical stages of the life experience—during advanced, serious illness and at the end of life. Authors Sandra L. Ragan, Elaine M. Wittenberg-Lyles, Joy Goldsmith, and Sandra Sanchez-Reilly posit palliative care—medical care designed to comfort rather than to cure patients—as an antidote to the experience of most Americans at the most vulnerable juncture of their lives. Applying communication theories and insights to illuminate problems and to explain their complexities, the authors advocate a patient-centered approach to care that recognizes and seeks to lessen patients' suffering and the many types of pain they may experience (physical, psychological, social, and spiritual) during life-threatening illness.

Multiple voices are present here: the patient, the medical professional, the family-caregiver, and the interdisciplinary health care team. The authors supplement their observations and analyses with ethnographic data gathered from clinical consultations with patients; palliative care team meetings; and interviews with team members as well as with physician fellows in a palliative care fellowship program.

As a work that highlights the role of communication in palliative care, the volume is required reading for students, educators, and researchers in health communication, communication and aging, and developmental communication. Health care professionals—physicians, nurses, and members of interdisciplinary palliative care teams as well as hospice professionals and volunteers will find this book essential to their clinical practice and research. It will also be an invaluable guide to anyone facing the prospect of serious or terminal illness and to their family members and caregivers.

Sandra L. Ragan (Ph.D. University of Texas at Austin) is Professor Emerita of Communication at the University of Oklahoma. She has studied communication and palliative care/end-of-life issues throughout her career.

Elaine M. Wittenberg-Lyles (Ph.D. University of Oklahoma) is an Assistant Professor at the University of North Texas.

Joy Goldsmith (Ph.D. University of Oklahoma) is an Assistant Professor at Young Harris College in Georgia.

Sandra Sanchez-Reilly (M.D., Colegio Mayor de Nuestra Señora del Rosario, Colombia) is an Assistant Professor of Geriatrics and Palliative Care and the director of the Palliative Care program at the University of Texas Health Science Center and the GRECC South Texas Veterans Health Care System and the Sam and Ann Barshop Institute for Longevity and Aging Studies in San Antonio, Texas.

LEA'S Communication Series
General Editors: Jennings Bryant and Doll Zillman

Communication as Comfort
Multiple Voices in Palliative Care

Sandra L. Ragan
University of Oklahoma

Elaine M. Wittenberg-Lyles
University of North Texas

Joy Goldsmith
Young Harris College

Sandra Sanchez-Reilly
University of Texas Health Science Center at San
Antonio; the GRECC, South Texas Veterans Health
Care System; Sam and Ann Barshop Institute for
Longevity and Aging Studies

Routledge
Taylor & Francis Group

NEW YORK AND LONDON

First published 2008
by Routledge
270 Madison Ave, New York, NY 10016

Simultaneously published in the UK
by Routledge
2 Park Square, Milton Park, Abingdon, Oxon OX14 4RN

Routledge is an imprint of the Taylor & Francis Group, an informa business

© 2008 Taylor & Francis

Typeset in Garamond by
HWA Text and Data Management, Tunbridge Wells
Printed and bound in the United States of America on acid-free paper by
Walsworth Publishing Company, Marceline, MO

All rights reserved. No part of this book may be reprinted or reproduced or
utilised in any form or by any electronic, mechanical, or other means, now
known or hereafter invented, including photocopying and recording, or in
any information storage or retrieval system, without permission in writing
from the publishers.

Cover painting: Circle of Friends © Carol Aust; used with permission of the
artist. www.carolaust.com.

Trademark Notice: Product or corporate names may be trademarks or
registered trademarks, and are used only for identification and explanation
without intent to infringe.

Library of Congress Cataloging in Publication Data
Communication as comfort : multiple voices in palliative care /
by Sandra L. Ragan ... [et al.].
    p. ; cm.
  Includes bibliographical references.
  1. Palliative treatment. 2. Terminal care. 3. Medical personnel and patient.
  4. Communication in medicine. 5. Death. I. Ragan, Sandra L.
  [DNLM: 1. Palliative Care–methods. 2. Terminal Care–methods.
  3. Attitude to Death. 4. Communication. 5. Interpersonal Relations.
  6. Terminally Ill–psychology. WB 310 C7346 2008]
  R726.8.C645 2008
  616'.029–dc22
  2007032506

ISBN10: 0–805–85808–3 (hbk)
ISBN10: 0–805–85809–1 (pbk)
ISBN10: 0–203–93867–4 (ebk)

ISBN13: 978–0–805–85808–2 (hbk)
ISBN13: 978–0–805–85809–9 (pbk)
ISBN13: 978–0–203–93867–6 (ebk)

616.029
C734

Dedications

My sister, Sherry Ragan Morehouse
(1945–2001)
—Sandy

My grandparents, Mildred and Alvin Pritchard
(1911–1978 and 1915–1989)
—Elaine

My sister, Janet Forts Goldsmith
(1968–2002)
—Joy

My "Abuelitas," Bertha de Rueda and Paulina de Sanchez
(1927–1985 and 1922–2003)

My father-in-law, Thomas Reilly
(1932–2007)
—Sandra

In memoriam

Dr. D. Larry Wieder
(1938–2006)

Contents

Preface

Vast numbers of Americans are dying in ways that contradict what they purportedly seek: a peaceful, pain-free death at home, surrounded by their loved ones rather than by medical personnel and invasive medical technology and granted the luxury of time to settle their affairs, to make their last wishes known, to recount the stories of their lives. As a recent (2004) article in the *Journal of the American Medical Association* attests, dying Americans receive inadequate pain management, little emotional support, and poor communication from their physicians.

The mission of this book is to describe the complexities of communication during advanced, serious illness and at the end of life and to posit palliative care, or medical care designed to comfort rather than to cure patients, as an antidote to the way in which most Americans are treated by the medical system at the most vulnerable juncture of their lives. We challenge the current, predominantly biomedical model that informs much of the communication between seriously ill or dying patients and their physicians, caregivers, and families and advocate instead the communication of palliative care—a patient-centered approach to care that recognizes and seeks to lessen patients' suffering—and the many types of pain they may experience (physical, psychological, social, and spiritual) during life-threatening illness.

No book that we are aware of ponders the problems of palliative care from a communication perspective, though many medical texts allude to the pivotal role of communication in the physician's delivery of palliative medicine. As communication scholars, we have unique theories and insights to illuminate these problems and to explain their complexities. This volume integrates the medical literature on palliative care with that of health communication researchers who advocate a biopsychosocial approach to health care: Austin Babrow, Marifran Mattson, Barbara Sharf, Marsha Vanderford, Dale Brashers, and others.

The book is co-authored by three health communication scholars and one physician who is certified in geriatrics and palliative medicine. The presence of a physician on the writing team provides valuable insight and experience into current medical thought and practice that most health communication volumes lack. Her experiences in palliative medicine inform this book, make it credible, and bring it into the realm of the practical/clinical rather than the merely academic. Too, we supplement our observations and analyses with several forms of ethnographic data; our largest data source comes from the clinical setting of the Geriatric Palliative Care Team at the South Texas Veterans Health Care System in San Antonio, Texas, where our fourth author, Dr. Sandra Sanchez-Reilly, serves as director of the Palliative Care Clinical Program. Data from this setting include clinical consultations with patients, palliative care team meetings, and interviews with team members and interviews with physician fellows in a palliative care fellowship program administered by Dr. Sanchez-Reilly. Additional qualitative data come from an Internet listserv of patients and caregivers experienced in adenocarcinoma of unknown primary site—a non-clinical gathering place for patient and caregiver stories that reveal a range of palliative communication needs. A third data source for this book is a collection of letters, stories, and interview responses from ill and dying patients and their family members who were willing to offer us their illness accounts. Finally, media and fictional resources that portray characters with advanced and terminal illness are interwoven in the chapters that follow.

Because of the complexity inherent in palliative care communication, we wanted to represent the multiple voices that comprise the context of palliative medicine. Thus, we have structured the book around these various voices and perspectives. After overview material in Chapters 1 and 2 that provides the reader with a rationale for palliative care and a history of the hospice and palliative care movements and a brief look at the communication theories that explain palliative care practices, we divide the bulk of the remainder of the book into the four perspectives that comprise palliative care: the patient's perspective (Chapter 3); the medical perspective (Chapter 4); the family-caregiver's perspective (Chapter 5); and the interdisciplinary health care team's perspective (Chapter 6). We end the volume in Chapter 7 by inviting readers to listen to the palliative care experiences of each of the four authors.

We believe that this book can teach a number of different audiences about palliative care communication and its importance. Because no other text exists that specifically highlights the role of communication in palliative care, the volume will be particularly useful to health communication students, instructors, and researchers. However, we also hope that health care professionals—physicians, nurses, and members of interdisciplinary palliative care teams (i.e., social workers, psychologists, chaplains, and the like)—and hospice professionals and volunteers will find this book useful to their clinical practice and research. Too, we think this volume could be an invaluable guide to anyone who is confronting (or might confront) serious or terminal illness (or both) and to their family members and other caregivers. In short, it has relevance for all of us mortals.

Foreword

The education and training of physicians in the United States (and most everywhere else) is governed by a fundamental hypothesis. The more training as a biomedical scientist, the better the physician (Bloom 1998). The health system in which they work has also been governed by a similar hypothesis. The more the focus on the disease, the better the care. These hypotheses are illustrated in a paraphrase of a comment made in 1975 in reference to hospitalization: "if only patients could leave their damaged physical vessels at the hospital for repair, while taking their social and emotional selves home" (Ryndes and von Gunten 2006). In other words, the behavioral sciences are unimportant to the modern health care enterprise.

The pursuit of these hypotheses has had two important consequences. First, as the paraphrase ironically makes clear, patients suffer. If the patient is not cared for as a "whole person" with physical, emotional, social and spiritual dimensions, the health system may actually cause suffering for both the patient and his or her family. Second, communication science suffers. If a patient is merely a collection of biochemical and biophysical processes requiring bioscientific expertise, then who needs communication?

Patients notice this deficiency. When patients waiting to see their doctors were asked what their doctors should learn as part of continuing medical education, only 12 percent of patients thought they should learn more about medical science. 56 percent of them thought they should learn more about communication. In contrast, when their doctors were asked what they thought they should learn as part of continuing medical education, 90 percent said they should learn more about medical science. None thought they should learn anything more about communication (Morgan et al. 2001).

How did this aberration come to pass? Why isn't whole person care the norm rather than the exception? Why isn't palliative care integrated into the plan of care from the day of diagnosis of a serious illness? The answer lies not in what is taught, but what is done. Who are the role models in contemporary medical education? Who is at the top of the food chain? In academic medicine, it is the researchers. They are the "rock stars" of academic medicine. How did they get there? By getting away from direct patient care as quickly as possible. Who are the role models at the top of the administrative management pyramid in contemporary health care in hospitals and health systems? Administrators trained in business schools where the lessons are drawn from factories producing identical products. Those who revolutionized the way we think about business from observing factory workers, observed that all systems are perfectly designed to achieve the outcomes they achieve. Physicians and health care professionals do what they are rewarded to do (and what they learn to do by watching others) by the current system. If we want different behavior we need to role model and reward the behaviors that yield the outcomes we want.

This book by Sandra L. Ragan, Ph.D., Elaine M. Wittenbert-Lyles, Ph.D., Joy Goldsmith, Ph.D., Sandra Sanchez-Reilly, M.D. advances the case for communication science as a way to discern the behaviors we want to see in health care professionals. In addition, they make a compelling case for a different approach to modern healthcare. While it is rooted in observations of patients with the most serious illnesses, including those who are expected to die soon, it would be a mistake to think it is limited in its implications. They make a detailed case for why communication science is a cardinal principle that should undergird contemporary evidence-based health care. To put it another way, why would you save up very effective health care and use it only for the dying? Wouldn't you want everyone to get it? In fact, it might even be more effective for those who have a better prognosis.

Charles F. von Gunten, M.D., Ph.D.
Provost
Institute for Palliative Medicine

Acknowledgments

In addition to citing individual acknowledgments, the authors express gratitude to the early pioneers of palliative care for their passion and courage to advocate for care of those who suffer. Their hard work and determination have created the beginning of better health care for everyone. We are also thankful for the many patients, families, and team members for allowing us into their most private moments, sharing their deepest thoughts, and teaching us about life, living, and the beauty that can be found in death.

This book took shape over several years and was influenced by many. I express thanks first to Linda Bathgate, Senior Editor at Erlbaum, with whom I first discussed the idea and who generously led me through the proposal process. Thanks also to two "anonymous" reviewers (one of whom, Elissa Foster, suggested several improvements in writing and over lunch!) Of course, I bent the ears of many friends over the years and also listened to their wisdom—particularly that of Athena duPre, Jane and Dick Smith, Martha and Perry White, Jill and Toney McMillan, Mike Nicolson, and Coleen Grissom. I thank my parents, Alex and Sherry Ragan, and my sister, Sherry Ragan Morehouse, each of whose lives and deaths contributed to my thinking about what constitutes quality of life. And, most of all, I'm indebted to my co-authors, Elaine, Joy, and Sandra, for sharing my passion and working tirelessly to make this book happen. Writing has never been so satisfying an experience.

—Sandy

My contribution to this volume would not have been possible without the love and support of George, chief cook and bottle washer at Casa de Lyles (and the hardest-working man I know), and Cody who gives me every reason to love life. I am also grateful for my mother, who continues to provide guidance, soothe my heart, wipe my tears, and believe in my dreams. A special thank you to Hope McClellan and Mary Roscoe, who provide voice and palliation at a moment's notice and are always ready to listen. Last, I appreciate the support provided by Katy Monath, who had the daunting task of working with me on a day to day basis.

—Elaine

I am grateful for the always willing and extremely fast database support of my good friend and researcher, Stephanie Short. Montana Miller of Bowling Green State University has provided top-notch participant consent and protection information throughout this project. Thanks to Karen Sheriff Levan for your partnership in thought and deed and our shared participant data. Thanks to my spouse, Donnie Kelley, for opening boxes and faxing documents in order that I might represent my own experience and passion in health communication through this project. I am indebted to Sandy Ragan for inviting me to be part of this project and recognizing the turn in my life toward palliative care communication. She has been and continues to be an incredible mentor and friend. Finally, I am infinitely thankful for the grace and love of my parents, Dale and Katy Goldsmith; this project has their care sewn in its fabric.

—Joy

To my husband, Michael, my loyal partner and the love of my life; our girls, Laura, Paula and baby Elizabeth, who are the light of my eyes and teach me so much about life. I am also thankful to my parents and my sister for their wisdom, support, and encouragement. Thank you to my Colombian family, friends, and heritage for making of me the woman I am today and to my American family and friends for their welcoming acceptance. I am grateful to my mentors and teachers for their influence in my career and to the pioneers of palliative care, who dedicate their lives to improving our field. Last, to my everlasting inspiration, my "Abuelita" Bertha, who taught me all I know about strength, patience, courage and, most of all, the beauty of dying peacefully.

—Sandra

1 The communication of palliative care

From Millicent Kramer, a fictional character in Philip Roth's *Everyman*, who has had three surgeries for back pain, each one making her pain worse:

> I can't take the pain anymore. It overrides everything. I think sometimes that I can't go on another hour. I tell myself to ignore it. I tell myself it doesn't matter. I tell myself, "Don't engage it. It's a specter. It's an annoyance, it's nothing more than that. Don't accord it power. Don't cooperate with it. Don't take the bait. Don't respond. Muscle through. Barrel through. Either you're in charge or it's in charge—the choice is yours!" I repeat this to myself a million times a day ... , and then suddenly it's so awful I have to lie down on the floor in the middle of the supermarket and all the words are meaningless. Oh, I'm sorry, truly. I abhor tears (p. 89).

> I do apologize for all this ... It's just that pain makes you so alone ... it's so shameful.
> ... The not being able to look after oneself, the pathetic need to be comforted ...
> The dependence, the helplessness, the isolation, the dread—it's all so ghastly and shameful. The pain makes you frightened of yourself. The utter otherness of it is awful (p. 91).

(Ten days later she kills herself with an overdose of sleeping pills.)

From a real patient: Mr M., a 75-year-old man with metastatic pancreatic cancer:

> Please help me!! I cannot take it anymore ... somebody help me!! Is this a hospital? Can you help me? You are supposed to help me, are you not? I want to go home, ahhhhh, please help me. ... My pain is unbearable, where? It is everywhere, are you asking me to rate it? It is a 20 out of 10. Confused? You bet, I can't think right. What are you showing me, a call button? Do you want me to call the nurse if I have pain? Why don't you call her, you are the doctor. I can't locate the call button, I can't see because I do not have my glasses on. Where are my glasses? Doctor, please help me, I can't take this pain.

Too many Americans, such as Millicent Kramer in Roth's fictional *Everyman* and the actual patient, Mr. M, live and die in pain. In the cases cited above, the pain expressed is mostly physical in nature, but patients also allude to psychological, social, and spiritual pain. The concept of total pain includes physical, emotional, spiritual, and social dimensions, as described by Dame Cicely Saunders, the founder of the modern hospice movement (O'Neill and Fallon, 1997). We know that, regardless of whether they explicitly express it, patients experience these various kinds of pain. We also know that in far too many cases, patients, particularly dying ones, do not attain relief from their pain. They live and die, feeling the shame, dependence, helplessness, isolation, dread, and fear that accompany unresolved pain. Communication fails them. They can't make anyone understand what they're experiencing. They believe that their need for comfort *is* pathetic.

The purpose of this volume is to explore the need for and the communication challenges of providing medical care that does bring comfort to patients, whether they suffer from advanced, terminal disease or have been given diagnoses of any medical co-morbidity (the presence of two or more medical conditions requiring care) that seriously threatens their quality of life and their ability to live largely free of debilitating pain, whether physical, emotional, social, or spiritual. We are concerned about current medical care that too often fails to offer palliative or comfort care but rather is solely intent on curing a patient. We describe the medical culture and the communication issues affecting medical providers that promulgate this current state, but we also focus on those communication challenges facing patients and their family members and caregivers who must confront serious or terminal illness—challenges that might prevent the acceptance of palliative care even when medical providers offer it.

Given the multiple voices in the interpersonal transactions that determine how serious illness-related suffering gets treated in our culture, we focus on four perspectives that we believe to be most critical in this determination: the patient's perspective, the medical perspective, the family-caregiver's perspective, and the interdisciplinary health care team's perspective.

Our goal, then, is to describe and analyze current health care practices that frequently fail to deliver compassionate care to chronically ill and dying patients; to offer palliative medicine as an antidote for this failure; to point out the communication dilemmas confronted by doctors, patients, family members, and health care teams in the delivery and acceptance of palliative care; and to posit a patient-centered approach to these communication challenges—one that elicits and privileges the patient's voice as the most important one in the health care interactions surrounding palliative care. We further challenge the current, predominantly biomedical model that informs much of the communication between seriously ill and dying patients and their medical providers and suggest new "scripts" for communication that would empower both patients and health care professionals.

The authors of these pages aim to make a positive contribution to end-of-life communication by including perspectives from all relevant parties. Therefore, this book is intended for all audiences: health care providers, patients, and caregivers and particularly for health care professionals and communication experts who could make a difference in changing health beliefs and communication practices in the field of palliative medicine.

Palliative care is vital to all populations, and it is therefore critical that we learn about the communication patterns and needs dominant in various cultural groups in light of the discussions encountered in this book. The detailed exploration of cultural communication in light of the complexities proposed throughout the volume must be left to another volume, though some essential issues must be mentioned in light of the reciprocal and most formidable burden carried by a family in the experience of palliative care communication.

As authors, we present a privileged Western stance in terms of a patient's knowing the status of her or his diagnosis and prognosis. Families and their loved ones living in Western culture but holding patterns of knowing that differ with the primary thrust of research we have emphasized here present further communication challenges for all parties facing palliative care interactions. Some cultural groups believe strongly that the family must assume the responsibility of knowing and decision making for a dying patient and thus protect a loved one fully from an awareness of dying (Ambuel and Mazzone, 2001). Obviously, medical caregivers and interdisciplinary team members in palliative care must be aware of and sensitive to cultural differences in providing care.

Readers of this volume will realize from its beginning that all four authors are advocates for palliative care and for the communication practices that would most facilitate its delivery. We do not pretend objectivity in this regard; though we offer evidence for our position from current medical and social science research, we are unwavering in our argument that the widespread teaching and practice of palliative medicine must become a foremost goal of universal medical care in the United States. Our values orientation is unabashedly reflected in our assertions and consists of the following premises:

1   We believe in a patient-centered, biospsychosocial approach to health care.
2   We believe that communication research and theory can inform and illuminate palliative care practices.
3   We believe that palliative care, though it may not be the antidote for all the ills that beset the American way of death, offers our best hope to date for compassionate, holistic treatment of seriously ill and dying patients.
4   We believe that palliative care must begin at diagnosis of serious illness, not just at end-stages—though we may center our discussion more frequently on terminal illness (and whereas the vast bulk of our data set is composed of discourse surrounding patients at the end-stage of their diseases), we nonetheless hold firm to the view that palliative care is an ongoing process.
5   We believe that doctors, health care providers, patients, and their families are complicit in producing the "scripts" that contribute to the American way of dealing with serious illness and impending death. Whereas it has been

popular for social scientists, health communication researchers included, to lambaste the medical profession for being chiefly responsible for the ineffective communication with the sick and dying and the absence of palliative care, we suggest that all parties would need to alter their health beliefs and communication practices before palliative medicine could become a dominant care mode.

6   We believe that palliative care should be introduced early in the education of all health-related trainees. Further, this education should not be limited to health care professionals but should be extended to include patients and families who can then advocate for such services. Communication training must be a crucial part of both educational processes.

The data included in this book represent several contexts. Our goal was not to locate consistency among the narratives, illnesses, and patients presented but rather to include stories of the seriously ill and dying from clinical and non-clinical settings. The Geriatric Palliative Care Team at the South Texas Veterans Health Care System in San Antonio provides a clinical backdrop for patients involved in conversations about a terminal diagnosis. Ethnographic data from team meetings, clinical consultations, and interviews with team members comprise the data set. An Internet listerv for patients and caregivers experienced in adenocarcinoma of unknown primary site provides a non-clinical gathering place for narratives revealing a wide range of palliative communication needs. The third data source for this project is an eclectic gathering of participants who learned about our research and offered their letters, stories, tellings, writings, and interview responses as patients and caregivers about serious and terminal illness for the construction of this book. All names of participants have been changed. Finally, media and fictional sources that portray the complex issues surrounding advanced illness are interspersed throughout the chapters.

The American way of death: dying in silence

Fiction can be instructive in informing us about the way in which we die—and the way in which we live with severe illness. Dr. Diane Meier, director of the Hertzberg Palliative Care Institute and Co-Director of the Center to Advance Palliative Care, Mount Sinai School of Medicine, and one of the leading proponents of the palliative care movement in U.S. medicine, explains in Bill Moyers's (2000) excellent televised series, "On Our Own Terms: Moyers on Dying," that she always uses the short novel by Tolstoy, *The Death of Ivan Illych*, in teaching her fellows about the need for palliative versus curative medicine. Illych is obviously dying, but no one—neither his family members nor his physician—acknowledges his impending death. As a result, he dies alone and without benefit of the conversations that might have granted him solace and vital connection to those he loved, conversations that might have eased his spiritual, emotional, and existential pain in his final hours. As Meier attests, it is the silence surrounding a patient's death experience that creates much of his or her loneliness and agony.

How we die in the United States and how we say we would prefer to die are at glaring odds. Whereas most Americans claim to wish to die at home, surrounded by their loved ones and with minimal invasive medical technology, most die in hospitals and in institutions instead ("The SUPPORT Investigators", 1995). Likewise, few of us would want to live with the unrelenting pain that serious illness may bring. Yet studies of ill and dying patients and of their family members' experiences with their illnesses and deaths manifest a scene replete with suffering. The SUPPORT Study, the largest ever multi-center study funded by the Robert Woods Johnson Foundation, revealed that of the 9,000 patients who were enrolled in the study, 50 percent died within six months of entry ("The SUPPORT Investigators", 1995). Shocking findings included the large percent of patients admitted to intensive care units during their last days of life; almost half of the patients reported uncontrolled symptoms prior to their passing.

Rather than receiving the benefits of palliative care, dying Americans instead are offered inadequate pain management, little to no emotional support, and poor communication from the medical providers attending them (Teno, *et al.*, 2004). Key findings from this study included: one in four people who died did not receive enough pain medication; one in two patients did not receive enough emotional support; 21 percent complained that the dying person was not always treated respectfully; one in four expressed concern over MD communication and treatment decisions; and one in three said that family members received inadequate emotional support. According to the study,

> high-quality end-of-life results when health care professionals (1) ensure desired physical comfort and emotional support, (2) promote shared decision making, (3) treat a dying person with respect, (4) provide information and emotional support to family members, and (5) coordinate care across settings (p. 88).

Of course, the factors that contribute to our culture's handling of serious illness, suffering, and death are many and complex, the lack of adequate palliative medical care being only one among these. Ethicist Daniel Callahan (2000), a leading critic of the American way of death, discusses the ambivalence between fighting death and accepting it: more than many cultures, the United States is a death-avoidant culture. The preeminence of medical science and advanced technology, which have led to the eradication of many diseases once considered death sentences, permit us the belief that we have conquered death, that it is no longer the inevitable, natural conclusion to life.

Such advances in medicine and medical technology have changed the way in which Americans are dying. Quick and intense deaths caused by infectious disease, accident, or injury are no longer the norm (Callahan, 2000). The ability to receive medical treatment and advanced testing has caused illness to become a permanent condition rather than a temporary state, further obscuring the medical community's ability to determine when death is imminent (Callahan, 2000). This prolongation of life has shifted the cause of death from infectious to chronic diseases. In essence, the act of death has been replaced by the medical process of dying. Callahan summarizes that this has resulted in "longer lives and worse health, longer illnesses and slower deaths, and longer aging and increased dementia" (p. 47).

As a result of this change, Americans are experiencing death differently today than in the previous century. For example, 50 percent of children in 1900 experienced a death in their nuclear family before the age of fifteen compared to 10 percent of children born in 1976 (Bern-Klug and Chapin, 1999). Of the 2.3 million deaths that occurred in 1995, more than two-thirds were people aged seventy years or older; opportunities for learning about death and how to communicate with dying persons thus are limited by this older population of dying persons. In addition, as more causes of death result from chronic conditions, people are living in a dying role longer, thus increasing the necessity of communicating more frequently with dying persons (Bern-Klug and Chapin, 1999).

Many Americans today see technology as an escape from the inevitability of death and believe that technological advances will be able to fix any bodily damage created throughout their lives (Ufema, 2004). The medical delaying of death contributes to our inability to discuss death explicitly. Moreover, the attempt to control death has resulted in a loss of understanding of the meanings surrounding death. "We must, in short, face and refashion our understandings of nature and death and ultimately of what it means to live a human life" (Babrow and Mattson, 2003, pp. 42–3).

Babrow and Mattson conclude that the dying process has thus become, paradoxically, even more agonizing; they discuss the issue as a manifestation of a dialectical tension between scientific and humanistic orientations, with the scientific, biomedical approach to medicine and health care centering on the disease and the humanistic, biopsychosocial perspective considering both the person who suffers the disease and the disease itself. Barriers to communicating openly about death are a result of a lack of experience with death, society's high expectations and emphasis on health and life, a materialistic culture, and the change from community-based religion to individualized religion (Buckman, 1998). In the United States, death has become a cultural taboo (Kearl, 1996).

Moreover, realistic views of death from practical experience have been replaced by "a voyeuristic, adolescent preoccupation" with death, as dying has been unrealistically portrayed (Littlewood, 1993, p. 70). This misrepresentation has contributed to the trepidation associated with communicating with dying persons who are seen "as living reminders of the unavoidable reality of death…[and] may be avoided rather than supported" (Littlewood, 1993, p. 70). As a result, many people are dying alone, and individuals are missing the opportunity to say good-bye to loved ones.

The fear of death and how and whether to talk about death affects how people communicate with a person with a terminal illness and with each other. The presence of someone who is dying is perceived to be highly threatening on both an individual and social level (Littlewood, 1993). As a result, many people experience communication apprehension when communicating with a dying person. This apprehension stems from a fear of one's own death or death of loved ones (or both), a fear of the new and untried, a fear of inadequacy, a fear of not being accepted, or a fear for one's health (e.g., in AIDS cases). Communication apprehension with the dying has been positively related to death anxiety, negatively related to chronological age, and independent of general communication apprehension (see also Servaty *et al.*, 1996; Servaty and Hayslip, 1997). It is also assumed that death education is a primary component to reducing death anxiety associated with communication apprehension with the dying.

The loss of public rituals and practices surrounding death and dying (both cultural and religious) has contributed to communication apprehension in these contexts (Callahan, 2000). Callahan argues that it is these practices that teach us "the comfort of knowing how to behave publicly in the presence of death—what to say, how to compose one's face, to whom to speak and when to speak" (p. 33). Without them, individuals do not know how to behave. Moreover, Mooney (2003) notes that the dying process is a very intimate time for families of a dying person. It is a time when "they are the most defenseless, dealing with circumstances that they have no control over" and they are "frightened or confused" (p. 16).

Specific discourse used to talk about death and dying also contributes to death anxiety. According to Corr (1997) as cited in Golubow (2002, p. 154):

> Prominent illustrations of ways in which death is forbidden in much of modern society include language of ordinary discourse, professional speech and communication about dying. It is important to pay attention to these linguistic practices because naming helps to define and to determine reality. How we speak says a good deal about who we are and the attitudes we hold … (p.36).

The use of euphemisms, such as "passed away" and "no longer with us," are examples of how our thoughts about mortality and the dying process are denied (Golubow, 2002). In one large city newspaper's daily obituaries, such euphemisms are commonplace: "fought his last battle," "went to be with the Lord," "entered into rest," "passed from this life," "was called home to the Lord," "was reunited with her husband and received by the Lord," "completed her journey on Earth and went to be with God and her husband " (*San Antonio Express-News*, February 6, 2007, Section B, pp. 6–7) and other similar phrases are replete. Though we would not deny that many of these phrases may give comfort to friends and family members of the deceased, (particularly those religious ones suggesting that the dead, in reuniting with God and loved ones who have predeceased them, find solace in death), we contend nonetheless that such euphemisms may also manifest our culture's failure to view mortality as normal and natural. Particularly in end-of-life care, health care professionals and dying patients often experience miscommunication as a result of "undisclosed fears and anxieties over an end stage diagnosis and feeling of mortality" (Golubow, 2002, p. 151).

Western medicine and the ignoring of human suffering

That Western medicine largely has developed from and is practiced through a biomedical perspective—one that privileges, even sanctifies scientific, evidence-based medicine—is inarguable: "The dominance and success of science in our time has led to the widely held and crippling prejudice that no knowledge is real unless it is scientific—objective and measurable" (Cassell, 2004, p. viii). Yet, as Cassell argues, the difficulties with medicine's dehumanization and impersonality do not rest with medical science or technology per se. Rather, he claims, what is lacking in current medicine is "an adequate consideration of the place of the person of the patient" (p. vi). Though Cassell acknowledges that sick persons *are* becoming more the focus of medical care, with disease gradually taking second place, this change is slow; though dissatisfied with the status quo, we still are resistant to transform current practices.

According to Cassell and others, our current medical system does not deal adequately with human suffering. Cassell writes in his recently published second edition of *The Nature of Suffering and the Goals of Medicine*:

> The test of a system of medicine should be its adequacy in the face of suffering; this book starts from the premise that modern medicine fails that test. In fact, the central assumptions on which twentieth-century medicine is founded provide no basis for an understanding of suffering. For pain, difficulty in breathing, or other afflictions of the body, superbly yes; for suffering, no. Suffering must inevitably involve the person—bodies do not suffer, persons suffer (p. v).

Many would concur with Cassell that twentieth and twenty-first-century medicine also deals inadequately with physiological pain (e.g., the findings from a 2004 study by Teno *et al.* would certainly indicate that far too many patients live and die in pain). Cassell further argues that MDs must learn to treat patients, not diseases, as patients present vast individual differences: "The scientific basis of medicine does not recognize nor provide a methodology to deal with such individual variations on the level of patient–doctor interactions" (p. 19). In addition, he contends that the relief of suffering, though considered a primary goal by patients and their family-caregivers, does not appear to be considered a paramount goal by the medical profession, given medical education and its scant concern with teaching medical students about suffering.

One of the problems rests with the disparate discourses of the physician's Voice of Medicine and the patient's Voice of the Lifeworld (Mishler, 1984): Patients and their caregivers do not categorize suffering as physical and nonphysical, as do MDs, who are chiefly concerned with the physical (Cassell, p. 31). Doctors see suffering as coupled with "pain" (and Cassell's search of medical and social science literature constantly demonstrated this pairing). Such pairing was reiterated in a review of palliative care literature by Ragan *et al.* (2003), which revealed a preponderance of studies in palliative medicine focused exclusively on a biomedical approach to patient care, particularly in regard to pain and symptom management. Cassell concludes that though medicine largely has conquered infectious disease and is fighting valiantly against cancer and heart disease, the elimination of suffering has not been much on the radar screen:

> In view of the long history of medicine's concern with the relief of sources of suffering, it is paradoxical that patients often suffer from their treatment as well as their disease. The answer seems to lie in a historically constrained and presently inadequate view of the ends of medicine (p. 31).

Cassell also attributes blame to the Cartesian notion of the mind–body dichotomy:

> As long as the mind–body dichotomy is accepted, suffering is either subjective and thus not truly 'real'—not within medicine's domain—or identified exclusively with bodily pain. Not only is the identification of suffering with bodily pain misleading and distorting, for it depersonalizes the sick patient, but it is itself a source of suffering" (p. 33).

Though the mind–body division may be anachronistic, its widespread acceptance divides the human condition into what is medical (or having to do with the body) and what is non-medical (everything else). According to Cassell, this gives medicine too narrow a definition of its mission and thus, MDs, in concentrating on curing disease, may cause patients as persons to suffer.

The medical obsession with what Cassell terms *survival* and what Nuland (1993) and other MDs have called *solving "The Riddle"* dominates much of the critique of Western medicine. Ironically, this criticism gets leveled most stridently and most poignantly by MDs themselves (e.g., Nuland, 1993; Cassell, 2004; Groopman, 2004). Particularly when writing about the treatment of cancer, for example, Cassell points out,

> The primary focus on survival, which so determines most people's behavior toward cancer ... orients the beliefs of our whole culture ... This concentration on survival, however, is as though there are no other goals in medicine. Actually the medical focus is on the disease cancer and not dying from cancer in general terms ... The slogan of one of the best cancer hospitals in the world, proclaimed in public advertising and on every computer screen in the institution, is "The Best Cancer Care ... Anywhere." Why doesn't it say "The Best Care of Patients with Cancer ... Anywhere" (p. 249)?

Cassell goes on to decry Western culture's obsession with survival, with the goal of saving life at all costs: "It is hard to imagine any population more concerned with keeping themselves from dying" (p. 249). Whereas the ubiquitous nature of death until the late nineteenth century in the United States (one that remains in the non-industrialized, third world) promoted the notion that death is commonplace and natural, fear of death and obsession with curing and surviving are now rampant.

Unfortunately, saving life at all costs has led to a disregard for advance directives, prolonging the process of dying when mercy would ask otherwise, failing to relieve suffering or actually causing it, and other excesses revealed by studies of end-of-life care (p. 250).

Cassell notes the irony of nineteenth and twentieth-century medical advances promulgating this survival mentality:

> Thus, the set of meanings, ideas, and beliefs associated with cancer and other potentially fatal diseases comes from the change in focus of medicine over the past century. It is possible to see things in other ways—for example, serious illness does not merely threaten death but provides the opportunity for patients to reassert what is personally important to them in their lives, besides just staying alive, and to pursue their goals with the help of their medical team. (In which case their doctors would have to concentrate on other important medical goals besides survival, such as the preservation and maximization of function and enabling patients to pursue their desires and purposes with as little interference from their disease or treatment as possible.) (p. 250)

Theoretical approaches to palliative care communication

The disparities between how we purport to want to be treated by our health care system, particularly at the end of life, and how we customarily die in the United States force us to question why. As stated at the beginning of this chapter, we do not intend this volume to be one that places blame solely on medical practitioners; that would be too facile. Rather, we believe that the dialectical tension between science and humanism (Babrow and Mattson, 2003), our death-avoidant culture (Nuland, 1993; Callahan, 2000), and the failure of Western medicine to adequately acknowledge human suffering (Cassell, 2004) are all major players in the reality of two-thirds of Americans dying in hospitals (52 percent) and nursing homes (24 percent) when ninety percent of us claim a preference for dying at home (von Gunten, 2002).

We argue as well that patients and their family members and caregivers also bear responsibility for exercising decision making that would help to ensure the kind of humane treatment advocated by proponents of palliative medicine. Medical care is interactive; doctors, patients, family members, and health care teams each contribute to the nature of enacted health care. One of the major functions of this book is to point out the communication obstacles inherent in the complex set of decisions that evolve in the treatment of seriously ill and dying patients.

We do that by examining the perspectives of the four primary players—patients, doctors, family members-caregivers, and the interdisciplinary health care team—in Chapters 3–6.

Throughout this volume, we discuss the communication theories and practices that help to illuminate and inform health care communication surrounding ill and dying patients. Chief among these theories are the social construction of illness (Sharf and Vanderford, 2003; Mishler, 1981, 1984); dialectical theory (Baxter, 1988, 1992); uncertainty management (Dillard and Carson, 2005); problematic integration theory (Babrow, 1992, 2001; Babrow and Mattson, 2003); dramaturgical and performance theory (Turner, 1982; Goffman, 1959; 1974), and narrative theory (Fisher, 1987, 1989). Each of these theories is briefly introduced below and referenced in subsequent chapters wherever relevant.

In discussing communication theory, we adopt the broad notion of theory advanced by Babrow and Mattson (2003): "Theory is a consciously elaborated, justified, and uncertain understanding" (p. 36). This definition appears germane to the study of health communication—and, in particular, to health communication in the specific context of ill and terminal patients.

Social construction of health and illness

The notion of reality as socially constructed permeates much recent research in the social sciences: sociologists Peter Berger and Thomas Luckmann (1966) discussed the concept as a dialectic between social reality and individual existence; the individual acts on accepted knowledge through language that creates for him or her an individualized world and its meanings. More recently, Robert Craig (1999) differentiated approaches to communication as either transmission (the transfer of information in the form of messages) or as constitutive (conceptualizing communication as a "process that produces and reproduces shared meaning" (Craig, 1999). According to health communication scholars Barbara Sharf and Marsha Vanderford (2003):

> In the context of health, illness, and medical care, the application of the constitutive model of communication reveals the complexities of moderating between scientific truth derived from the physicality of organic disease and the materiality of bodies, and the meanings of human suffering experienced by patients, their loved ones, and the health professionals who care for them. (p. 11).

Sharf and Vanderford explain further that the social construction approach to health communication has emerged as a reaction to the predominant biomedical perspective, a perspective in which science—the objective, verifiable, and measurable—has been valorized over the subjective, nonverifiable experiences of ill people. Mishler (1984) further amplified this notion in his discussion of the two discourses in health care—the objective, scientific and the subjective, humanistic—

or, as he terms them, the *Voice of Medicine* and the *Voice of the Lifeworld*. The presence of two voices is predicated on Mishler's assumption that

> the world as a meaningful reality is constructed through human interpretative activity [and] whether or not a particular behavior or experience is viewed ... as a sign or symptom of illness depends on cultural values, social norms, and culturally shared rules of interpretation (Mishler, 1981, p. 141).

Dialectical theory

Interpersonal relationships are an initial starting point for examining communication in palliative care. Though relationships continually experience constant states of change, a health crisis such as a terminal diagnosis exacerbates this fluctuation (Baxter, 1988). According to dialectical theory, there are four major components to relationship fluctuation: contradiction, change, praxis, and totality (for an example of the application of dialectic theory in communication research, see Johnson *et al.*, 2003).

Dialectical theory is derived from Bakhtin's (1981, 1984, 1986) dialogism, which premises that dialogue is characterized by the opposition of centripetal (unifying) and centrifugal (diversifying) forces (Baxter, 1992). The meaning of the communication results from the interactive practices of the two partners. Thus, according to Baxter (1988),

> a contradiction is formed whenever two tendencies or forces are interdependent (the dialectical principle of unity) yet mutually negate one another (the dialectical principle of negation) (p. 258).

These are known as dialectical tensions.

Contradiction, the first component of dialectical theory, exists in the context of end-of-life care. This contradiction is best illustrated through the values and assumptions between the scientific and humanistic study of medicine (Babrow and Mattson, 2003). On one hand, the scientific perspective, also known as the *biomedical model*, focuses on prolonging life through medical technology and pain management. On the other hand, the humanistic perspective, which is characterized more by the biopsychosocial model (Engel, 1977), concentrates on psychological and social aspects of care. Though the goal of providing health care is the same, the contradiction can best be summarized as the dialectical tension between length of life versus quality of life.

The attitudes and practices related to death and dying demonstrate the dialectical tension between science and humanism (Babrow and Mattson, 2003). A scientific perspective illustrates medical advancement, as research on disease and treatment has prolonged life for many Americans. A humanistic approach, however, reveals that these advances have ironically increased the time it takes to die and the suffering associated with the dying process.

Overall, death has become less definitive as advances in technology have generated life-support systems that allow individuals to continue living. What has not been taken into consideration, however, is the quality of life associated with such "living." From a humanistic perspective, individuals kept alive through technology may be all but dead (or at least their quality of life is severely compromised), yet scientifically they are considered to be alive.

The second component of dialectical theory is change. According to dialectical theory, contradiction triggers change in the relationship; therefore, relationships never sustain a stable state (Baxter, 1988, 1994). The centripetal pole typically symbolizes normative social conventions whereas the centrifugal pole represents non-conventionalized behavior (Baxter, 1994). In terms of end-of-life care, the scientific perspective would be considered the normative social convention and would be characterized by advanced testing and treatment options. Conversely, the humanistic perspective would be considered non-conventionalized behavior and would consist of refusing potential treatment options and focusing on advanced planning arrangements. Brown *et al.* (1992) note that both poles of contradiction are necessary for the existence of either. Each contradiction takes place in an interactive moment and is thus fluid (Baxter, 1994). Therefore, in the context of end-of-life care, the tension between the biomedical and psychosocial models is reflected by discussions of medical treatment options and by psychosocial treatment options.

The third component of dialectical theory, praxis, characterizes the reactions to dialectical tensions. As change is inherent, according to Baxter (1994), one pole may dominate only temporarily. Therefore, communication in palliative care should reveal shifts between biomedical and psychosocial emphases. A physician, for example, would likely experience the tension between biomedical and psychosocial care when evaluating a patient's pain. The physician's primary emphasis will initially be on the patient's biological pain. However, palliative care physicians are also trained to acknowledge and recognize the psychosocial elements of pain that include spiritual pain [Where am I going when I die?], emotional pain [I have not spoken with my son in twenty years], and social pain [I feel so lonely, I cannot go out the way I look, or the way I feel]. Differentiating between the four aspects of patient pain illustrates praxis of this tension.

Finally, the fourth component of dialectical theory, totality, must be taken into consideration. That is, the focus is on the relational situation (Baxter, 1988). Health communication takes place within the context of the larger culture, such as the organizational culture of the health care setting. Equally as important, dialectical tensions can be unconsciously felt or expressed within relationships because tensions occur between individuals (Montgomery, 1993). For example, these tensions can occur within and among patients, family members, and health care providers with different focuses on biomedical care and treatment versus quality-of-life comfort measures. Though all parties are committed to patient care, the dialectical nature of care goals can cause tension.

Uncertainty management theory

Though dialectical theory provides a framework for understanding the interpersonal nature of the nuances of communication in palliative care, it does not provide insight into uncertainty management at the end of life. When a loved one is given a terminal diagnosis, there is uncertainty about prognosis, treatment, identity, and social support issues for the patient and for family members and health care providers. Especially for patients, uncertainty also includes relational uncertainty, lack of uncertainty management assistance, and the burden of others' uncertainty management (Brashers *et al.*, 2004).

Uncertainty management rests on three assumptions (Dillard and Carson, 2005). First, an individual determines the meaning of uncertainty, wherein uncertainty can be viewed both positively and negatively dependent on the outcome. Second, the appraisal of the consequences of uncertainty has an associated emotional response. For example, terminally ill patients often question exactly when and how they will die as a means of managing their uncertainty, which then triggers an emotional response such as fear of death or hope for a comfortable and peaceful death. Third, appraisals and emotions prompt various behaviors, such as control. "Appraisals and corresponding emotions motivate behavioral and psychological actions directed toward managing uncertainty" (Brashers *et al.*, 2004, p. 306). Maintaining communicative control over the uncontrollable biological ramifications of disease is manifested by the selection of certain individuals for support and by maintaining boundaries (Brashers *et al.*, 2004).

The maintenance of these boundaries is expanded on through communication privacy management theory. According to communication privacy management theory, private information is owned by individuals, and boundaries are maintained by sharing information with others under certain conditions, known as *boundary conditions* (Petronio, 2002). Once private information is self-disclosed to another individual, that individual assumes co-ownership of the information. Boundaries are then managed through rule management processes that are negotiated between individuals. Terminally ill patients and family members must ultimately manage collective boundaries as a means to managing uncertainty. Particularly among their social support networks, personal boundaries between dyadic partners can be expanded to become collective boundaries between multiple persons, each with different boundary conditions. Thus, individuals manage personal, dyadic, and group boundaries of private information through privacy rules that dictate boundary conditions. Originally proposed as a way of understanding organizational culture, this rule management process is also applicable to family systems and is highly influential in determining family culture during the last months of life (Petronio, 2002).

In addition to maintaining boundaries, individuals also engage in either active or passive information seeking to manage uncertainty. Such information seeking often involves the use of social support systems. Yet, social support systems can both alleviate and cause uncertainty; this is known as *dilemmas of support* (Brashers *et al.*, 2004). Thus, contrary to normative assumptions regarding uncertainty management, not all individuals desire to reduce uncertainty. Rather, some communicative acts facilitate increasing, decreasing, or maintaining uncertainty.

Problematic integration theory

Problematic integration theory (Babrow, 1992, 2001; Babrow and Mattson, 2003) explains how individuals attempt to manage uncertainty, and it offers a theoretical basis for understanding the process of end-of-life decision making. Communication in palliative care is considered a collective dilemma among patients, family members, physicians, and other health care providers (Hines *et al.*, 2001). That is, there are variances among the individual parties involved, ranging from open communication to limited or absent communication about the factors that contribute to the decision-making process (i.e., patient placement factors, such as incontinence, pain management, independent feeding). The dilemma thus arises when communication is nonexistent or limited and life-prolonging treatment continues as a means to managing the uncertainty about the prognosis.

Problematic integration theory outlines the "collective communicative dilemma in end-of-life decision making" (Hines *et al.*, 2001). It includes two components used in producing and coping with subjective uncertainty: probabilistic judgments, the likeliness of the event-issue occurring, and evaluative judgments, an assessment of the goodness of the outcome. Probabilistic orientations are based in cognition, whereas evaluative orientations are based in emotion. For terminally ill patients and family members, probabilistic judgments might be seen in the extent to which they accept the prognosis. Evaluative judgments might include individual perceptions of a patient's life or the relationship with the patient in general. These two components are integrated in the minds of patients and family members through messages that are sent and received as part of the health care experience (Babrow, 1992, 2001). Likewise, probabilistic judgments for physicians and health care providers involve knowledge and experience with similar diagnosis and prognosis.

Probabilistic and evaluative judgments are integrated and reciprocally related. Babrow (2001) illuminates probabilistic judgments as "associational webs of understanding that we form through more or less thoughtful engagement with the world" (p. 560). In examining communication in palliative care, it is important to consider the role of probabilistic orientations in end-of-life decision making. For example, probabilistic orientations are essential for physicians and health care providers who assist patients and family members with managing uncertainty about the prognosis. Additionally, probabilistic judgments ultimately serve as an assessment of patient care because family members gauge real-life events with estimates given by a physician and health care team.

The integration of probabilistic and evaluative judgments is problematic and creates uncertainty. As a result, problematic judgments produce alternative strategies for handling the integration of both judgments. There are four forms of problematic integration. Divergence occurs when there is a discrepancy between what we want (evaluative) and what is likely (probabilistic). In the health care setting, this occurs when we want the patient to get better and be pain free, yet this outcome is unlikely. Ambiguity transpires when the probability of the event is unknown or uncertain. Particularly near the end of life, the desire is for the patient to die comfortably according to his or her preferences; however, many factors ultimately determine whether that is viable.

Ambivalence takes place when two equal evaluations are present or an event produces two contradictory responses. Patient placement is an important part of palliative care; ambivalence arises when there are recognizable benefits of a specific patient location yet simultaneous concerns about the emotional and cognitive risks of such placement. Impossibility occurs when an individual feels absolutely certain that an event will not happen. This is problematic for seriously ill individuals who maintain hope that they will get better and live longer. "In short, the challenge in improving end-of-life decisions is understanding a volatile, dynamic mix of interrelated expectations and desires, a mix that is undoubtedly different for patients and for care providers" (Hines *et al.*, 2001, p. 331). Parrott *et al.* (2004) have suggested that humans' spiritual lives explain why health situations might cause greater feelings of ambiguity, ambivalence, impossibility, or divergence.

Ultimately, communication is the source of problematic integration and a resource for coping. Communication and decision making are easier when probabilistic and evaluative judgments merge. Likewise, when judgments conflict, communication and decision making are much more difficult. Using problematic integration theory as a backdrop illuminates that interconnectedness between uncertainties and communication conflicts that occurs as part of the decision-making process.

Performance and dramaturgical theories

Erving Goffman (1959) adopts the lexicon of the theater in his seminal work, *The Performance of Self in Everyday Life*. The theatrical lexicon Goffman employs labels all people as performers—noting that participants in any social interaction are at once aware and unaware of their efforts to play a part. "Ordinary social intercourse is itself put together as a scene is put together, by the exchange of dramatically inflated actions, counteractions and terminating replies" (Goffman, 1959, p. 71). The projection of self, community interaction, inequalities, and deviant behavior create a complex rubric through which the medical setting can be explored. Goffman considers all social activity as performance and all participants in a setting as role players enacting observed and practiced scripts.

Goffman claims that, as performers, we all produce and observe impressions. All humans are skilled, at some level, in the art of impression management. At the same time, we work readily at crafting ourselves for others to perceive, and we readily see through the performances that others have built. Goffman describes communication as an information game with a potentially unending cycle of concealment, discovery, and rediscovery.

Building on the work of Gregory Bateson (1972), Goffman defines frames as a way of categorizing social experience; they are a recognized understanding of what is happening in a particular social context. Ceremonies and technical re-doings (i.e., practicings of any event) are frames that may transform; the rehearsing of a robbery actually becomes a robbery, and the practicing of dog grooming actually becomes dog grooming as a paid service. At its most basic definition, frames and their analysis are a way of organizing experience.

Richard Schechner's life work in the area of performance studies further fleshes out the concept of performance as it relates to this volume's examination of palliative care communication.

> "To perform" can also be understood in relation to: being [cancer patient], doing [receiving chemotherapy], showing doing [nurse instructing a cancer patient on self-administered chemotherapy], and explaining showing doing [a nursing student being taught how to instruct a cancer patient on self-administered chemotherapy]. … Performances are made up of "twice-behaved" behaviors, "restored behaviors," performed actions that people train to do, that they practice and rehearse.
>
> (Schechner, 2002, p. 22)

Schechner articulates that performance, as a concept, occurs in action, inter-action, and relationship. To study performance is to investigate, for example, how a conversation breaking difficult health news serves as an interaction with recipients, how it relates to the intended audience, how it identifies the actor and audience, and how it affects the relationships it informs.

Narrative theory

Finally, an understanding of the narrative paradigm (Fisher, 1989) is useful to the study of palliative care communication. In short, the narrative paradigm is a philosophical statement that is meant to offer an approach to interpretation and assessment of human communication—assuming that all forms of human communication can be seen fundamentally as stories, as interpretations of aspects of the world occurring in time and shaped by history, culture, and character (Fisher, 1989). Illness, like narrative, occurs within context at the same time that it reshapes context, within relationships at the same time that it reshapes them, and within a person's life at the same time that it reshapes that life. Narrative also occurs in time, but time accumulates at the same time it passes; there is always part of a narrative that is present in a meaning-making sense without being present within the moment. One of Fisher's aims is to gain practical knowledge concerning how people use stories to guide behavior—or to put it in his words, "to account for how people come to adopt stories that guide behavior" (p. 87). Fisher (1987)

introduces these ideas when he distinguishes his narrative paradigm project from
that of Jurgen Habermas:

> Habermas posits persons as arguers; I see them, including arguers, as
> storytellers. … His [Habermas's] concept of the end of communication is
> understanding; my concept of the end of communication is practical wisdom
> and humane action (p. 92).

With such practical knowledge, doctors, patients, families, and medical care teams
may, as Richard Carson suggests, "work together to accomplish what neither one
can individually" (Carson, 2002). These co-created stories give order to human
experience.

Fisher argues that there is not one solitary form of human communication that
creates knowledge. "Narrative is the foundational, conceptual configuration of ideas
for our species" (p. 193). His philosophy describes that narration is the context
for understanding and valuing all human communication. Human life experience
joins with literature, which merges with stories of culture, history, and character;
in all of these, conflict and struggle is embedded. Narration is omnipresent in any
and all human communication, and as humans we respond to narrative.

The narrative paradigm proposes four primary tenets. First, humans should be
reconceptualized as *Homo narrans* (i.e., essentially story-telling animals). Second,
all communication is, at its core, a story that has been shaped and reshaped by time,
culture, and character. Third, an individuated idea or motive should be considered
as a "good reason" to differ from others and develop a separate thought as a valid
action. Fourth, the narrative logic principles of coherency and fidelity should be
the valuation by which meaning is coordinated and expressed (Fisher, 1987).

Fisher's interest centers on how people come to adopt narratives that direct
action. He points out that many of the dominant social science theorists and
theories take up an interest in prediction of behavior. Narrative paradigm moves
beyond a predictive occupation by employing the idea of narrative rationality
consisting of coherence and fidelity; these are the tools that are used to discern the
worth of stories.

> The narrative paradigm advances the idea that good communication is good
> by virtue of its satisfying the requirements of narrative rationality, namely
> that it offers a reliable, trustworthy, and desirable guide to belief and action
> (p. 95).

Fisher's ideas mark a clear break with rational positivism by naming all people
as creators of knowledge that guides action. Decisions are made on the basis of
good reasons instead of mavens' pronouncements. Stories are constantly growing
and being remade as opposed to the grand narrative or puzzle that is solved with
one essential truth or reality. The narrative paradigm is not a rhetoric nor a set of
tenets about criticism nor a genre on its own. Instead, the narrative paradigm

celebrates human beings, and it does this by reaffirming their nature as storytellers. ... Regardless of genre, discourse will always tell a story and insofar as it invites an audience to believe it or to act on it, the narrative paradigm and its attendant logic, narrative rationality, are available for interpretation and assessment.

(Fisher, 1989, p. 56)

Personal narratives serve as building blocks for public knowledge about illness and palliative care (Frank, 2005). The stories of individuals cannot be built and understood separately from public narrative. Serious illness presents a desire and necessity to make sense of this change in a life. Narration is a way to organize, understand, make meaning, and reduce uncertainty in the course of an illness; it is a communicative vehicle to perform these tasks. All these tasks named take on particularly heavy weight when facing the end of life. Sharf and Vanderford's (2003) development of the five actions of illness narrative, including sense making, asserting control, transforming identity, warranting decisions, and building community, exemplify how the seriously ill and dying story their journey. Narration provides those living with serious illness and their families a way to interpret, change, understand, manage, and respond to their diagnosis or diagnoses.

Though much health communication research has focused on the voice of the patient, more than one account of reality needs to be explored to ascertain key points of divergence and commonality in an illness experience. Illness narratives (e.g., those stories that involve a patient's experience of the disease or ill health) illuminate an understanding of the illness for providers and caregivers (Sharf and Vanderford, 2003). These narratives incorporate the humanistic perspective of disease and illness as they extend beyond biological suffering and include the patient's experience with illness as related to changing roles, relationships, and identities (Sharf and Vanderford, 2003).

The inclusion of narratives in an exploration of health communication is one approach that challenges the assumptions of scientific knowledge, thus enabling us to highlight and focus on the communicative domain of such care (Geist and Gates, 1996). These vignettes of human experience provide a shift from a biomedical model to a biopsychosocial one that includes a sociocultural, political, and historical understanding of end-of-life care (Geist and Gates, 1996). Overall, such an examination views health communication as a social construction of reality, defined by Sharf and Vanderford (2003) as "a dialectic between social reality and individual existence" (p. 10).

Webbed throughout each chapter in this volume are the voices of physicians, health care providers, patients, family, and caregivers in an attempt to illustrate the challenges, complexities, and nuances of communication during severe illness and at the end of life. By presenting the multiple perspectives of patient (Chapter 3), doctor (Chapter 4), family member (Chapter 5), and interdisciplinary care team member (Chapter 6), we hope to highlight the often disparate voices in the wide range of individuals involved in the communication of palliative care.

2 The history and practice of palliative care

Before I came here the pain was so bad that if anyone came into the room I would say, "Please don't touch me, please don't come near me." But now it seems as if something has come between me and the pain, it feels like a nice thing wrapped round me.

(Saunders, 2003, p. 5)

By 2030, 20 percent of the U.S. population will be older than age sixty-five. For most Americans, the years after that age are a time of good health; however, many elderly adults will develop several chronic illnesses with which they will live for years before death. These years are characterized by physical and psychological symptom distress, progressive functional dependence and frailty, and high family support needs. Literature suggests that medical care for patients with advanced illness is typified by inadequately treated physical distress; fragmented care systems; poor communication between health care professionals, patients, and families; and enormous strains on family caregiver and support systems (National Hospice and Palliative Care Organization, 2007).

That traditional Western biomedical medicine increasingly has not met the needs of these suffering patients—whether critically ill or dying—can be attested to by the numerous medical and academic journals devoted to hospice and palliative medicine. Such titles as *Journal of Palliative Medicine, Journal of Palliative Care, Palliative Medicine,* and the *American Journal of Hospice and Palliative Medicine,* along with multiple organizations for those physicians, nurses, non-medical staff, and volunteers who work in the arenas of hospice and palliative care (organizations such as the American Academy of Hospice and Palliative Medicine and the National Hospice and Palliative Care Organization) bespeak the growing field of patient care with its primary aim of comforting more than curing, though these are not mutually exclusive. In addition, it is important to note that centers of palliative medicine, such as the Center to Advance Palliative Care (2007), exist at this writing, and that palliative medicine is now a board-certifiable area of medical specialization by the Accreditation Council for Graduate Medical Education (ACGME, 2006).

The purpose of this chapter is to introduce the reader to a brief history of the hospice and palliative care movements in the United States, to distinguish between hospice and palliative care—two words often used interchangeably, even by the medical profession—and to provide a rationale for why we see palliative medicine as a potential antidote to many of the problems posed in Chapter 1 and often encountered by critically ill and dying patients. Though we acknowledge that the communication challenges of practicing palliative medicine in the United States are many and complex, we contend nonetheless that it is our best hope for diminishing the suffering of sick and dying patients.

A brief history of hospice and palliative medicine

The goals of both hospice care and palliative medicine are to relieve patients' suffering—at end of life (hospice) and during the entire course of serious, advanced illness (palliative medicine)—while also maintaining an acceptable quality of life for such patients. The focus is on patients' comfort and physical needs and on their emotional, social, and spiritual needs. This health care approach is patient-centered, as patients are able to dictate what they need and want during both critical illnesses and in their last days or weeks. These two types of care—hospice and palliative— are inextricably tied together while at the same time distinguishable. In short, palliative care subsumes hospice care, which is specifically designed for patients at the end of life. This chapter highlights the history of care for the very ill and dying, points to the shifts between home and professional care, and details the differences between hospice and palliative care.

In tribal and pre-Christian eras (prehistory–AD 500) when there was a life-threatening illness, the community as a group responded because death often posed a direct threat to the entire community. As individuals worked for the common good of the group, when someone was sick or had sustained an injury requiring care, that person's family and the group would support him or her. In some societies, ill persons would be excluded from the group and left to die on their own or to be supported by a close loved one, if any (Amitabha Hospice Service, 2007).

The earliest form of hospice care dates back to the sixth and seventh centuries with the spread of Christianity in Europe. Though end-of-life care was provided at home, many monasteries accepted sick and dying people who did not have family to care for them. Care was provided by monastery nurses who were wealthy women and widows. This type of care for the dying provided at the monasteries continued throughout the Middle Ages and the Crusades and well into the seventeenth century as ill and dying travelers often spent their last days being cared for by monks, nurses, and lay women. As the field of medicine began to evolve and formal hospitals were established, ill and dying people were treated and cared for in hospitals.

Care for the dying, often provided through services of the church, shifted to institutionalized care in hospitals. Unfortunately, early hospital environments were primitive, and a lack of understanding about germs and disease often meant that hospitalized individuals contracted and died from diseases other than those for which they were admitted. Thus, early hospitals garnered a poor reputation and were viewed as death houses. Early end-of-life care thus shifted again to home care provided by family members and neighbors.

Care for the dying continued at home despite advances in medicine and the established effectiveness of hospitals after World War II. As knowledge of germ theory and the origins of disease became apparent, medical treatments flourished, and the focal point of health care turned exclusively to saving lives and curing diseases. Individuals who were dying were seen as medical failures; as they had no hope of advancing medical knowledge, their care was not considered within the scope of medicine.

Consequently, religious groups and organizations embraced home care for dying persons. The term *hospice* is of Latin origin, "hospes" meaning to be a guest or stranger. The term was first used by Madame Jeanne Gernier who founded the Dames de Calaire in Lyon, France in 1842. In 1879, the Irish Sisters of Charity opened their hospice, Our Lady's Hospice, in Dublin, Ireland. Mother Teresa, who is also noted as one of the founders of hospice care, opened the Kalighat Home for the Dying in 1952. Shortly thereafter, Dame Cicely Saunders started the first hospice program at St. Christopher's in London in 1967. The religious roots of hospice care facilitated the growth of the movement and formalized care of the dying as hospice care. The movement spread, and the first hospice program in North America was established in 1974 in New Haven, Connecticut.

Dame Cicely Saunders, the founder of the hospice movement, writes compellingly of the patient experiences that led to the opening of the first modern research and teaching hospice, St. Christopher's in London, in 1967:

> While working at St. Joseph's Hospice in East London with the Irish Sisters of Charity, where I spent seven years on an extensive study on The Nature and Management of Terminal Pain (Saunders, 1967), I began making tape recordings of many of my patients … As I wrote then and many times since, what was being talked about was "total pain" – "all of me is wrong." Without any further questioning [other than "Tell me about your pain"] she had talked of her mental as well as her physical distress, of her social problems and of her spiritual need for security. Then, as now, I know that listening to a patient's own tale of their troubles can be therapeutic in itself. As another patient said, "It seemed the pain went with me talking."
>
> (Saunders, 2003, pp. 4–6)

Even though, according to Saunders (2003), the hospice movement, yet unnamed, had begun earlier than in 1967 when despairing medical staff began taking a "fresh look at end-of-life care" (p. 6) in the 1950s, it was the intentional listening to suffering patients' voices that inspired the first real hospice, St. Christopher's, in 1967. Saunders concludes, "the patients are the founders of the now accepted development of the specialty of palliative medicine" (p. 8).

The medicalization of grief and bereavement that occurred during the 1950s prompted yet another transition in the place of death from home to hospital. The medical community believed it was their responsibility to keep death away from the community (Littlewood, 1993). Yet, little attention was paid to the dying process, and little care was given to those who were terminally ill. In her 1969 best seller, *On Death and Dying*, Dr. Elisabeth Kübler-Ross launched nationwide attention to the care of hospitalized dying persons. The book detailed the need for care rather than just treatment for individuals with terminal conditions. The popularity of the book sparked a 1972 U.S. Senate meeting on death and dignity in the United States.

By 1982, eight years after the first hospice program began in the United States, the Medicare Hospice Benefit was introduced as a cost-saving measure under the Tax Equity and Fiscal Responsibility Act. This was preceded by the establishment of the Palliative Care Unit at Montreal's Royal Victoria Hospital in 1976 and the creation of the National Hospice Organization (NHO) in 1977. The NHO later became the National Hospice and Palliative Care Organization (NHPCO, 2007). Thus, it has been only within the last thirty years that health care professionals began to focus on end-of-life care.

In 1983, the Medicare Hospice Benefit became available to all Medicare recipients. To be eligible for hospice care, patients must meet three criteria: (1) a patient's doctor must certify that the patient has a terminal illness with a life expectancy of six months or less; (2) a patient must choose hospice care rather than curative care; and (3) a patient must enroll in a Medicare-approved hospice program. By enrolling in a hospice program, patients waive the standard Medicare benefits for treatment of the terminal illness. Patients can receive hospice care as long as their illness is certified by a physician as terminal. The enrollment period is two ninety-day periods that are followed by an unlimited number of sixty-day periods.

Medicare's hospice program pays almost four-fifths of all hospices in the United States and, in 1997, spent $2.7 billion on hospice care (Gage *et al.*, 2000a, 2000b). In 1995, there were 390,000 patients in hospice, and 96 percent were receiving routine home care at about $114 a day (Gage *et al.*, 2000a; NHPCO, 1995). The National Center for Health Statistics reported in 1998 that almost 80 percent of all hospice users are aged sixty-five and older, many of them dying from some form of cancer (Gage *et al.*, 2000a). Though 5 percent of the elderly population dies each year, only 18 percent of these individuals enroll in Medicare hospice (Gage *et al.*, 2000a). Furthermore, from 1987 to 1990, more than 40 percent of patients in all health care settings were enrolled in the hospice benefit program for fewer than fifteen days. In a thirty-year period, the number of hospices in the United States grew from one in 1974 to 3,650 in the year 2004.

The 1982 legislation established four levels of hospice care: routine home care, continuous home care, inpatient respite care, and general inpatient care (Gage *et al.*, 2000b). According to the National Hospice and Palliative Care Organization (NHPCO, 2007), the Medicare Hospice Benefit provides for physician services, nursing care, medical appliances and supplies, drugs for symptom management and pain relief, short-term inpatient and respite care, homemaker and home health aide services, counseling, social work service, spiritual care, volunteer participation, and bereavement services. To facilitate the offering of these various services, hospice uses a team approach wherein everyone has equal input on all issues pertaining to affected patients. The hospice team is available twenty-four hours a day, seven days a week.

Overall, hospice is a care service that excludes curative treatment of illness, opting for holistic care of terminally ill patients. The primary goal in hospice care is pain and symptom management at the end of the disease progression. Today, most hospitals in the United States have affiliations with several hospices, and some even have inpatient hospice units. The majority of hospice care, however, is provided at a patient's home with assistance from nursing staff who make regular visits. The paramount goal of hospice care is to provide patients with the opportunity to die at home, surrounded by loved ones, with as little pain as possible.

What is palliative care?

Though many, including some health professionals, use *hospice care* and *palliative care* interchangeably, palliative care encompasses a broader range of patients and services. "Pallium" is a Latin term for a cloak or mantle worn by the ancient Greeks and Romans to symbolize comfort and respect. The term *palliative*, from the verb "to palliate," means to make comfortable by treating a person's pain and other illness-related symptoms. A leading proponent in the palliative care movement in the United States, Charles von Gunten, served as Medical Director of the Palliative Care and Home Hospice Program at Northwestern Memorial Hospital, Chicago, from 1993 to 1999 (and is currently the medical director at the Center for Palliative Studies at San Diego Hospice). In a recent article in the *Journal of Palliative Medicine*, von Gunten and Romer (2000) provide a succinct definition of palliative care:

> Palliative care is interdisciplinary care that focuses on the relief of suffering and improving quality of life. I like this simple definition because it leads to a host of manifestations of how you actually operationalize that. You notice in this definition it does not say anything about how long you have left to live, or whether you are terminally ill, whatever that means. It is simply focusing on relief of suffering and improving quality of life.
>
> (von Gunten and Romer, 2000, p. 115)

Through this "simple definition," von Gunten and Romer provide us with a rudimentary understanding of the goals of palliative care, yet they also allude to several of its complexities: What is suffering? What is quality of life? Is *palliative care* about care for the terminally ill only? How can we reach any sort of consensus on these questions? These dilemmas and others, both philosophical and pragmatic, pose some of the quandaries for researchers in and practitioners of palliative care. Though this volume cannot purport to answer these questions in ways that would satisfy all patients and their caregivers, we do intend to grapple with them throughout subsequent chapters. We fully realize, of course, that they may be answered differently by affected patients, their medical staff, family, and loved ones, and their interdisciplinary care team—hence our organizing scheme of representing these four unique perspectives in Chapters 3–6.

There are several tenets of palliative medicine that are commonly expressed in the literature:

- Patients and their families constitute the unit of care (because patients don't suffer in isolation but in a constellation with their families).
- Suffering includes four components: physical, psychological, social, and spiritual.
- Communication is a critical skill in palliative care.

Some writers further note that the principles underlying the practice of palliative care include autonomy or the ability of individuals to exercise choices about their lives; open and sensitive communication about the issues facing patients; quality of life being defined by affected patients; and a holistic approach to dealing with the whole person, not just the diagnosis or presenting problem (Sheldon, 1997).

A fundamental issue in the practice of palliative care, however, has concerned the question, when should palliative care commence in a patient's treatment? Von Gunten and Romer (2000) note that the Canadian health system first advocated "that relieving suffering and improving quality of life is not something that just should happen at the end of life" (p. 115). The World Health Organization also adheres to the belief that palliative care is not just for the terminally ill; as von Gunten and Romer assert, "the relief of suffering and attention to quality of life need to be appropriately integrated across a spectrum of illness and the lifespan" (p. 115).

Though many U.S. practitioners of palliative care also advocate such a view, there are numbers of volumes dealing with palliative care, particularly those published in the United Kingdom, that view palliative care as tantamount to care for the dying, as indicated by these recent titles: *Psychosocial Palliative Care: Good Practice in the Care of the Dying and Bereaved* (Sheldon, 1997); *The Dying Process: Patients' Experiences of Palliative Care* (Lawton, 2000); and *Crossing Over: Narratives of Palliative Care* (Barnard *et al.*, 2000). Yet, most of the prominent research voices in palliative medicine now advocate that palliative care should begin when serious illness is diagnosed and certainly for all patients with advanced illnesses. Morrison and Meier (2004), for example, note that the National Consensus Project for Quality Palliative Care, which is a collaboration of five national palliative care organizations, has set out guidelines for palliative care for patients with advanced chronic illnesses. These guidelines parallel and encompass those of The National Comprehensive Cancer Network, which recently developed guidelines for patients with advanced incurable cancer (as cited by Morrison and Meier, 2004), yet they also include recommendations for spiritual, religious, and existential aspects of care, and cultural aspects of care and care of patients whose death is imminent. As Morrison and Meier (2004) explain:

> Although the guidelines of the National Comprehensive Cancer Network are targeted to patients with terminal cancer, many patients who have early stages of the disease or uncertain prognoses or who are undergoing active curative or life-prolonging therapies can benefit from the organization's recommendations. The application of those recommendations should not be restricted to patients with a limited life expectancy (p. 2587).

Despite its beginning as a home hospice program, palliative care grew out of the hospice movement before the Medicare Hospice benefit in 1982. Originally it was called *supportive care* by the medical staff who didn't want to use hospice and didn't want to have a service for dying patients (von Gunten and Romer, 2000). As opposed to hospice care, palliative care programs concentrate on the relief of suffering and improving quality of life; they do not take into account an individual's diagnosis or prognosis. Palliative care is primarily hospital-based, whereas hospice care is provided at home or at an inpatient facility, such as a nursing home or hospice unit.

Both hospice and palliative care are provided by a team of health care professionals and volunteers. There are more than 3,600 palliative and hospice care teams in North America (Finlay *et al.*, 2002). These teams are responsible for coordinating care and improving communication among health care professionals, patients, and families (Finlay *et al.*, 2002). A palliative care team is called in by a physician when a disease is not responsive to treatment, whereas a physician refers a patient to hospice when a patient has been given a diagnosis of a terminal condition and has a life expectancy of less than six months. "Hospices coordinate the care of the terminally ill acting as a gatekeeper to manage treatment of the terminal condition" (Gage *et al.*, 2000b, p. 5). With hospice, the focus is on care, not cure, and patients no longer seek curative treatment.

Conversely, one of the distinguishing features of palliative care is that palliative care patients may receive curative treatment for their terminal conditions. Both hospice and palliative care are delivered by a team of interdisciplinary professionals who determine a plan of care for the patient, the location of the care, and the team members who will provide end-of-life care.

Specific features of palliative care

Palliative care is interdisciplinary care that aims to relieve suffering and improve quality of life both for patients with advanced illness and for their families. It is offered simultaneously with all other appropriate medical treatment and thus is not for dying patients exclusively, as many laypersons and professional caregivers believe. The primary focus in palliative care is symptom management, comfort, and improved quality of life for patients. Palliative care involves an interdisciplinary health care team led by a physician and including nurses, social workers, chaplains, psychologists, dieticians, and pharmacists, among other health care professionals. The unit of care is the patient and the family member (with palliative care often involving bereavement services). There are three primary objectives of palliative care: (1) the first goal of patient care is to relieve physical and emotional suffering; (2) the second goal is to improve patient–physician communication and decision making; and (3) finally, the third goal of palliative care is to facilitate the coordination of continuity of care across all care settings.

Historically, the cure–care model, one calling for life-prolonging care and treatment, has been used throughout the progression of a disease. On medical consensus that the patient was in the last six months of life, palliative and hospice care were introduced. The latest trend has been to include palliative care for the entire course of the illness. Thus, on initial diagnosis of a serious illness, palliative care is introduced in conjunction with life-prolonging therapy. Ultimately, as patients near the terminal stages of a disease, the hospice benefit (commonly provided by Medicare, but also by other insurance companies) is offered in the last six months of life. Thus, palliative care encompasses modern medical treatments and regimens and hospice care services. As one oncologist put it, "Palliative care is the superheading and hospice is the sub-heading. Hospice is a form of palliative care" (C.K. Daughtery, personal communication, October 18, 2005).

Globally, palliative care has expanded its services from hospice and the management of pain primarily for dying persons, such that the centralized focus of palliative care is symptom relief, the art of paying attention to those who are suffering, and the relief of suffering for individuals at any age, stage, or setting. Palliative care practitioners serve patients, families, professionals, and community organizations. This shift away from hospice has redefined palliative care as an overall holistic approach to pain and symptom management in general. In short, palliative care involves the relief of suffering.

Though specific boundary delineations such as these have been important in demarcating palliative care, they have also been problematic. Defining palliative care as pain and symptom management is so general as to be interpreted as applicable to all patients and to all physicians. Using such an all-encompassing definition suggests that all patients require palliative care services and that all physicians practice some element of palliative care. From one oncologist's point of view, palliative care begins at diagnosis by paying attention to the emotional response of diagnosis (C.K. Daughtery, personal communication, October 18, 2005). Thus, an oncologist can say that he or she is practicing palliative care. In essence, non-hospice and non-palliative care staff can and must deliver palliative care, assuming their training is adequate.

Palliative care practitioners assert, however, that palliative care goes beyond general symptom relief. Rather, palliative care physicians practice specialized pain management. Though Meier (2000) argues that there should be a palliative care physician on every hospital staff to ensure that adequate pain control is maintained, it is unlikely that this will happen any time soon, as hospital resources are limited, and the United States continues to experience a health care crisis. Still, health care practitioners have called for increased training in palliative care among all disciplines as one approach to meeting this need ("Hospitals embrace the hospice model," Forbes.com 2007).

A rationale for palliative care

Palliative care is critical to U.S. health care for several reasons. First, it is clinically imperative to offer palliative care services. There is a need for better quality of care for persons with serious and complex illnesses. The 1997 National Mortality Followback Survey found that 56 percent of individuals died in the hospital, 19 percent in nursing homes, and only 21 percent died at home (National Center for Health Statistics, 1998). More important, individuals with a serious illness spend at least some time in the hospital. A recent study reported that 98 percent of Medicare decedents spent at least some time in a hospital in the year before death (Dartmouth Atlas of Health Care, 1999). Moreover, 15 to 55 percent of decedents had at least one stay in an ICU in the six months before death (Dartmouth Atlas of Health Care, 1999). Overall, the care of people with chronic illness accounts for more then 75 percent of all U.S. health care expenditures (Dartmouth Atlas of Health Care, 2006).

The preponderance of deaths occurring in hospitals was one of the triggering forces for initiating palliative care services. Hospital death frequently involves physical suffering and also has a serious fiscal impact on hospitals. Moreover, hospital deaths typically occur due to poor communication about the goals of medical care and care that is discordant with patient and family preferences. In addition to patients and hospitals, family members and caregivers are also impacted financially, physically, and emotionally.

In 1995, the seminal SUPPORT study provided national data on the experience of dying in five tertiary-care teaching hospitals (The SUPPORT Investigators, 1995). The study consisted of a multi-center controlled trial to improve care of seriously ill patients and was funded by the Robert Wood Johnson Foundation. Of 9,000 patients with life-threatening illness, 50 percent died within six months of entry. Phase I results of the study found that 46 percent of do-not-resuscitate orders were written within two days of death, and of the patients preferring do-not-resuscitate orders, fewer than 50 percent of their physicians were aware of their wishes. Even more alarming, 38 percent of those who died in the hospital spent more than ten days in ICU, and half of all the patients had moderate to severe pain in the last three days of life. Morrison and Meier (2004) summarize the effectiveness of palliative care programs:

Referral to palliative care programs and hospice results in beneficial effects on patients' symptoms, reduced hospital costs, a greater likelihood of death at home, and a higher level of patient satisfaction than does conventional care (p. 2586).

Second, palliative care is a necessary component for ensuring concordance with patients' and families' wishes. A recent study of family caregivers of terminally ill persons at six sites across the United States revealed that 72 percent of caregivers are women, 96 percent are a close family member, 33 percent are older than age sixty-five, and 33 percent are in poor health themselves (Emanuel *et al.*, 1999).

Recent research has illustrated that patients with serious illnesses are concerned with their own care and are worried about care for their family. One study documented a desire for pain and symptom control, the avoidance of inappropriate prolongation of the dying process, and the achievement of a sense of control (Singer *et al.*, 1999). Patients also emphasized concern for relieving the burden on their families and strengthening relationships with loved ones.

Family caregivers, conversely, emphasized concern with patient care and priority placed on patient desires. Caregivers wanted their loved one's wishes honored, to be included in the decision processes, and to be given honest information. They also expressed a need for support/assistance at home, a desire for practical help (such as transportation, medicines, equipment), personal care needs (bathing, feeding, toileting), and being remembered and contacted after the death of their loved one (Tolle *et al.*, 1999).

Third, palliative care is necessary to meet growing patient demographics. Hospitals need palliative care to effectively treat the growing number of persons with serious, advanced, and complex illnesses. The median age of death is rising as medical advances and treatment options continue to prolong life; it is estimated that there will be more than 10 million people older than age eighty-five in 2030—this trend will exacerbate the need for palliative care.

Fourth, palliative care facilitates educational opportunities. Teaching hospitals are the site of training for most clinicians. Research has illustrated that there are deficits in skills and knowledge and attitudinal barriers to assisting those who are critically ill (Meier *et al.*, 1997). Moreover, current medical school curricula offer little to no instruction in palliative care. An overview study of medical education found that 74 percent of residencies in the United States offer no training in end-of-life care and 83 percent offer no hospice rotation (Billings and Block, 1997). In addition to revealing limited educational exposure, the study also found that 41 percent of medical students had never witnessed an attending physician's talking with a dying person or family members, and 35 percent never discussed the care of a dying patient with a teaching physician.

Fifth, the health care model of delivery has changed to meet the demands of a consumerist culture. Today's consumers are better educated and more informed. The traditional health care model that placed the physician at the top of a hierarchy has transformed to a consumer model of delivery. Better care and services are demanded. Contributing factors to this change include increasing costs of health care, a large number of uninsured patients, the nursing shortage, and federal and state health care funding. Palliative care does provide a venue for adequate care because it relieves physical and emotional suffering, improves patient–physician communication and decision making, and coordinates continuity of care across settings.

Finally, palliative care services are fiscally imperative for hospitals. Several factors are contributing to the growing financial crisis for health care. The population is aging, thus increasing the number of patients in need. Though new technologies exist, many hospitals and health care organizations still use an antiquated payment system. Taken together, experts project that this is a recipe for a serious health care financial crisis. Between 2001 and 2011, health spending is projected to grow 2.5 percent per year faster than the gross domestic product, so that by 2011 it will constitute 17 percent of the gross domestic product (Center for Medicare and Medicaid Services, 2002). Meanwhile, current reports illustrate that the burden of care rests on Medicare. Aggregate spending for health care on behalf of Medicare's 39.6 million enrollees reached $267 billion in 2002, 8.25 percent higher than spending in 2001 (Cowan *et al.*, 2004). Additionally, total Medicaid spending increased to $250 billion in 2002, an increase of 11.7 percent over the previous year (Cowan *et al.*, 2004).

Numerous studies have illustrated the cost-effectiveness of palliative care (von Gunten, 2002; Schneiderman *et al.*, 2003; Campbell and Guzman, 2003; Smith *et al.*, 2003). Palliative care lowers costs for hospitals and payers by reducing hospital and ICU length of stay and direct (such as pharmacy) costs. Palliative care facilitates these cost-saving measures by clarifying goals of care with patients and families, helping families to select medical treatments and care settings that meet their goals, and assisting with decisions to leave the hospital or withhold or withdraw death-prolonging treatments that don't help to meet their goals (Smith *et al.*, 2003). More important, palliative care improves continuity between settings and increases hospice, home care, and nursing home referral by supporting appropriate transition management. A huge cost difference exists between palliative care and hospice; palliative care needs to be included in hospital insurance coverage (von Gunten and Romer, 2000). Though some hospice professionals may view palliative care as a threat to their service and revenue, the two models provide different yet similar care as both seek to comfort the patient (von Gunten and Romer, 2000).

The vital role of communication in palliative care

At the root of hospice and palliative care practice and philosophy is communication: communication between physicians and patients, between patients and relatives, and between health care professionals, all of whom contribute in the dying experience (Doyle *et al.*, 1998). De Montigny (1993) characterizes the palliative care unit as "strengthened by the sharing of tasks, helping one another, and reciprocity" (p. 13). These communicative processes are all affected by contact with dying persons (Servaty and Hayslip, 1999).

There are several communicative goals to accomplish in practicing palliative care. Palliative care teams are primarily concerned with a holistic assessment of pain and symptom management. The completion of advance directives and living wills by all patients is equally important. Palliative care physicians must also assess where a patient is in terms of understanding and accepting diagnosis/prognosis, and they must convey hope. Physician–patient communication involves helping patients to transition from cure and reframing their goals to meet their situation (Kaur, 2000).

After the SUPPORT study, it became apparent that physicians were in need of additional training in communication skills, ethics, and palliative care. The American Medical Association developed Education for Physicians on End-of-Life Care to facilitate training at medical schools. Palliative care is now a subspecialty recognized by eleven boards of the American Board of Medical Specialties (Internal Medicine, Family Medicine, Emergency Medicine, Anesthesiology, Surgery, Neurology and Psychiatry, Pediatrics, Rehabiliation, Radiology, and OB/GYN; American Academy of Hospice and Palliative Medicine, 2007).

It is evident that communication plays a vital role in the delivery of palliative care and at the end of life. As de Haes and Teunissen (2005) report,

> The quality of communication with patients, family, and team members was indeed found by medical specialists to be fundamental to the quality of care for the dying. Ineffective communication was found to be one of the major barriers to optimal end-of-life care at the health care provider level (p. 345).

Curiously, however, most studies of communication with the seriously and terminally ill have been conducted by medical professionals and not by health communication scholars. In fact, the authors are aware of no studies by communication researchers that deal specifically with palliative care communication. Even communication at the end of life is an understudied area in health communication research, as few studies have explored the complexities of this particular setting for health care. Recently, however, communication research has investigated communication and information sharing between health care staff and patients in end-of-life contexts (Egbert and Parrott, 2003; Hines *et al.*, 2001) and has explored the relational aspects of communication with terminally ill patients (Keeley, 2004a, 2004b; Foster, 2006; Wittenberg-Lyles, 2007).

End-of-life communication is complicated by patient informational needs and wants, which often result in prolonging life under extreme circumstances. By juxtapositioning the perspectives of elderly dialysis patients and nurses regarding communication about treatment and outcomes, Hines *et al.* (2001) found vast differences among quality-of-life issues and uncertainty of patient outcomes. Overall, their study found that patient preferences for type of information were drastically different from the nurses' beliefs about the type of information patients should be given. Specifically, patients desired information that facilitated coping, whereas nurses wished to impart the seriousness of long-term treatment. The authors conclude that problematic integration theory suggests that nurses frame the problematic integration differently than do their patients. Though nurses view dialysis treatment for elderly patients as "coping with death," patients view treatments as "coping with life." In this regard, information needed to make informed decisions regarding death and dying is the same information that is deemphasized to facilitate coping. Thus, patients seek information that will help them to cope rather than information that will help them to make informed decisions regarding care (Hines *et al.*, 2001).

Additional research on communication between health care professionals and patients investigated differences between hospice and hospital volunteers on providing empathy and social support to patients. Egbert and Parrott (2003) found that hospice volunteers were more likely to provide emotional support and less likely to feel comfortable and willing to provide physical helping behaviors. Overall, hospice volunteers were less likely to provide instrumental support and more likely to provide emotional support.

Other communication research in the end-of-life context has focused on the relational aspects of end-of-life communication. Keeley (2004a) has devoted considerable attention to the study of remembered final conversations between survivors and the terminally ill. She defines final conversations as "all interactions (verbal and nonverbal) that a participant had with the loved one that was dying, between the point of a terminal diagnosis and the moment of death" wherein both individuals were aware that one was dying (2004a, p. 35). The relational approach to studying the end-of-life context reveals communication patterns specific to this setting. Keeley's initial work (2004a) in this area explored the religious and spiritual dimensions of final conversations. The study concluded that memorable messages of religion and spirituality were characterized by validation and comfort and consisted of messages that confirmed long-held belief systems, resurrected dormant belief systems, and triggered a perceptual shift in belief. She concludes that final conversations often prescribe behavior. Specifically, Keeley concluded that memorable messages often include encouragement about coping, survivor involvement in the death and dying process, and enactment of the survivor's religion or spirituality. In subsequent research, Keeley (2004b) focused on memorable verbal and nonverbal messages of love during final conversations, which involve affirmation of love, love and reconciliation, and altruistic love. She highlights that the end-of-life context is a unique relational turning point that allows for the sharing of love, often for the first and last time.

Foster's book (2006), *Communicating at the End of Life: Finding Magic in the Mundane*, also uses relational communication theory as a backdrop to studying communication at the end of life. Drawing on her experience as a hospice volunteer and on the perspectives of other hospice volunteers, Foster illustrates the relational dynamics with dying patients. Through ethnographic storytelling, she applies communication theory as a means to understanding the final stage of life. Subsequent research on the narratives of hospice volunteers has revealed that experiences with patient deaths provide volunteers with examples of good deaths and the opportunity to become hospice educators and to learn more about their own mortality and acceptance of death as part of life (Wittenberg-Lyles, 2007).

The purpose of this book is to amplify the research in palliative care communication that has been conducted solely by medical providers. We intend to frame and reframe communication issues and challenges in the light of communication theory and also to include ethnographic data gathered by the authors in palliative care contexts. The remainder of this volume will deal with the communication challenges and perspectives of affected patients (Chapter 3); the physician (Chapter 4); the family and lay caregivers (Chapter 5); and the interdisciplinary palliative care team (Chapter 6).

3 The patient's perspective

Not often enough do we have the opportunity to access patients' words, thoughts, experiences, questions, and narratives at their weakest and most impaired states. Here, we consider what the perspective of the patient is in light of their *perpeteia*— Aristotle's reference to the event that changes your course suddenly and swiftly. At the core of interest here are palliative care communication scripts and narratives that emerge from the patient experience of serious and terminal illness. Recognizing a new identity through the changes in their life to suppressing the reality of those changes are the ends of the continuum of response to illness. Presented with illness, a patient is faced with a formidable number of communication challenges and participants. A patient's performance of self in the face of grave illness teaches all of us how we might be better stewards of those navigating the grueling demands of severe illness, survival, and dying.

Research in a palliative care setting is known to be difficult in terms of access and content. We believe the seriously ill patient's perspective is largely underrepresented and unknown, particularly from a communication studies lens. The application of communication theory, including uncertainty management, problematic integration, social construction of illness, narrative, and performance of self, will allow us to provide descriptive insight into an experience that is often quantified when studied.

Reconsidering illness narratives

Theater artist, literary scholar, and essayist Peter Brooks (1984) describes narrative as "one of the large categories or systems of understanding that we use in our negotiations with reality," specifically "with time-boundedness and with the consciousness of existence within the limits of morality" (1984, p. xi). The unfolding of the sequence of the narrative gives it meaning, but also the "anticipation of retrospection" is central to making sense of narrative as well, or projecting how things will end (Brooks, 1984). A need to make sense of time and project the outcome of an experience shapes our discussion of narrative and terminal illness.

Glaser and Strauss (1965) performed seminal end-of-life ethnographic research; their book, *Awareness of Dying*, was the result of research in response to the

American cultural shift from dying at home to dying in the hospital. One of their primary questions was whether seriously ill Americans were experiencing the social process of death in addition to the biological process within the medical context and what this meant for human relationships. The result of their work centers on the term *awareness context*. Suspicion awareness is a short-lasting modality in which a patient learns indirectly that she or he is dying. From suspicion awareness emerge two possible interaction contexts: the ritual drama of mutual pretense or open awareness.

The ritual drama of the mutual pretense context is established when medical staff, family and friends, and patient agree to communicate as though the patient is not dying. To accomplish this context, a complex, mutually achieved but often unspoken coordination is a necessity (Glaser and Strauss, 1965). If one participant in the context is unable to pretend, the context will end. The pretense begins when either the patient or the medical staff produces talk indicating that the patient will not be dying. Nearly forty years after Glaser and Strauss performed their research, Groopman (2004) affirms the same phenomenon and its devastating impact on patient–physician trust:

> The evasions, the elliptical answers, the parsed phrases were all supposed to be in the service of sustaining hope. But that hope was hollow. … Once a physician lied to a patient, even if he told the lie with good intentions, then he could not be trusted again … As time passed and the disease advanced, the truth became irresistible, and the patient's illusions evaporated, leaving her and her family with nothing but resentment and anger (p. 53).

The instances and levels of awareness included in this chapter and in Chapter 5 demonstrate brutalities and loss still present forty years after Glaser and Strauss's work. Even in the instances of open awareness, insensitive communication can be addressed more inclusively with an appreciation of the patient's perspective.

The "restitution narrative" of Frank (1995) is a commonly employed alternative to Glaser and Strauss's mutual drama of pretense for the patient who is enduring a terminal illness. For the very sick person, the restitution narrative can become "I was not sick before, today I am sick, I will recover and be whole again." A longing for restitution at the brink of death is exemplified in these quotes from patients in the midst of end-of-life conversations with the doctor who is one of our co-authors. Both patients are being referred to hospice in this conversation yet are still using the language of restitution.

> Stage 4 cancer patient: I've never really asked anyone—how long do I have to live. I have faith. I feel really positive I'll overcome this.

> Stage 4 cancer patient days away from death: I don't know if I'll ever be able to use my legs again. I live 200 miles away but once I get on my own again I'll probably go and live with my daughter in Indiana.

The chaos narrative of Nietsche *et al.* (1967) is polar to the restitution story and what many patients and families experience on a terminal diagnosis. The chaos narrative might sound something like this: "I have a devastating terminal disease that will cause only suffering and sorrow. I will never know a peaceful life again." The chaos narrative makes the restitution narrative seem a far saner and comforting alternative. However, in so many instances, restitution is a lie for the patient and family—limiting the possibilities that life, illness, and treatment have to offer.

Meador and Henson (2000) suggest the quest narrative, a story in which there is a claim on hope grounded in living, suffering in the company of others openly, dying well, and planning for the gifts of life after death. The quest narrative is reflective of the integrated awareness of palliative care that we as authors believe is essential for the patient early on in any serious diagnosis. The ethnographic notes and narratives of patients included in this chapter demonstrate very little of the quest narrative. Patient perspectives most often point to a drive for restitution, a lack of information, a failure of open communication about their condition and disease path, and little preparation in the direction of living well with family and friends once curative treatments are curtailed.

Diagnosis, recurrence, prognosis

The majority of terminally ill patients in Western culture do want to know their condition and their life expectancy (Hagerty *et al.*, 2005). More commonly, patients come away from a diagnosis with an overestimate on survival, which impacts treatment decisions. At the point of diagnosis, very often there is the promise of curative treatment. New science is described with the latest medicine. The shock and anxiety of learning about life-threatening illness is mitigated by the hope of treatment options. Fueled by relief, patient and family are often eager to begin treatment with great commitment.

Many patients enter a perceived curative therapy phase of treatment after diagnosis unaware that their disease process is not curable. Explicit conversations of prognosis might not occur between physician and patient once discussions of curing therapies are underway. During the curative care period, patients are fully engaged in treatments they might believe will restore them to their way, or close to their way, of life previous to diagnosis.

The recurrence of cancer or the worsening of any terminal diagnosis defines the entry in a new period of illness for the patient. Several patients in McCormick and Conley's (1995) study thought even in this new phase of treatment that they were in clear communication with their physician and proceeding as though the disease were curable. Two of the patients learned from nurses that they were terminal. Several of them self-initiated conversations with their physicians to clarify their terminal prognosis as their condition was weakening and therapies were becoming too physically costly.

A palliative care period is the next phase of illness; many of the terminally ill cancer patients in McCormick and Conley's (1995) work speak of "being incurable" during this level of awareness. Ann, a thirty-four-year-old woman with end-stage metastatic breast cancer, writes about her interpretation of the words incurable and terminal:

> Being incurable meant that I would have to live with it. I knew that I was going to die, but I regarded that as something in the future. I didn't know when that would happen. I was more concerned with living as much as I could, getting as much done with the amount of illness and discomfort I had. Incurable meant that I had to face dying, but I could face it in the same sense that everyone does. … Terminal meant that I had less time. It meant that dying was not countable. It was not time to prepare myself to die (p. 241).

Late palliative care is the terminal period in a patient's life and disease. Not surprisingly, patients rarely found out that they were in this stage from their physicians and, if they did, the discussion was initiated by the patient (McCormick and Conley, 1995). Each of the six terminal patients in the study was able to describe "the" conversation with their physician, but most often it was not the initial way in which they learned of the news but rather a confirmation of their suspicions. Typically, patients are most satisfied when they can receive information directly from their physician concerning diagnosis and prognosis (McCormick and Conley, 1995).

> Fay: It happened so quickly. I just heard him talking to a nurse in the hall, and he said, "Let's see if we can get her into the program." That's the first I ever knew of hospice being around.

> Ken: I quit chemo because it was making me sick three days a week and there was no change in the tumor.

> Nan: I think that the medical profession knows it's the end of the line, but they don't come out with it. They feel they have to keep going or they aren't doing their job.

> Ann: Talking with nurses has helped a lot. I get tremendous support from them, but I don't think it makes up for talking to my doctors. It's frustrating, because these are excellent doctors, yet they can't talk about dying (p. 242).

Wresting physician communication

Sam is fifty-four, married and with grandchildren. After spending most of his life building a successful business, he and his wife sold their company to pursue careers in the academy—theater specifically for Sam. Nearing the end of his doctoral program, he describes his experience of laboring with a physician to attain his diagnosis after struggling with odd and persistent symptoms. Sam is also a thirty-year survivor of melanoma. In this transcription, he describes his stage 4 prostate cancer diagnosis:

> It was almost like he, he would rather send a letter or have one of his uh have one of the nurses tell us. It was almost like he was uncomfortable and didn't want to meet with us himself. We sort of had to wrest the information from him so it was not a good experience.
>
> From my standpoint it was all very confusing and I didn't have the information I felt I needed. Now we were left to do a lot of the research on our own. The whole process of diagnosis took about three months over the summer of 2004 from June to about August from the time I first went to the doctor ahh having symptoms. Then those symptoms checked out ahh to the time we had a biopsy umm was about three months into it when the diagnosis actually was wrested from the doctor ahh something we had to work kind of hard at. Ahh so during the process before I just thought I was having typical problems in a man as he ages might have, ah I was having difficulty with frequent urination and uhh just what I thought was a function of getting older as it turns out it was enlarged prostate which was restricting and causing ah frequent urination and also that we eventually found out that the prostate was ah ah there was cancer there. And so before ah I was just hoping that case wasn't going to be the case I did know the repercussions but I was hoping that it wasn't the case. He was rough and brusque and although he was the head of the uhh urology division in the teaching Hospital at _____ University he's very uhh very blunt and not very tactful and he was rough with his physical handling. Uhhm and he was very blunt and without a lot of information forthcoming in his conversations with us. In fact after the biopsy he said check back in what? Three of four days. Something like that. Check back in three or four days, you should have information in three or four days if not contact us. Well we waited over a week and did not have information and we called and didn't seem to be able to find any information so we finally just decided one day to go into his office at _____ Hospital and uh march in and plunk ourselves down until we were able to find out what were the results of that biopsy. And that's exactly what occurred. We sort of took over one of those examination rooms until they ahh were able to track down this doctor and have him come in to meet with us to give us the diagnosis that the biopsy uhh was was a ahh cancer.

For many patients, navigating medical treatments is predicated on a diagnosis and prognosis. The myriad ways in which this information is uncovered and then relayed to patients is of great interest to health communication scholars because of the impact this information has on patient care. Cancer is a frequent example in our text, as it lends itself so readily to the many complexities of palliative care communication.

Lamont and Christakis (2001) find that physicians would provide an estimate on life only for 37 percent of patients who have a diagnosis of cancer and requested a prognostic projection. In the remaining 63 percent of the instances, physicians would provide no estimate, a conscious overestimate, or a conscious underestimate, leading to large differences in expectations between the patient and physician. With inaccurate information at the point of diagnosis-prognosis, a patient might make a decision to aggressively employ chemotherapy and radiotherapy treatments that will not, in the end, extend life and that will increase the possibility of a "bad" death that might include intubation, resuscitation, end-of-life intensive care, and death precipitated as a result of treatment without patient and family end-of-life planning.

Selie is 64, married and with grandchildren and also living with Type I diabetes since her early teenage years. She worked as a bookstore manager and buyer for two decades until her multiple sclerosis began to interfere too heavily with her day-to-day activities. This is her tape-recorded diagnosis narrative:

> I began to have what's called trigeminal neuralgia. It is terrifically painful. It's pain that comes in the-in the middle of a tooth and then just goes through the top of your head uhhm it's-it's in the face but it starts I mean the only way I know how to describe it is it starts in a tooth .hhh and then goes up. I've had a number of different dentists look at it and they say there's nothing wrong with it; this has to be what they call trigeminal neuralgia. Over two year period that came and went for me and I still was just not able to to uhhhm realize that that this could be MS. I-I just, it was something I could deny. Uhhm I-I, after having quite an extreme trouble with the trigeminal Dr. Amold, who was my neurologist at the time, said [as doctor] we need to do some more tests [as Selie] uhh that's when I went to the hospital. I had the MRI several things—several tests were done. I waited a week while he looked at the outcome of those tests and it seemed like he just never would call and finally on a Sunday evening the call came from him and his first words were that I had quite an impressive. Impressive progression. Progression's the word. I had impressive progression of of MS. You know impressive is uhh-uh positive term and it took me probably one or two seconds to realize what he was actually saying to me that yes indeed I did have more signs of the MS in my brain. I found that *very* difficult to ac-accept.

These narratives of diagnosis reveal an intense need to reduce uncertainty in the face of potential new identities as seriously ill individuals and the creative ways in which our participants went about seeking more information.

Pat was in her late forties and a resident of Missouri when her Internet narratives were created. She worked for the local school district on issues of student transportation. She was a wife and mother of two teenage sons. In one of her early postings on a listerv for her particular type of cancer (adenocarcinoma of unknown primary site), she describes some of the very confusing diagnosis communication she experienced:

> The tumor in the sciatic notch that was removed had been with me for at least a year. I went to [Medical Center] April 2002 because something was wrong with my right calf. I asked him to do an MRI of my right buttocks because I had complete atrophy. The [Medical Center] basically refused telling me it wouldn't show anything different. I have copy a of drs. notes on that also. Then April 8, 2003 [year later] I went to ER because I couldn't hardly walk at all—and was using crutches. He stood over my bed and told me it was "chronic pain and neuropathy and I'd have to learn to live with it." A kind orthopedic dr. sent over for most recent MRI film and told me the tumor was located so close to the sciatic nerve he didn't feel like he should even touch it and thought I should see a neuro-surgeon. So, I transferred hospitals. The neuro-surgeon thought it could "possibly" be a nerve sheath tumor and sent copies of the MRI and CT scan to a nerve graft specialist in another city— who asked an orthopedic oncologist to take the lead in surgery. All of that was in April 2003—3 hospitals in 3 different cities—in one month … but I can see by everyone else on the ACUP board we'll do anything and everything we need to get answers and treatment.

Decision making and quality of life

The news of a morbid or comorbid diagnosis is life-changing and sometimes immediately life-reducing. Theologian Stanley Hauwerwas (2005) reflects on medical ethics and a patient's autonomy. He notes that a very sick person never has autonomy. They need their friends, family, and especially the medical world to help them journey through illness. Despite the need and reliance on medical expertise for therapies in disease progression, many patients feel as though they must navigate treatment choices and decisions with their families in spite of rather than in chorus with medical support. Here Sam describes his awakening and understanding of himself as navigator after he received his diagnosis of stage 4 prostate cancer:

> I vividly remember him saying that your job now is to keep yourself alive, (deep breath) and it's really true that a lot of the impetus fell on us. We had to do a lot of the research to find out what this disease entailed, what it was about, what happened to you, how it progressed, how to treat it. We were not given any of that information by the original urologist … .This pathologist said do as much as you can now; take responsibility. Don't listen when the doctors tell you they can't see you. You've got to be aggressive and get yourself taken care of. That's what we began to do.

In a study of hospitalized AIDS patients, researchers framed quality of life as the impact of illness and health care on a person's daily life and sense of well-being (Ragsdale *et al.*, 1992). In the context of catastrophic or chronic illness, other scholars have incorporated the access, administration, and delivery of health care, social support, and socioeconomic status as vital conditions in patient self-evaluations of quality of life in the midst of disease (King *et al.*, 1997).

The choices that actual cancer patients with life-ending illness would make concerning their treatment reveal a great deal about their willingness to sacrifice quality of life for a slim chance of life extension. Davies *et al.* (1996) found that patients with malignant cerebral glioma would still choose to receive radiation to the brain knowing that it had no effect on survival. Taburnini *et al.* (2000) learned from terminally ill non-small-cell cancer patients that they would again opt for chemotherapy, knowing that there was a very slim benefit, even if their physician had presented it as an unattractive option. Patients seem to demonstrate a willingness to suffer to continue living, despite the cost to their bodies, additional hospitalizations and elements of suffering they might endure, and suggestions from their doctors that it will not be beneficial. Patients enduring chemotherapy carry an expectation of suffering to treatment and brace for the possibility of at least nine different symptoms (Hoffman *et al.*, 2004). As they move into their second- and third-line chemotherapy options, patients might be more willing to accept aggressive side effects, pain, weakness, and complications. Might this be due to the fact that there have been no clear intercepting discussions of alternatives along the way?

These numbers and narratives point to the quality-of-life elements missing in scripts that doctors and patients are using in communication. Recent research reveals that 98 percent of cancer patients wanted a realistic description of their disease and prognosis, a chance to ask questions about their illness, and to be treated as an individual as opposed to a statistic/group with illness when discussing these issues (Hagerty *et al.*, 2005). It is likely that many oncologists are gently directing patients with new and grave diagnoses in the direction of curative therapies when those treatments do not always or often (in the case of some diseases) offer such patients the best option. Oncologists are taught to offer lines of treatment with 20 percent anticipated response, possibly prolonging the life of a patient for a few weeks to a few months. For many patients, the chance at even an additional day of life would be enough motive to persuade them to accept aggressive treatment.

There is a precious exchange of time for treatment that does call into question the value of life that the patient is extending. Yabroff *et al.* (2007) culled the records of 763,000 Medicare cancer patients and their treatment wait times to better understand the monetary value and lost opportunities of a patient receiving curative therapies. This project measured the time that patients with the eleven most common cancer types spent traveling to, waiting for, and receiving treatments. It did not measure the time spent recovering from therapy, feeling too weak or sick to be productive or performing job tasks, interacting with family and friends, or enjoying day-to-day activities. It is estimated that those with gastric cancers spend more than 500 hours, lung cancers near 500 hours, and ovarian cancers near 400 hours receiving curative care treatments in the last twelve months of their lives (Yabroff *et al.*, 2007).

To pursue curative or palliative treatments

Individuals with diagnosed advanced metastatic disease present a curious dynamic for consideration in the overall discussion of patient perspective and palliative care. In a recent article in the *Journal of Clinical Oncology*, researchers report that chemotherapy is used more frequently in the United States than in any other place in the world, with patients receiving these therapies nearer the end of their life and hospice referrals nearer death (Matsuyama *et al.*, 2006). Medicare data from 1996 reveal that chemotherapy and radiotherapy two weeks previous to death jumped from 13.8 percent in 1993 to 18.5 percent in 1996. During these years, there was also an increase of hospice use but additionally a spike in use during the last three days of life for patients (Earle *et al.*, 2004). In a 2003 study, researchers found that many Medicare patients received chemotherapy during the last six months of their lives, regardless of the type of cancer they had (chemotherapy-responsive or chemotherapy-non-responsive; Emanuel *et al.*, 2003).

Patients likely facing the most difficult news of their life will look to their diagnosing physician for guidance in making a curative/palliative treatment choice. Matsuyama *et al.* (2006) describes the trend of oncologists to overestimate patient prognosis and express overoptimistic views about how their patients will fare the disease process.

Faced with a looming decision of whether to pursue life-extending therapy or palliative care, patients who understood that they had a chance at living for at least six months opted for aggressive chemotherapies. These patients experienced the same survival rate as those who opted for palliative care but incurred more hospitalization, intubation, ventilator support, and intervention in general (Weeks *et al.*, 1998). The (2002) identifies a repeated pattern of false optimism among non-small-cell lung cancer patients—a diagnosis that is grave with a prognosis of less than six months for those with diagnosed stage 4 disease. Despite receiving a diagnosis, all patients observed opted for very aggressive chemotherapy treatment and spoke about their treatment as though they were receiving curative therapy. They learned the truth about their conditions through their own physical failings and discussions they shared with other patients and family members in waiting areas over the weeks and months of their treatment.

Internet access has provided patients and families alike ready access to government and organization descriptions of their illness in an effort to gain an understanding of the changes they will encounter. These sources are also a place many turn to in an attempt to navigate what can be overwhelming decisions concerning treatment in the early days after diagnosis. Matsuyama *et al.* (2006) point out that Web sources considered rigorous and sponsored by researching organizations do not provide the information patients need to make decisions about anticancer versus palliative treatments. The National Cancer Institute, for example, has an entire set of pages for non-small-cell lung cancer, and they include stage descriptions, the segment of the population affected, and myriad treatment options—but none include palliative care without some active anticancer treatment or hospice care alone. Additionally, there is no information on the effects of treatment, the possible outcomes of treatment, how well the treatments will work, some ways to choose among myriad anticancer and palliative care options, or what patients might expect from the options they do choose. Even less specific information on disease staging and life expectancy for decision making is found at the American Cancer Society and other specific cancer Web sites, including the Lung Cancer Alliance and the Susan G. Komen Breast Cancer Foundation.

Online support groups

Online support groups span the world of illnesses. Davison and Pennebecker (1997) note that different illnesses generate varied themes and patterns in listerv communication. The level of severity and complication from an illness will likely produce a need for specific forms of social support from the group in an online community.

Despite this growing area of research, literature revealing data about patients' access to cancer care information beyond the health care environment is minimal (i.e., their feelings about their care, their outstanding needs; Balmer, 2005). Dickerson *et al.* (2006) analyzed patients' narratives about ways in which they used the Internet. Two of the five themes identified in patient talk about their Internet usage included (1) meaningful information regarding symptom management, and (2) peer support, including stories, chat rooms, message boards, and e-mail. Shaw *et al.* (2000) performed a phenomenological study of interviews with breast cancer patients about how they received social support from participation in an online support group. Participants shared that the asynchronous nature of the online support group was positive. Schedules did not have to be shaped around meetings, nor did additional efforts need to be made to travel out of the home when patients were not feeling well. The somewhat anonymous nature of the computer-mediated context also positively influenced participants' willingness to share and ask for support. Interaction in the group made symptoms seem less harrowing and language of the illness less foreign, and it decreased uncertainty.

Dealing with doctors: a lack of control

Victor Turner coined the term *liminality* to refer to the place betwixt and between, when we are straddling between two worlds. This is the place where many seriously ill patients live: in no-longer and not yet (Turner, 1982). The doctor–patient relationship holds its liminality in the hyphen that connects the two. The patient's life is changing, and the doctor has medical information that will inform that patient. The hyphen that connects the two parties points to the possibility of joining together two narratives; the hyphen also points to the possibility of two separate conversations.

Clem is a member of the ACUPS listerv (adenocarcinoma of unknown primary site). He is the primary caregiver for his spouse, who is living with the illness. The overall prognosis of ACUPS is poor. The median survival for these patients as a whole is three–five months, and fewer than 25 percent are alive after one year. People with multiple sites of involvement, including lung, brain, and liver, have a life expectancy measured in weeks (Hoskin and Makin, 2003, p. 256). Kagan and Steckel (2000) note that ACUPS is incurable, as it is unidentifiable until it is overwhelmingly metastatic, and in most cases there is still no effective oncological palliative treatment available. The writing from Clem below reveals the very difficult communication challenges faced by the patient, family, and physician in light of this diagnosis.

> I will always remain badly irritated by oncologists who approach ACUP as a mortal diagnosis from the start. Point of fact, they have given up before the fight is even waged. And when you fight, after all, you sometimes win. But we must. And we certainly can't let someone else yield our lives because they are too lazy to help us fight.

The order is tall and demanding for the physician imparting the news of a terminal illness. Both honesty and hope are communicative components highly valued by patients and physicians alike. The tightrope act involved in cultivating honesty and hope in the midst of life-ending news is perhaps one of the greatest challenges medicine presents and one of the greatest needs a patient can ever experience. The resources demanded of both physicians and patients are enormous if the subject is to be addressed with honest and careful communication. A patient needs honesty and hope but not an overestimation of survival as a place-holding substitute.

Patient's body and its interpreter

Part of the sheer power doctors hold over a catastrophically ill patient is their ability to interpret what is happening inside the patient's body. For the very sick, not trusting feelings about their own bodies is a confusing betrayal. The tools used by the well person no longer seem to work or provide reasonable data for the severely ill person. Tremendous trust is placed in the individual performing the part of the well-bodied doctor, the person who likely never knew this patient's body without disease.

Patients' body alienation can begin early in the course of the disease while they are feeling well. The technologies of the medical world outrace the body in communicating with the senses.

The measure of "how well they are" is, from [diagnosis] on, no longer how they feel but the results of laboratory tests and X-rays, and the interpretations that the doctors attach to these. As one patient put it during a bad news interview, "It's the X-rays that tell me that I'm sick, not my body."

(The, 2002, p. l2)

In this moment, a patient's body is no longer a reliable communicator, according to medical technologies. This betrayal steals away the part of a patient that has identified her or him as a healthy person, a person in possession of his or her own physical faculties.

For terminally ill cancer patients, the course of their treatment, if they opt for it, takes them down a path that further disconnects them from their physical selves. Chemotherapies for the most aggressive cancers are physically destructive, permanently debilitating the factories producing blood. Surviving the ravages of these chemicals is a stunning effort in its own right. Patients in treatment for terminal cancers are often shocked in diagnosis and confused about their sense of wellness. How can they be so sick and feel so well? Conversely, in midtreatment, they have never felt worse. "The doctor says [to the patient] that things look fine on the X-rays but the patient often does not feel well at all. This is all very confusing and alienating for patients: they cannot trust their own bodies" (The, 2002, p. 87). As tumors shrink in response to treatment, whether by chemotherapy, radiation, or other methods, affected patients feel very sick, but the news they receive from the doctor is positive. This positivity can vary wildly from the dark news of the diagnosis when patients feel physically stronger.

Pat describes a communication with an oncologist, and more specifically her attempt to understand her disease progression and treatment:

I asked my oncologist "what next?" He said he was just going to "follow me": and of course nurse will keep my prescriptions filled … my oncologist just wants to do CT of pelvis and I want him to continue the chest, abdomen, and pelvis, to get those organs on a regular basis. Oncologist won't do a scan of brain—that's the 2nd time I've asked—that same response—NO. Said unless I have symptoms it's not cost effective. I've always been forgetful but onc. says I'll know if I have mets in brain—balance will be off and eyesight screwed up, headaches, etc. UGH. I don't think he should wait for symptoms but I'll fight that one when I'm stronger and just keep track of brain problems (if any).

I'm having a hard time accepting the fact that all happened under the "watchful eyes" of my oncologist. Maybe I'm being too hard on him…but for heaven's sake…do any and all tests to prevent the spread of cancer … NOT just treat it. Many times it's too late if you wait to treat. I'd just like to shake my oncologist by the ears. Sounds like the tumor in my butt is growing. UGH.

I just have the strangest feeling that I don't have a lot of time left … that's why I'm pushing everyone so much. It's VERY hard and I can't explain it … just a feeling.

No physician was direct with Pat in explaining her terminal status. Her sense of treatment seems to be that her medical team is several steps behind her disease and her job is one of trying to keep them on task. In fact, no one knows better than an oncologist about the progression and course of adenocarcinoma of unknown primary site, but no one would spend the thirty minutes explaining to Pat that she was terminal and might consider palliative care. Her narrative reveals a struggle to make sense, make decisions, and make choices about her identity as a dying person.

Patient communication in the SPIKES strategy

Robert Buckman is a medical oncologist at the Princess Margaret Hospital and Professor of Medicine at the University of Toronto in Ontario, Canada. His research agenda has fixed on breaking difficult news to patients with cancer and other life-changing illnesses. In 2000, Baile *et al.* published a six-step protocol for delivering bad news to cancer patients with the chilling acronym of SPIKES (setting, perception, invitation, knowledge, empathy, strategy-summary). Setting guides the physician to create the best physical circumstances for conferencing with the patient; the details of the protocol even address proxemics, nonverbal leakage (though in different language), and the presence of family in the conference space. Perception addresses the "ask before you tell" principle; here physicians are to route out the patient's understanding of their own medical situation. Invitation asks the patient how much information they would like to have concerning their diagnosis-prognosis. Knowledge is the step in which physicians actually impart "bad" news. Alignment with the patient is encouraged in this step and the use of non-technical language in small units of meaning. Empathy follows the breaking of the bad news; here the physician is encouraged to listen for and identify the emotions of the patient and identify the cause of those emotions—making a connection between the two. The intention here is to validate the patient's feelings and experience. The final element in the protocol is to summarize and strategize a plan for the next step of care (pp. 139–41).

Buckman cites the need for SPIKES by noting the stress experienced by physicians who must share difficult diagnostic information with patients on a regular basis. The protocol, which Buckman (2005) asserts is not a script, is meant to relieve the effects of stress for physicians. Though he does not view the protocol as a script, it is a structured performance meant to take place in a particular context and order. Buckman has provided a rehearsed structure for physicians to follow, though the wording they select can take many forms. By following a set of structured communications maneuvers, a patient is also obliged to acquiesce to this protocol administered by a physician. SPIKES is built in the best interest of physicians—to relieve their stress related to delivering bad news. It is not built with patients first in mind; if it were, the research detailing and justifying SPIKES would be framed quite differently.

Buckman writes, "It is important to define the central element of bad news—that is, to try to identify what makes it so bad for the patient" (p. 138). "Badness" is the gap between what patients expect and the impact on them and their families. "As a clinician, you cannot know how patients will react to bad news until you ascertain their perceptions of their clinical situations. Hence, a valuable rule is 'Before you tell, ask' " (p. 138). The protocol thinly disguises an assumed patriarchal omniscience. The physician decides what is "bad news" and is also entitled to determine the impact of the news on an affected patient and family.

SPIKES is a giant leap forward in palliative care communication education in the medical school setting. Anyone can now download the strategy from the M.D. Anderson Web site for health practitioners. It is widely consumed and taught and executed; previous to SPIKES, there was no structured "help" available for practitioners to use while sharing difficult information with their patients. Despite this advancement, the patient can be taken by surprise and put "on the spot" in the interrogation of their illness perception. As physicians pursue a patient's perception per the SPIKES strategy, a feeling of near entrapment can be read into the language of patients. The dialogs presented within this section are exemplars of the SPIKES protocol; in the first example, we include protocol labels as a guide to follow the process of interaction between our palliative care physician and patient.

[Setting established]
[Perception]
MD So, why are you in the hospital?
P I have a brain tumor.
MD What's going to happen?
P Well, it sounds like to me a twice failed attempt to remove it (two prior surgeries). This distress is creating like headaches that I have because I'm thinking and I shouldn't be.
MD What's gonna happen to you?
P I believe I'm going to come out of this as well as normal because I believe this because I have never stayed …
MD What did they tell you about the tumor?
P Similar comments from the doctor—it seems I'm going to come out of this.
MD But the tumor is not going to go away—and you don't want chemo.
P But during the last operation they put a chemo disk in my brain to reduce the size of the tumor.
[Invitation]
MD Yes, but the tumor will not go away, sir. Your doctors asked me to come to see if you can do rehab … .
 [at this point, the patient stirs in his bed and is mumbling]

[Knowledge]
MD The tumor is not going to go away.
P If you can monitor the tumor…

MD Yes, but the tumor will not go away.

P The treatment I am receiving now, whatever prognosis you can come up with … but I don't know one way or the other the best treatment.

MD We can give you treatment but we cannot cure you—but we want to take care of your headaches.

[long pause]

MD Do you know what I'm saying, sir?

P Yes, I know what you are saying. If I am able to ambulate then that is a good step?

MD Yes, then the next step is to go home with your wife on hospice. Do you know what hospice is?

P Yes, it's like a hospital.

MD Yes, and more than that. It's for people who are very ill and their illness will not go away. They provide a lot of help.

P I don't have a problem with that. The only problem I have with hospice is that I …

[Empathy]

MD Let me give you some juice, sir, because your mouth is getting very dry.

[she gives him juice to drink]

P I'm not trying to act like I don't know more than I should know and I'm thinking … I think about the tumor all the time. I especially think about my body. I know when something is wrong with my body. It almost brings me to tears because of a plan I made years and years ago because I tried to maintain a friend who … .[patient begins to cry openly] The reason I tried drugs and alcohol … it hurt my temperament. [patient begins to sob]

MD How can we help you? [she reaches over and touches his shoulder when talking]

P I have a headache.

MD We are going to help you [she turns to an MD fellow and instructs him to "please go ask the team to get something right now"]. I think your family loves you and they want to be with you. I think that's wonderful. What do you think?

P [continues to cry]

[Strategy-Structure follows with a discussion of advance directive]

It is difficult to read the words of this patient, imagining the effort to integrate his own perception and hope of restoration in the midst of this interview process in which he discovers turn after turn that his conceptions are incorrect. For the physician, the protocol fills an outstanding need; research has not revealed the same for patients. McCluskey *et al.* (2004) studied diagnostic disclosure satisfaction among amyotrophic lateral sclerosis patients and their caregivers who learned about their diagnosis through SPIKES. Results of this study reveal that what patients found most helpful was the time that physicians shared with them on diagnosis rather than the actual structure of the SPIKES protocol.

The palliative care team's discussion about Tim reveals the following background information. He is fifty-six years old and has metastatic lung cancer. Given the diagnosis in November, he did not see an oncologist until January. On January 11, he was admitted to the hospital by the oncologist. He is able to walk and suffers no incontinence. The team assesses that the patient does not understand what is happening to him. He has posttraumatic stress disorder, anxiety disorder, and depression and is an active drug user. His diagnosis is stage 4, prognosis 6 months. What follows is the patient consultation in which Tim learns he is dying of cancer. On entry into the room, Tim appears healthy and is walking around the room. The MD decides to let Dr. J (fellow) handle this consult-breaking bad news.

The team greets the patient and moves into the family meeting room on the hospital floor.

T [shares that he is very depressed but has faith] I have read the literature on my condition. I think I'm at the final stage. I want more information on remission.

DR. J [interrupting] Yes, you are at a stage 4.

T I've never really asked anyone—how long do I have to live? I have faith. I feel really positive I'll overcome this. [he talks about his disease—he's not sure where it all is and how it is affecting his body]

DR. J They told you it was bad but you don't feel bad …

T Yes. I can take a lot of pain and that's not done me any good. I have a lot of faith. Once they get it stable then I can go on with my life.

MD [takes over for Jane] What are you hoping for? You said you have faith, what are you hoping for?

T A normal life—to be happier, my family, be normal.

MD You like fishing?

T Yes, I love the water, I love flower beds, gardening [he continues to recall his medical history leading up to diagnosis of tumor]. I'm glad they discovered it. I feel positive. I've got a lot of faith.

MD What is your understanding of your disease—what is stage 4?

T The worst it can get.

MD You understand that we cannot cure you.

T [long pause]. A pretty good life, I'm thankful. I worry about my kids, my grandkids, my daughter crying. I don't want to lie to them. To me, I'm ready for anything. This fourth stage is where it's at. I don't feel like it but I don't know how long. I wonder about it all the time.

DR. J Would it make a difference to know?

T No.

MD We are meeting today to discuss a plan.

T With my family [referencing Jane's questions].

MD What's going to happen to you with radiation?

T Shrinkage and containment. That's positive and made me feel good. As long as I'm mobile and healthy. I like to walk.

MD [focuses on plan, which is better pain control] The other part of the plan, once radiation is complete, you want to go home. Have you heard of the term *hospice*? What do you think it is?

[Chaplain enters room to join group]

MD Hospice is a benefit and could happen at home. It's for people who have incurable diseases.

T Like mine.

MD Yes. Now we have to think about later at some point you won't be doing so well. We need to think about somebody who will represent you and what you wish. Do you have someone in mind?

T [names someone]

MD Can a social worker come today to do paperwork? Please let _____ know what you want.

MD Right now you are doing well but say that you become sick and your heart stops beating

P Like being a vegetable?

DR. J Being kept on a machine.

P I'd rather just go.

DR. J [discusses advance directives]

P I feel like—I've just got such a faith. It feels like a challenge to beat this. I'm sick but you know it's a challenge to me.

MD It's important to focus on the quality of life.

P I feel like it's hard to hold me down. I have a lot of faith.

MD [explains that his radiation is for palliation]

DR. J It's not to cure it, just to make you feel better.

Bob is a 53-year-old man who is in the midst of a prolonged hospital stay due to metastatic prostate cancer, liver failure, and a history of alcohol abuse. He is presently on restraints because he has pulled out his tubes four times. He is married and has three children. The palliative care team discusses that his liver problem is not curative and hospice does need to be introduced. The team concludes that it is likely the patient will return to a nursing home for care. What follows is the patient consultation in which the idea of hospice is first proposed.

B Please cut it off [referring to leg].

MD Why? Because it hurts so bad?

B Yes.

MD Did you fall? [turns to male nurse: did he fall? Answer: no]

MD [examines patient and determines by looking at bruises that he did indeed fall] We need to contact the wife.

MD We are just here to say hello.

B Hello, good-bye.

MD I knew you would say that. What is your understanding of what's going on with you?

B I have prostate cancer that has spread to my bones.

MD May I sit down? [on patient's bed]

B Yes.

B I don't know if I'll ever be able to use my legs again. I live 200 miles away, but once I get on my own again I'll probably go and live with my daughter in Indiana. [Patient goes on to talk about transportation problems-issues with current living situation]

MD Let's go back to talk about your cancer. At this point, the cancer is not curable.

B Well they haven't actually said that.

MD Well, it's not curable. [Pauses]. But it is a very slow cancer. What we are concerned about is pain. Are you in pain?

B No. I'm okay.

MD You'll need to get stronger. Have you heard of hospice?

B Yes, it's for your last days.

MD Well, actually it's for individuals with advanced disease. And your disease is considered advanced.

B God, you are an optimist.

MD It's not about being an optimist; it's about being real.

[Patient was walking up until a week ago]

B But I want to go home. A couple of days is okay but I want to go home.

Pain

Eric Cassell describes suffering as the "challenges that threaten the intactness of [a] person as a complex social and psychological entity." Cassell believes that when a person's cultural, emotional, and spiritual elements are placed in peril, suffering results (as cited in Abraham *et al.*, 2006, p. 659). The body, the mind, the spirit cannot be in a state of harmony near the end of life; self-regulatory systems are not working with any sort of unity or grace. Pain and suffering are partners to the end-of-life experience. Founder of the hospice movement, Dame Cicely Saunders, coined pain connected with dying as total pain. Total pain consists of four components: physical pain, anxiety, interpersonal interactions, and non-acceptance.

Physical pain is composed of acute, chronic, somatic, visceral, neuropathic, and breakthrough pain. Each of these can be addressed with medication, though not necessarily fully abated. The second major contributor to overall end-of-life pain is anxiety. Anxiety can be produced by physiological imbalances or myriad concerns that might only begin with fear of physical pain, abandonment, death, loss, and change. The pain of interpersonal interactions can be caused by family strain and isolation in illness. Non-acceptance is the fourth component in the definition of pain. This component addresses a patient's awareness of his or her own disease process and likely outcome (Lelszi and Lewandowski, 2005). Together, these four elements build total pain—what any patient at the end of life faces in various degrees, depending on the illness and life situation. The palliative care team studied in this volume also uses the concept of total pain from Dame Cicely Saunders; physical pain, psychological pain, social pain, and spiritual pain are rated by the patient on a daily basis.

Our palliative care team consults with a 46-year-old mother living with metastatic breast cancer and discusses her pain. The discussion reveals the inability to separate the four areas of pain and concern in the terminal phase of illness.

MD [Introduces the team as we enter the private hospital room]

MD Are you in pain?

L Yes, a 10.

MD Okay we can do something about that … [asks questions to assess pain]

MD What have your doctors told you about your cancer?

L Am I stage 4? Yes.

MD It's spread to your bones and everywhere.

MD Have you been taking chemo?

L Yes, at home. [not in area where hospital is located; different city]

MD Are they trying to cure or kill it?

L Trying to kill the cancer.

MD Well we might not be able to get rid of the whole cancer, just try to control it.

MD [begins to discuss current arrangements for taking care of 8-year-old son]

MD Do you know what hospice is?

L It's when they come and take care of you to the end. I'm not ready for that. I'm not ready for hospice.

MD Can I ask why not?

L I'm not ready for hospice. I'm not ready to leave yet.

MD Well, let's talk about your pain … [re-assesses pain]

[following pain assessment, she brings up topic of power of attorney] Do you know what that is?

L Yes.

MD Who would that be?

L My daughter.

MD [brings up code status topic] Do you know what you would like?

L [begins crying] … kept alive as long as my little boy needs me.

MD I can't imagine how hard this is for you [touches patient's hand]. What is his name?

L Thomas.

MD Is he doing good in school?

L [shakes head yes—still crying]

MD [in low voice] How can we help you besides controlling your pain? [MD reaches over and touches her hand again] … Tell me about Thomas.

L He is feisty. I don't want him to have anything to do with his father [son is currently staying with older sister].

MD　Well, that's why it's so important to get paperwork done, so he'll stay with your daughter.

MD　Are you depressed?

L　Yes.

MD　Would you like anything for it?

L　I already take something.

MD　Do you have thoughts of killing yourself?

L　No.

[Brief pause]

MD　Has anyone ever talked to you before about these things?

L　No.

MD　Does it feel good to talk about these feelings?

L　[begins crying again] Yes.

MD　Would you like to see a chaplain?

L　No.

MD　Okay. I'm going to do something about your pain. We'll talk more later.

Many more conversations follow this one in which the team attempts to alleviate all kinds of pain for this patient. She endures the social pain of leaving her little boy "unprotected," the psychological pain of letting go, and the burden on her spiritual life. Our team meets with her on several occasions. Some issues are resolved, but her pain is still profound. The team had the sense they had failed as she was unable to say good-bye.

What follows next are a series of excerpts of letters from Pat as her physical pain is increasing from disease progression from adenocarcinoma of unknown primary site. It is nearly impossible to separate the physical, spiritual, social, and psychological pain in these writings, as one links directly to the next. The excerpts of her writings showcase the uncertainty and anxiety of her thoughts in addition to her physical pain.

December 19, 9:17 AM

I've been feeling bad lately. My leg is hurting, almost at the same level before surgery. CT last week shows the tumor has not changed … but the location is still on or near sciatic nerve OR the crap in the nerve is causing lots of problems.

I just started crying this AM and couldn't stop thinking about the boys graduations etc … but I don't want to get started on my stuff … you are dealing with a lot too.

December 19, 6:43 PM

Drs. want to know where the pain is coming from so try to figure that out … I say … give me the pills … make me comfortable … and then figure it out. I'm not hard to get along with☺ If they need to do surgery, do it after

Christmas—if they need to do more radiation do it if after Christmas—but personally I think they need to do MRI first.

I just called my husband and told him if I don't hear from the nurse before 8:00—we're driving to [the city].

January 11

I'm still trying to get used to the look of this foreign object in my belly [pain pump] … but I guess the important thing is it works. There are some portable ones you can't shower with etc … and you have to carry a bag with them…and sleep with the bag, etc. I'm hoping this surgical implant is the right choice for me.

Even though the original tumor was adhered to the bone, and the surgeon said something about it … I just never thought about it being in the bone. It's actually in about 3/4 … all in the pelvic area … so still "localized" … as my oncologist puts it. One of his partners wanted to know if I had a "living will" filled out … and another one wanted to know if I had my boys in counseling … kind of scared me. So, I asked my dr. how aggressive this was and he said "moderate" … none of that tells me anything.

January 22, 10:19 PM

A friend of mine bought me a book about dying—which is what I need to read. I'm not much on talking to people about my feelings but I love to read … not that life follows certain patterns … but it keeps my active mind busy.

My hip/butt is hurting more than usual today. Who knows why. I've just taken a few break through pain meds … but think I'm going to find some ibuprofen and take some of that. So, I'm in a little more pain today—up towards my waist on right side … I'm keeping a pain journal so I'll be able to give a good description of how I felt and when for this appt. on Feb. 11.

February 11

Just got out of hospital yesterday. I'm not going to write much today, but will tell you more tomorrow. More mets in spine and arm. Arm tumor is what's causing the non-functional hand. Plus, after asking, almost begging my onc. to do brain mri for months, he finally did it, and have one tumor there, surrounded by edema. He couldn't even look me in the eye. I asked my neuro-surgeon to do it and he said give me a reason and I'll do it. Told them both my memory was bad. Not good enough. The reason I finally gave my onc. was for my peace of mind. He reluctantly ordered it. Anyway, long story. Radiation starts tomorrow here in my home town with the radiation onc. I trust and like, then more chemo. My neuron-surgeon said he'd do surgery, so that may still be in picture, but need to get rid of edema first. I'm on steroids for that. I'm really tired…so need to go lay down, but didn't want you to worry. Thanks for prayers.

Bob, declining with metastatic colon cancer, skillfully articulates the mitigating role of communication in alleviating pain for the dying patient. "You can tolerate a difficult situation if you have a doctor who can sit down and explain and tell you where you are" (McCormick and Conley, 1995, p. 242). The quest after their physicians' time is a recurrent theme for patients in terms of their articulated need; this will be an identifiable component in Chapter 5 as well.

Reciprocal suffering: anxiety over family burden

A reciprocal suffering shared by patient and family is a central factor in the experience of dying and is also reported as such by patients. Affected patients endure two worlds of suffering: the intrapersonal effort to deal with loss and pain and the interpersonal effort of caring for others in the midst of family transitions. Patients consistently share a major anxiety in illness equal to their own distress about death, experience of pain, or loss of a well identity in the suffering experienced by their family (Loscalzo and Zabora, 1998).

> [Caregivers] spoke of patients' concerns about ensuring matters were in order and that the family was provided for after their death. Others raised issues about suffering with symptoms, in particular pain, loss of functioning, wanting to be at home, losses associated with life events that they would miss, such as children and grandchildren, and uncertainty about the future.
>
> (McPherson and Addington-Hall, 2004, p. 109)

If patients experience an open awareness of their illness trajectory, Yurk *et al.* (2002) note a shift from concern over medical issues to a need to express some control over what might happen to them during end-of-life care and how they might be a lesser burden on their family during this period through planning.

Conclusion

Sam tape records his thoughts about his terminal diagnosis:

> So I haven't really, I haven't had any-any ahh epiphanies or life changing moments or big changes that I can think of other than the fact that I've had to, ah it's-it's more it's more become into a little more realistic comprehension of the fact that we all die and I'm going to someday too and it might be very soon. Um but I'm in good company John Kerry had ah had prostate cancer and he hasn't died of it and Nelson Mandela had cancer, so you know it's-it's not an unusual disease among men and ahh I lived a very rich and full life and have been very lucky in terms of having someone to love me who I've been with for so many years and ahh the-the beautiful children that we have. I feel I've been really lucky. So if something happens tomorrow and I'm gone then

I'm happy, I'm satisfied. But ahh I've come to ahh a more realistic evaluation of that process.

In a conversation between Rita Charon and Jerome Bruner (2002), they exchange ideas about the terror and plight of illness. Charon asks Bruner, "Aren't there plights … that you don't want to be true to but rather free from?" Bruner responds with "Yes, and the freedom usually comes from someone else's recognition" (p. 6). This idea is essential to each patient narrative included in this chapter. Every patient's words reveal some element of their communication experience as a seriously ill or dying person. Pat travels to an online cancer support community to find freedom from her pain and anxiety and to aid in decision making. In her words, we see the quagmire and constant struggle created by the lack of information communicated about her prognosis. She is trapped in a terror of not knowing her identity as a surviving person or dying person. Some of the patients engaged in end-of-life conversations with our palliative care team members did experience an open awareness about their terminal status; the truth of their prognosis had been previously unspoken until these conversations. Yet many of them continued to hang on to the restoration narrative even at this late stage in their illness.

Bruner describes the exchange of narrative over plight as the creation of a local community. The specific communities to which we commit shape us and our ability to manage and cope. This is another reason why physician abandonment is so devastating. Without the conversation and exchange of narratives about the loss of health and life and ways to care for the very sick more openly, there is no community but the opposite of freedom: imprisonment.

The patient perspective to opt for aggressive treatments in light of bleak benefits seems to be the prevailing phenomenon. The increasing trend of patients opting for aggressive chemotherapies closer to death with the unintentional outcome of hospitalization and very late hospice referrals demonstrates a gap in care and communication for the terminally ill. This pattern will change if there is more conversation about prognosis, the individual patient, and the options and inclusions of care; most patients do not receive this information from their physicians but instead from interactions they or their caregiver initiate. The information passed on to patients via specialists and public information sites concerning side effects of treatment and palliative care options are minimal, leaving a vacuum in which patients and carers must decide how to address their treatment, often in moments of acute physical crisis.

4   The medical perspective

Case study

An eighty-four-year-old white man with dementia is in bed, restrained because he was physically aggressive with the nurses, as the interdisciplinary palliative care team enters his hospital room. A twenty-four-hour nurse assistant has been assigned to his room to monitor his care around the clock.

PATIENT: I've been in pain all morning.
MD: Do you know where you are?
PATIENT: Hell yeah, I'm in the hospital. I'm in miserable pain.
MD: Do you know who Paula is?
PATIENT: [confused, asks MD a question]
MD: Who do you live with, sir?
PATIENT: I live with my wife, stepdaughter, and adopted son. OHHH my wrists.
MD: [inquires about his belly and wrists]
PATIENT: Hell, if it gets too bad then I'll let it hurt.
[Patient and team continue discussing his belly and wrists]
MD: Do you know why you are in the hospital?
PATIENT: I was hurting a lot.
MD: Can I examine you?
[Patient nods yes and MD begins examination]
MD: Why did they tie you up?
PATIENT: We got in an argument.
MD: Who?
PATIENT: I don't know. One of these nurses around here.

The MD examines the patient more and discovers that his belly is rigid, indicating a need for a bowel movement; the nurse watch says, however, that the patient had a bowel movement the day before. After the exam, the team meets in the hallway outside the patient's room. The doctor explains that the patient is "very impacted" (meaning that the patient's bowels were not moving). The patient's chart shows renal problems. The doctor explains that in these cases, patients typically get agitated, go into a coma, and subsequently die. This patient is already in the last stage of pancreatic cancer. The doctor advises that his restraints need removing, a bowel regimen needs to be prescribed owing to the constipating opioids he is receiving, and he needs to be transferred to the hospice inpatient unit. According to the doctor, also one of the authors of this book, such a case scenario illustrates perfectly the importance of palliative care from the medical perspective.

It is daunting to begin a chapter that claims to detail the "medical" perspective of the communication challenges inherent in palliative care. Even with a physician on the writing team whose specialties are in geriatrics and palliative medicine, we cannot hope to present the multiplicity of voices among physicians who are daily encountering very ill and dying patients. We also do not claim that there is a univocal agreement among physicians as to how to approach patients with advanced, chronic illnesses or with end-stage disease. A myriad of communication issues confront physicians as they encounter the most difficult challenges of their professional practice: breaking bad medical news to patients; determining how much information to disclose; influencing patient choices regarding treatment options; dealing with the communication ramifications of pain and other symptom management; discussing difficult topics with patients, such as advance directives and "do-not-resuscitate orders"; and confronting professional and ethical pressures to cure the patient rather than to palliate him or her. In this chapter, we focus on how physicians convey medical prognoses to seriously ill and dying patients, why they are reluctant to fully disclose "bad news" to their patients, and what challenges they confront in switching from curative to comfort care as several of the most critical communication junctures between physicians and their ill and dying patients. In addition, we deal briefly with the extreme stressors that seriously ill and dying patients exert on physicians—and with the resultant depression and burnout that result from the futility of trying to save all patients, regardless of age or severity of illness.

Overview: the medical backdrop

Drs. Sean Morrison and Diane Meier, two prominent proponents of palliative medicine, note that the need for palliative care rests on the premise that many patients with advanced illness do not receive adequate medical care, primarily because of a prevalent medical philosophy that focuses "almost exclusively on curing illness and prolonging life, rather than on improving the quality of life and relieving suffering" (2004, p. 2582). They further assert that traditional medicine has had two mutually exclusive goals: to cure disease and prolong life *or* to provide comfort care (this dichotomy driven by the current insurance reimbursement system with regular Medicare covering curative therapies and Medicare hospice benefits covering comfort care). As a result, they argue, "the decision to focus on reducing suffering is made only after life-prolonging treatment has been ineffectual and death is imminent" (p. 2582). The division of services reinforced by this dichotomy has resulted in an interesting and painful irony: patients are given life-prolonging treatments that are costly and not beneficial to them; furthermore, such treatments have augmented rather than reduced suffering during all stages of advanced illness (Fisher *et al.*, 2003). As a result of the medical philosophy and the reimbursement system that have promoted curative rather than palliative medicine, Morrison and Meier (2004) conclude that "patients would benefit most from care that included a combination of life-prolonging treatment (when possible and appropriate), palliation of symptoms, rehabilitation, and support for caregivers" (p. 2582).

Von Gunten and Romer (2000) illustrate dramatically the differences between traditional medical care and palliative medicine in a hypothetical patient scenario. A patient with metastatic breast cancer is admitted to the hospital for treatment of decreased mental status and bone pain. Pain medication is begun, but little is addressed about advance directives or overall treatment goals. "Life at all costs" is the predominant treatment mode. The patient will be given a CT scan, an MRI, and x-rays of all her bones, in addition to extensive blood testing. A complete blood count will be drawn every day, and she'll also have an SMA-20 (a chemistry panel) every day. If, on the other hand, the palliative care team is consulted and, together with the family, determine that the primary goals are the relief of suffering and improvement of quality of life, this question is asked before any medical test is performed: "Why? Why should we do this test? What will it tell us that will help us relieve this patient's suffering or improve her quality of life?" (p. 120). In a palliative care unit, von Gunten and Romer explain, that question is always asked, but it goes unasked in a general hospital setting. With the hypothetical patient in question, then, there would be no reason for a blood draw every day, as this would make her quality of life worse, and the data from the blood draw would not be used to change anything. This transformation in medical mind-set from curative to palliative care also drastically affects patient charges; von Gunten and Romer (2000) claim that, on average, charges for patients decrease by 50 percent in the palliative care unit.

Though patient charges are decreased with palliative care, according to von Gunten and Romer (2000), the amount of time that medical staff spend with patients is increased; both patients and family members alike report that a palliative care unit is the first place in the hospital where patients believe they've gotten sufficient information and interaction time, where they were treated as if they mattered. Communication is at the heart of this transformation from traditional medical to palliative care.

Steinhauser *et al.* (2000a) contend that communication with patients is a core skill of palliative medicine. Morrison and Meier (2004) cite several empirical studies that support this assertion:

1   In typical clinical encounters, fewer than half of patients' concerns are elicited, nor are patients' values, care goals, and treatment preferences discussed adequately (Steinhauser, *et al.*, 2000a; Tulsky, 2003).

2　Specific clinical communication skills are effective in enhancing disclosure of issues of concern to patients, decreasing anxiety, assessing depression, improving patients' well-being, and increasing both the patients' and family members' satisfaction with treatment (Tulsky, 2003).

3　A patient-centered communication approach (e.g., making eye contact, asking open-ended questions, responding to patients' affect, and demonstrating empathy) rather than a traditional, closed physician-centered interview style is associated with improved satisfaction for both patients and their families (Dowsett *et al.*, 2000).

Though Morrison and Meier (2004) assert that the communication guidelines developed for palliative care treatment—establishing goals of care, communicating bad news, and withholding or withdrawing treatment—have not received adequate empirical testing to confirm their efficacy, they are nonetheless useful in clinical practice. De Haes and Teunissen (2005) concur that it is striking how few studies focus on "what happens in communication in palliative care" (p. 348) and that observer-based studies are indeed rare: "This is unfortunate not only because the practice of palliative communication thus remains unseen but also because the mechanisms behind what happens in real life are more difficult to study" (pp. 348–9). Certainly the belief that appropriate communication skills are effective with patients with advanced and terminal illnesses is the rationale for the offering of communication skills training courses across a number of medical specialties (Harvard Medical School; American Academy on Communication on Healthcare; as cited by Morrison and Meier, 2004).

The challenge of informing patients that they are seriously or even terminally ill is one that most physicians face with trepidation. As a result, it is an area that has received much research attention by both social scientists and physicians. The communication task of "breaking bad news" must be prefaced by a brief discussion of the history of medical disclosure. The paramount questions include: what do patients want to know? How do physicians ascertain this? Do physicians tell patients all that they know about their disease and its probable course (i.e., do physicians communicate a patient's prognosis honestly)? To answer these questions, we must begin first with a look at the history of medical disclosures.

Medical disclosure, decision making, and information exchange between doctors and patients

According to Gillotti (2003), the literature dealing with bad news delivery, informed consent, and patient autonomy "appears to reflect a tug-of-war between necessary paternalism and patient self-determination and autonomy" (p. 167).

Thomasina (1994) wrote a classic work exploring the ethics of doctors telling the truth to their patients about their medical conditions and prognoses. Though he noted that the "truth" is ultimately revealed by most physicians, regardless of whether they are attempting to conceal or distort it for their patients' benefit,

Thomasina also noted that there are many reasons why the truth is occasionally hidden from patients, the primary one being the physician's paternalism. Dating back to Hippocrates, the history of medical disclosure is replete with the ideology that physicians are responsible for determining just how much information patients should be told about their medical situations. Though many modern patients might find such a belief system abhorrent in the face of their right to be fully informed, individual and, especially, cultural differences make medical disclosure a complex topic: the overwhelming majority of patients, at least in the United States, wish to be fully apprised of their medical conditions and prognoses, but not all patients want all the information. Doctors are called on to make difficult judgment calls in determining the information needs of their patients. Admittedly, many physicians continue to operate under traditional, paternalistic constraints even when informed consent is a basic patient right.

Waitzkin (1985) studied the problems of physicians' withholding of information in a consumerist age of patients demanding information. Though he discovered that physicians provided more information to patients when diagnoses were more uncertain and that patients of higher social class received more information, he also concluded that "even though the concern 'to do no harm' was the original principle on which physicians decided whether to withhold information, it does not necessarily influence information dissemination decisions in the same way today" (Gillotti, 2003, p. 165).

Clearly, a patient-centered or biopsychosocial approach (or both) to medical care relies on a patient's being fully informed so as to participate appropriately in medical decision making. Goldman (1980) and other ethicists have written of full disclosure, informed consent, and patient self-determination as paramount to protecting patient rights. Goldman proposes two conditions for withholding information: "one is where the truth will cause direct harm—depression or loss of continued will to live. The other is where informing may be instrumentally harmful in leading to a choice of wrong treatment or none at all" (Goldman, 1980, p. 171). Yet Goldman countered these conditions by stating that it is improbable that safeguarding patient rights will lead to harm, that great harm is committed in denying a patient his or her rights to full disclosure. Many current studies conclude that patients do wish to know the truth about their diagnosis and prognosis (e.g., Sell *et al.*, 1993; Davis, 1991).

Yet the research on disclosure reveals that, for myriad reasons, doctors do not tell their patients the whole truth. One of the most telling research studies investigating the complexities of full medical disclosure was undertaken by a Dutch ethnographer, Anne-Mei The (2002; also referenced in Chapters 3 and 5 on patient and family communication, respectively). The, a cultural anthropologist, spent many months in a lung cancer clinic and meticulously analyzed the interactions between the clinic physicians and their patients, all of whom had been given diagnoses of a generally fatal type of lung cancer: non-small-cell lung cancer. Her research focus was the curious paradox she had observed among the clinic's patients: "When confronted with a disease that is almost invariably and often swiftly fatal, patients nevertheless maintain a remarkable sense of optimism about the future" (p. xi). The (2002) discovered many possible explanations for this paradox, the chief one being a collusion between physician and patient in which both pretend that the patient's medical situation is not as dire as it is. (Others, including Quill, 2001, and Groopman, 2004, also speak of this collusion, as discussed in the next section of this chapter.)

The (2002) first notes that physicians rarely discuss what she calls the "long term perspective" of patients' illness but rather concentrate solely on short-term consequences; she cites the work of Costain Schou (1993) and Costain Schou and Hewison (1999), who reported that physicians constantly focus on the short term and do not discuss long-term aspects of illness with their patients:

> Into the patient's existential uncertainty the doctor introduces order, occupying his time with activities (treatment, check-ups) and suggestions of certainty (treatment schemes, laboratory tests). Specialists inform their patients mainly about these fixed aspects of treatment, and this diverts the patient's attention from the more general uncertainties of his condition (pp. 194–5).

Research by de Swaan (1985) amplifies this notion: patients are given the impression by their doctors that long-term prognosis can only be addressed after it is known how the initial treatment is working; the long-term perspective is completely dependent on the short-term consequences. Yet, according to de Swaan, after the first round of treatment, explanation and long-term prognosis is again postponed and made dependent on future treatment and further tests. "Because the patient is continually promised something, he never really has the chance to prepare for death" (de Swann, 1985, p. 19 as cited by The). de Swaan goes on to say that this concentration on the short-term perspective of illness structures the process for patients and their families, rendering the medical crisis orderly and manageable; treatment itself has a sedative effect.

The (2002) also notes that patients' concerns about the long-term course of their disease are handled by doctors from a medical perspective only; when patients raised psychological and medical complaints, only the medical issues were dealt with. Maguire and Faulkner (1988a, 1988b) term this reaction "the distancing technique" and believe it to be an unconscious way that medical caregivers distance themselves from their own psychological suffering, thus enabling them to cope emotionally with their seriously ill and dying patients. The (2002) notes in her own research in the lung cancer clinic that she observed some doctors and nurses enlarging their roles beyond the medical-technical to the psychosocial; moreover, the psychosocial support extended to patients varied by patient and by practitioner. Most patients became aware of how the system worked—that physical complaints were almost always taken seriously and investigated whereas doctors might not have the time or inclination to pursue emotional distresses. Thus, when patients somatized their psychosocial problems, they received their doctors' attention—a process of somatization and medicalization was set in motion. As The explains,

"The system is self-perpetuating; in a totally medicalized context the focus of specialists on the physical and medical aspects of illness and treatment is to be expected" (p. 196). This, in turn, leads to what The found most striking about the communication in the physician–patient interactions she studied: the imbalance between the relatively short conversational time spent on the large, long-term problem (i.e., that the patient's incurable illness will soon kill him despite treatment) versus the larger amount of talk devoted to relatively trivial matters (i.e., the short-term problems related to treatment). Concludes The (2002), this phenomenon is related to the need in Western culture to see all problems as controllable and solvable and to avoid confronting what we cannot solve: "From large problems we make smaller ones, which are solvable, or at any rate manageable. Because of our problem solving optimism, we transform the dying trajectory into fragments that are emotionally convenient" (p. 196).

What is particularly of interest to us, the authors of this text, is that The (2002) and other researchers have noted that both doctors *and* patients collude in the dramatic performance described above. Patients are more comfortable telling the "recovery narrative" (Frank, 1995), in which the patient fully recovers her previous good health (also see a discussion of illness narratives in Chapter 3), than any other story: "They learn to recite the socially propagated recovery narrative" (The, p. 222), though they may be living simultaneously with chaos (and other) narratives. Through these diverse narratives, The (2002) explains,

> patients gradually develop an ambivalent realization of approaching death. Patients (and their loved ones) know what is happening, but at the same time they are unaware. Patients use this condition of "knowing and not knowing" in their communication with others, and in this sense it is functional for them (p. 222).

The acknowledges as well that what she'd initially believed to be the patient's "unjustified optimism" in the face of a dire prognosis was the product of a collusion between patient and doctor, that patients had considerable power and influence over their communication and thus over the "unjustified optimism":

> The optimism about recovery stems to a large extent from a collusion between doctor and patient in which more attention is devoted to the short-term perspective compared to the long-term. Both parties are ambivalent. The doctor both does and does not want to inform the patient of the death sentence; the patient both does and does not want to hear it. Both are afraid of the confrontation with the medical truth and with each other. In their communication each has the other in a "hold": the doctor wants to "spare," the patient wants to be "spared." In this way the doctor avoids informing the patient about the long-term perspective and escapes into the details of the short-term perspective. For their part patients do not ask questions and do not force doctors to provide information about the final stages of their illness. As a

result of this collusion the wider picture of the illness—that it almost certainly recurs in the short term and is fatal—is only made clear in its final stages. In this way both doctor and patient collaborate in a way that is understandable at the time but regretted by patients and loved ones retrospectively. On the one hand, optimism gives both patients and their relatives the strength to persevere and cope with the situation. On the other hand, the realization that this is an illusion is experienced as painful, and the acceptance of approaching death and the saying of goodbyes are constrained by the sudden realization that time is limited (p. 222).

Jerome Groopman, an MD at Harvard Medical School and a staff writer in medicine and biology for *The New Yorker*, also speaks of this "painful" realization by the dying in his brilliant discussion of how people cope in the face of serious illness (2004). He tells of a dying patient, Frances, who was given false hope about her condition: When the tumors in her liver shrank after a round of chemotherapy, she asked her physician if she were "partly cured." He responded: "You are well on the way to a remission," to which she responded with an uncorrected, "Thank God. It's going away" (p. 14). Even though her doctor had spoken the literal truth, "remission" was misunderstood by the patient as "cure"—and Frances's doctor informed Groopman, then an intern, that "sustained ignorance is a form of bliss." Yet when her cancer returned in force, both Frances and her daughter, Sharon, bemoaned that they hadn't been completely informed of the prognosis of her metastatic colon cancer. Sharon stated, "I guess he [her mother's MD] didn't think people like us are smart enough, or strong enough, to handle the truth" (p. 41). Groopman learns from this experience that "ignorance was not bliss, not when it mattered. By abandoning the truth, Richard [Frances's MD] and I had abandoned Frances, and through our deception we left Sharon alienated and bitter" (p. 42).

What Groopman learned in part from the experience of dealing with Frances and Sharon is that patients *do* and *can* manage uncertainty, as the tenets of problematic integration theory (Babrow, 1992, 2001) teach us (see Chapter 1 for a more complete discussion of this theory). He questioned whether patients were capable of hope in their confrontation of significant uncertainty about their diseases:

> Doctors like Richard and me doubted not only the resilience of our patients but also our own capacity to hope. If we did not believe in our hearts that there was something to hope for, then we either pretended there was ... or made explicit that there wasn't ... we never gave [our patients] the opportunity to choose what to hope for (pp. 52–3).

Groopman's thesis is that physicians must find a way to communicate hope to their patients in a way that is neither false nor totally shattering to them:

> You didn't have to shatter a person by frankly citing statistics … these cold numbers were handed down the way a judge designates the days to be spent on death row, leaving the person with nothing but fear. Nor did you have to sustain sins of omission … The evasions, the elliptical answers, the parsed phrases were all supposed to be in the service of sustaining hope. But that hope was hollow. It was false, a seductive but only temporarily satisfying illusion.
>
> (Groopman, 2004, p. 53)

This "illusion," though well-intentioned, betrays the patient; as disease advances and the truth becomes evident, patients feel abandoned, angry, and resentful. Groopman thus advocates a "middle ground where both truth and hope could reside" (p. 57). He believes strongly that physicians should never "hand down a fixed sentence of days or weeks or months of remaining life" (p. 79) and that "omniscience about life and death is not within a physician's purview" (p. 79), but that physicians should encourage and facilitate a patient's right to hope: "To hope under the most extreme circumstances is an act of defiance that … permits a person to live his life on his own terms. It is part of the human spirit to endure and give a miracle a chance to happen" (p. 81). Groopman further distinguishes between "true hope" and "false hope," asserting that "an equilibrium needs to be established, integrating the genuine threats and dangers that exist into the proposed strategies to subsume them" (p. 210). Thus, when a patient tells Groopman that he doesn't wish to know about the problems and risks of his disease, that ignorance is needed for bliss, Groopman nonetheless gives him some information about his illness and its course to avoid giving false hope:

> … false hope is an insubstantial foundation upon which to stand and weather the vicissitudes of difficult circumstances. It is only true hope that carries its companions, courage and resilience, through. False hope causes them to ultimately fall by the wayside as reality intervenes and overpowers illusion (p. 210).

In fact, Groopman, Christakis (2001) and others believe that the inherent uncertainty of a prognosis is the grounding for real hope "because nothing is absolutely determined, there is not only reason to fear but also reason to hope" (Groopman, 2004, pp. 210–11). Thus, they likely would subscribe to the belief that patients sometimes cope favorably with uncertainty that sustains their hope rather than striving totally to reduce uncertainty, which might extinguish hope. (This phenomenon is explained by the communication theories of uncertainty management and problematic integration, as discussed in Chapter 1.) Groopman also wrestles with the notion of hope, as delivered through medicine, and hope that resides in the patient:

Hope does not arise from being told to "think positively," or from hearing an overly rosy forecast. Hope, unlike optimism, is rooted in unalloyed reality. Although there is no uniform definition of hope, I found one that seemed to capture what my patients have taught me. Hope is the elevating feeling we experience when we see—in the mind's eye— a path to a better future. Hope acknowledges the significant obstacles and deep pitfalls along that path. True hope has no room for delusion (p. xii).

Dr. Diane Meier, a leading proponent of palliative care, discusses a reframing of hope for seriously ill patients in the videotaped series on death and dying hosted by journalist Bill Moyers, "On our own terms: Moyers on Dying" (2000). Meier contends that though patients may not be able to hope for a cure, they still can hope for other, important things: for living long enough to witness a special occasion or the birth of a child; for enough time to make peace with relatives and other loved ones; and for dying in relative comfort and without pain. Helping patients to reframe hope, from hope for cure to hope for comfort, thus becomes a guiding principle in the implementation of palliative care. This sort of hope also permits doctors—oncologists, surgeons, and other specialists, in addition to palliative care doctors—to remain connected to their patients throughout the final stages of their disease. Kübler-Ross (1969) writes of the necessity for a patient not to be abandoned by her physicians in any stage of illness; many patients fear and experience abandonment when a physician is no longer able to treat their disease but must resort to treating them and their family. In a partnership relationship between patient and doctor, the relationship begins at diagnosis and continues through treatment and either recovery or decline; it remains until death (Quill, 2001). This open-ended commitment over time both holds and manifests hope. (For a further discussion of how patients reframe hope, see Chapter 3.)

Medical prognosis

One of the most eloquent proponents of the necessity for accurate medical prognosis is Nicholas Christakis, an MD who had long practiced what he wrote about in 2001 in a volume entitled *Death Foretold: Prophecy and Prognosis in Medical Care.* In this volume Christakis outlines, from the perspective of medical practitioners, why prognosis is so difficult for most physicians. Yet his thesis is clear from the beginning: "Over the course of my clinical training, I came to regard explicit, precise, and compassionate responses to patients' requests for prognosis to be a key part of my role as a physician" (2001, p. xi). His medical experience, however, taught him that most doctors avoided prognostication, rarely talked explicitly to patients about their futures, and "avoided even thinking about prognosis explicitly, except occasionally in the most benign and casual ways. I noticed that textbooks omitted prognosis, journals avoided it, and medical schools ignored it" (p. xii). Further, Christakis notes that the:

muffled presence of prognosis had a lot to do with the raging authority of death ... I came to regard the avoidance of prognostication as a sort of advertent and inadvertent self-deception, as an almost ideological, and not merely utopian, commitment in the medical profession. Physicians avoided prognostication, both consciously and subconsciously, because they did not want to deal with its unpleasant aspects or to think about the limits of their ability to change the future. But they also avoided it because they wanted to deceive themselves about death, as if in not predicting death they could avoid causing it or witnessing it (p. xii).

Though doctors apparently withheld terminal prognoses from their patients much of the time in the 1960s and 1970s (Novack *et al.*, 1979), they now report telling the vast majority of their patients the complete truth of their prognosis (The, 2002). Yet Christakis (2001) and others report a contradiction between what doctors assert about prognoses and what they actually do: Christakis cites a recent study in which 25 percent of 504 patients referred for hospice care were denied prognostic information about the course of their diseases. Doctors reported giving their best, most objective prognostic estimate to only 34 percent of these 504 cases. Prior research has found that cancer patients overwhelmingly wish to be fully informed about their diagnoses and prognoses, and this finding is corroborated repeatedly by subsequent research (Richards *et al.*, 1995). However, according to Christakis (2001) and The (2002), doctors rarely communicate their actual beliefs about a patient's prognosis to the patient; rather, they may find it more acceptable to communicate their true opinions to their colleagues (other medical personnel, including nurses) or even to the patient's family members. Christakis and other physicians write compellingly about why doctors find it so difficult to give their patients the whole truth about the probable course of their illness; for example, Christakis (2001) writes of some physicians' belief that making predictions about a disease outcome can actually influence that outcome through self-fulfilling prophecy:

> Making predictions—especially given the conviction that they influence the outcome through self-fulfilling prophecy—is a source of role strain and anxiety for physicians. The tension is this: to have optimistic, positive expectations may be hubristic but to have pessimistic and negative ones may indicate helplessness and ill will. On the one hand, physicians are afraid of being omnipotent; on the other, they are afraid of not being powerful enough. The necessity of prognosticating in medical practice can, given physicians' belief in predictions' effectiveness, be seen to conflict with the professional obligation to "do no harm" (p. 161).

Christakis (2001) concludes, given the findings of the 1995 SUPPORT study, one of which was that patients had unduly optimistic expectations about prospects for recovery, that physicians are able in many instances to predict mortality and certainly better able to estimate prognosis than are patients; the problem is that physicians are apparently failing to communicate prognosis to their patients. He cites the SUPPORT study's conclusions that

> To achieve the goals of making care at the end of life consistent with patient values and [to minimize] futile therapy, we may need to change what physicians tell patients about their prognoses and be sure that patients hear and understand what their physicians have said (p. 189).

Yet Christakis (2001), The (2002), and Nuland (1993) realize the difficulties that physicians face in communicating accurate prognoses to their seriously ill and dying patients. Nuland (1993), in his much acclaimed volume, *How We Die*, discusses a medical phenomenon termed *The Riddle* as a force gravitating against a prognosis that informs the patient that further curative treatment is no longer a viable option. Doctors are socialized early to address medical problems with medical treatment in a quest to cure the patient. As Nuland (1993) writes:

> This quest I call The Riddle, and I capitalize it so there will be no mistaking its dominance over every other consideration. The satisfaction of solving The Riddle is its own reward, and the fuel that drives the clinical engines of medicine's most highly trained specialists. It is every doctor's measure of his own abilities; it is the most important ingredient of his professional image (p. 248).

Though Nuland writes that The Riddle is the motivation for medicine's most talented physicians—those regularly found in research institutions who have the challenge of caring for an entire group of people suffering with a particular illness, not the individual patient—he also notes that once a patient needs care that is non-curative, the physician may retreat when The Riddle cannot be solved:

> The doctor creates order from chaos and finds power to exert control over disease, nature and his personal universe. When there is no longer a Riddle, such a doctor will lower his interest or lose it entirely. To stay and oversee the triumph of unrestrainable nature is to acquiesce to his own impotence.
> (Nuland, 1993, pp. 258–9)

Attitudes such as the one Nuland speaks about help to create further problems for many patients who both need to be referred to palliative or hospice care (or both) earlier in their disease course and who fear that they will be abandoned by their primary care physician when "there is no longer a riddle" and curative care ceases for them. David Weissman, editor of the *Journal of Palliative Medicine*, refers to himself as a "recovering oncologist" (2003, p. 859). After fifteen years of medical oncology, he transitioned to palliative medicine. He observes that hospice, palliative care, social workers, nurses, and non-oncology physicians complain that oncologists recommend chemotherapy long after it is useful. So why are patients not spoken to about palliation and not treated palliatively early on instead of a few days or hours before death? Weissman suggests the following: (1) Cancer patients come to the oncologist hoping for a cure or life prolongation; if they do not find it with that oncologist, they go on to another; (2) oncologists prescribe chemotherapy in the hope that it will improve quality of life, and the patient will require less analgesic; (3) despite the fact that oncologists, by far, have the more accurate information concerning prognosis and survival, they withhold direct prognosis information and provide hope through chemotherapies; and (4) training programs in oncology are dominated by research into the development and application of chemotherapeutic agents. Weissman notes that "95 percent of the questions on the Oncology Board Examination focus on cancer diseases, their diagnosis and chemotherapeutic and radiologic management" (p. 860). This emphasis on treatment leaves little room for teaching end-of-life care and palliation.

Collaboration is another point of consideration in the gap between oncologists and palliative care doctors. In work by Cherney and Catane (2003) that explores the attitudes of medical oncologists toward palliative care for terminal patients, only 35 percent of respondents indicated that they collaborated often with a palliative care specialist. A majority of oncologists responding believed that the oncologist should coordinate palliative care for their dying patients. The overall acceptance and integration of palliative care physician practice on the part of oncologists surveyed was more positive for those in private practice and much less so for those oncologists working in comprehensive cancer centers. The gap is real, and it exists for good reason. Specialization is partially to blame, and a lack of recognition of the importance of palliation for patients in general is also at great fault. These factors collude to produce patient narratives that reveal the gap.

Pat e-mails an ACUPS listerv friend about the abandonment she feels from one of her oncologists as her disease progresses:

> well, I've lost the function of my left hand. I'm left handed so it's very hard for me. I wrote another letter to dr g. I wasn't impressed that he didn't respond to the last letter. anyway, he said he's not going to intercede and that my oncologist seemed to have it under control … he did say he'd do an mri of the brain. would be a good thing now. I felt like just dumped me. he said he can't practice medicine over the phone, even though he's gotten every report.

The growing awareness of the need for palliative care and communication training among all physicians is represented through changes in medical school curricula (Ragan *et al.*, 2005). A survey of critically ill patients reveals important issues for these participants, including "being at peace with God," "feeling one's life is complete," "planning a funeral," and "freedom from pain." Physicians also surveyed for the study did not rank these same issues as important, leading the researchers to note that doctors need more communication training to teach them how to locate and discuss patients' values to truly provide the care needed (Steinhauser, *et al.*, 2000a).

Han and Arnold (2005) identify one likely cause that might often facilitate the abandonment of patients who move into palliative care modality. As primary care physicians or oncologists (or both) "sign off" medical cases (people dying of their illness) to palliative care physicians or teams, patients report experiencing abandonment owing to the failure of physicians to maintain relationships with patients who expected the relationships to continue or who were unaware their case was being "discontinued." This phenomenon, which occurs frequently in the United States, creates an environment of uncertainty and abandonment for patients and families (Han and Arnold, 2005). Two cases explored in the research reveal that primary doctors/oncologists withdrew their patients surreptitiously and unilaterally without prior discussion with patients or families. Han and Arnold report that the new and growing field of palliative medicine can actually enable and perpetuate patient/family abandonment by primary physicians by providing a place to "send" patients at the end of life. A fragmented system of care in which management of patients' problems is passed from one narrowly focused specialist to another might result in worse clinical outcomes. Important clinical tasks and considerations may end up falling through the cracks, and the lack of longitudinal involvement of individual clinicians might limit their understanding of patients' needs and values.

Research findings on "breaking bad news"

Even more prolific in the literature than medical prognosis are discussions and advice about how doctors should disclose bad news to their patients. One of the seminal works in the area of communicating bad news is Timothy Quill's (2000) article on initiating end-of-life discussions with seriously ill patients. Quill refers to the complexity of this challenging discourse with patients as "addressing the elephant in the room," acknowledging the collusion among patients, family members, and medical staff that develops in an attempt to avoid mentioning death or dying, even when the patient is obviously suffering and perhaps even when death is imminent. It is this silence surrounding a patient's death experience that palliative care specialist Dr. Diane Meier (2000) believes creates much of the loneliness and agony of death. Deploring this loneliness that our death-avoidant culture frequently imposes on the dying and believing that we all should have the opportunity to confront our own deaths, Meier requires her palliative medicine interns to read the novella by Leo Tolstoy, *The Death of Ivan Illych*, which depicts a patient forced to die in silence.

Quill's (2000) article is based both on observational research and on in-depth discussions with patients, family members, and physicians who each can contribute to the conversation on how to approach death and dying with an ill patient. Ironically, he explains that it is the very successes and advances in medicine in the last several decades that have contributed to patients' spending more time in dependent states of progressive debility (Faden and German, 1994; LaPuma and Lawlor, 1990), with almost 80 percent of U.S. residents dying in hospitals or long-term care facilities (Field and Cassel, 1997) rather than at home with their families and friends. Patients, who fear dying with unnecessary pain and suffering, had these fears partially warranted with the results of the 1995 SUPPORT study (discussed more fully in Chapter 1), which found that many patients do indeed die in moderate to severe pain.

Quill (2000) contends that "timely, sensitive discussions with seriously ill patients regarding medical, psychosocial, and spiritual issues at the end of life are both an obligation of and privilege for every physician" (p. 3) and that they may help shift treatment from curative to palliative care. He laments, however, that palliative care is generally offered too late in a patient's disease course for patients to fully benefit from it.

Whereas there is much literature on bad news delivery, Gillotti (2003) and others contend that it reveals "minimal theory development and little insight into the connection between bad news delivery and medical decisions" (p. 168). In other words, as Morrison and Meier (2004) and de Haes and Teunissen (2005) point out about communication in palliative care in general, not much research has explored what happens to patient treatment options and the like after bad medical news has been delivered. The paucity of such research has not squelched efforts to offer guidelines for the effective communication of bad news, however, and on the basis of results from investigations of the experiences and desires of both medical providers, patients, and their families in many medical contexts, such guidelines are widely incorporated into medical training (Rosenbaum *et al.*, 2004; Back *et al.*, 2003). Yet, as Eggly *et al.* (2006) report, "formal evaluation of the effectiveness of these guidelines has been primarily limited to self-reports by physicians or evaluations of simulated scenarios" (p. 2). For example, in a study of fifty physicians who had suffered serious illness, interview data suggested several techniques for improving communication with patients, including communicating directly about taboo topics and being more sensitive in discussing bad news. Such techniques might indeed improve the delivery of bad news, but the data in this study were limited to self-report. Even the doctor-patients questioned the degree to which empathy could be taught (Klitzman, 2006).

Eggly *et al.* (2006) further contend that the complexity of the setting of the delivery of bad news and the inherent difficulties in studying it may account for the lack of observational data to support the teaching of the communication guidelines in question. (These guidelines are reported in Ptacek and Eberhardt, 1996; Fallowfield and Jenkins, 2004; Baile *et al.*, 2000; and Girgis and Sanson-Fisher, 1995.) Note that the SPIKES model (Baile *et al.*, 2000) is critiqued from the patient's perspective in Chapter 3.

The guidelines include communication strategies for what is assumed to be three linear phases of bad news delivery: preparing to disclose the news; disclosing the news, and responding to reactions to the news (Eggly *et al.*, 2006). The strategies include (1) preparing for the difficult interaction by finding a comfortable and private setting and uninterrupted time; (2) using lay language, speaking in small chunks of information, adjusting their pace to the patient's and probing for patient understanding in the second phase; and (3) allowing for and responding to emotions, providing answers to questions, and concluding the interaction by summarizing and identifying next steps in the third phase. In addition, some guidelines also consider ethical and cross cultural concerns (Eggly *et al.*, 2006).

Von Gunten *et al.* (2000) offer a seven-step approach for physicians in acquiring competence in communication, decision making, and building relationships for competent patient care in end-of-life patient encounters. These guidelines, similar to those described above, can be used in breaking bad news, setting treatment goals, advance care planning, and the like. The authors note, "Effective application as part of core end-of-life care competencies is likely to improve patients' and families' experiences of care" (2000, Abstract). Beyond the guidelines, physicians offer one another such helpful advice as this: "To manage bad news well, the clinician must place his or her relationship with the patient, the strength and reality of their human bond, over the insecurity of disease, the threat of dissolution, and the fear of death" (Rabow and McPhee, 1999, p. 263).

Many of the current articles in medical journals that deal with how physicians can better handle the critical communication exigency of having to give bad news to patients apparently subscribe to the communication guidelines mentioned above without demanding more solid empirical evidence for their efficacy. Several researchers (e.g., Arnold and Koczwara, 2006) mention merely that the benefits of good communication skills for physicians are evidenced by studies that show, for example, that patients' satisfaction with their doctors' communication style increases their cancer-related self-efficacy and reduces their emotional stress (Zachariae *et al.*, 2003). Arnold and Koczwara go on to suggest that communication skills for breaking bad news can be acquired, most notably through experiential training, even though "the evidence for the efficacy of various strategies remains limited" (p. 2). Other researchers report the effectiveness of short courses designed to improve residents' communication skills at delivering bad news and eliciting patients' preferences for end-of-life care (Alexander *et al.*, 2006).

Though it is certain that physicians receive little to no medical school education in the communication skills needed for breaking bad news to their patients (von Guntenn *et al.*, 2001), it is far less certain that these skills are as effective as advocated since they have undergone scant empirical testing. Eggly *et al.* (2006), in a study of twenty-five video-recorded interactions between oncologists, patients, and their companions at two outpatient cancer clinics at two comprehensive cancer research centers, conclude from their analysis of these interactions that the current communication guidelines for the delivery of bad news bear rethinking. More specifically, they suggest that three of the assumptions commonly undergirding such guidelines may be oversimplified, that they may not reflect the intricacies and complexities of physician–patient interaction in the challenging context of delivering and receiving negative medical news. These three assumptions include (1) physicians can plan a bad news interaction, (2) bad news interactions focus on one central piece of information, and (3) bad news interactions consist of a physician–patient dyad.

Rather, their observations and analyses revealed that:

1   Information is defined as bad news by the recipient, not necessarily by the MD. Thus, doctors cannot always plan for disclosures that might be perceived negatively. The researchers thus argue:

> Rather than suggesting that physicians should anticipate and plan for bad news interactions, we suggest that physicians prepare for all interactions in which they will disclose any information, from the most momentous to the most trivial, by engaging in communication behaviors appropriate for delivering potentially stressful information. Current guidelines already suggest that physicians ensure adequate time and privacy, elicit patients' perspectives on the current medical situation and expectations for the visit, and tailor the information delivery process to the needs of the participants in the interaction. Existing guidelines for giving information should apply to all interactions in which information is delivered and discussed. This step should be the universal precaution of patient–physician communication.
>
> (Eggly *et al.*, 2006, pp. 3–4)

2   As interactions often involve numerous pieces of information given patients—details about diagnosis and staging, necessity for and consequences of further testing, various treatment options, adverse effects and logistical complexities of such treatment options, availability of clinical trials, and prognostic probabilities related to diagnosis and treatment of their disease—these researchers suggest that doctors prepare for delivering numerous bits of information in the "bad news" encounter rather than focusing on one central piece of news. Thus, the current guidelines—that physicians deliver information in lay language, speak in small chunks, adjust their pace to the patient's, and probe for patient comprehension—need adjustment so that this process is repeated for each piece of information given. Most important, relationships between pieces of information require clear explanation (Eggly *et al.*, 2006).

3   Because their observations revealed that "bad news" encounters rarely consisted of doctor and patient alone in that patients were accompanied by at least one companion, and as these companions asked significantly more questions than did the patients, the researchers suggest that guidelines for discussing bad news also "include strategies for facilitating effective interactions with multiple participants" (p. 5).

Thus, the researchers conclude that the delivery of bad news is far more complex than most communication guidelines have acknowledged. They urge that "future analyses of medical interactions and related guideline development should incorporate theoretical perspectives beyond the notions of linearity and causality, which currently predominate in the field of medicine" (p. 6). Further, as the interactions observed and analyzed were "nonlinear, unscripted, and highly complex," they advocate that the theoretical perspective of symbolic interactionism guide future development of communication guidelines for physicians in the context of bad news delivery. Such a perspective, aligned with the social constructivist view of health care discussed in Chapter 1, makes the assumption that meaning emerges from interaction and relationship, that preordained and predetermined behaviors and interpretation of behaviors can be misguided. Eggly *et al.* (2006) thus conclude, and we concur:

> From this perspective, we cannot plan for a bad news discussion before it occurs because its interpretation as bad and news results from the discussion. From this perspective, health care providers should not be trained to anticipate and engage in scripted encounters such as "the bad news encounter." Instead, communication training should provide physicians with the skills to adapt their behavior appropriately in response to the fluctuating informational and emotional needs of all participants during all stages of the interaction (p. 6).

We present the following algorithm in Figure 4.1 as a conceptual model for understanding Eggly *et al.* (2006) and propose our own recommendation.

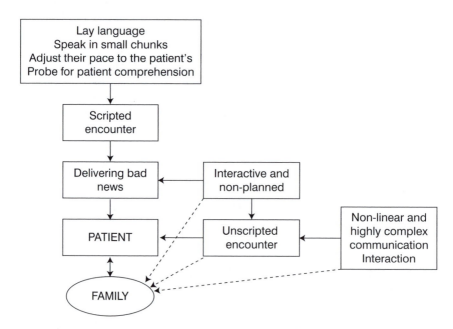

Figure 4.1 Recommended model for variables associated with breaking bad news.

One of the themes of this volume (as we outline in Chapter 1 and discuss under performance and dramaturgical theories) is that both doctors and patients have been socialized to adhere to "scripts" that prescribe their communication behaviors in health care settings, particularly in those challenging contexts in which they must inform or be informed about serious or terminal illness (or both). Eggly *et al.* (2006) suggest strongly to us that adaptive rather than scripted behaviors might better serve both parties in all medical encounters but most especially in those involving the communication of palliative care.

Challenges to the practice of palliative care: medical socialization, emotional turmoil, stress and burnout

Job-related stress, professional burnout, alcohol and substance abuse, and even suicide are legend in all walks of the medical profession (duPre, 2005), but emotional stressors are likely to be felt most intensely by those health care professionals who are on the front line in dealing with seriously ill and dying patients: oncologists and palliative care doctors. A 2001 article in the *Journal of the American Medical Association* by palliative care proponents Meier *et al.* entitled "The inner life of physicians and care of the seriously ill" delineates the emotional vulnerability of those physicians who care for very ill patients.

During the typically protracted course of a disease, patients' own emotional vulnerability and needs affect their physicians' emotions concurrently. These emotions "may reflect a need to rescue the patient, a sense of failure and frustration when the patient's illness progresses, feelings of powerlessness against illness and its associated losses, grief, fear of becoming ill oneself, or a desire to separate from and avoid patients to escape these feelings" (Meier *et al.*, 2001, Abstract). The authors contend that such feelings are problematic in that they may affect both the quality of patient care and the physician's sense of well-being in that "unexamined emotions may also lead to physician distress, disengagement, burnout, and poor judgment" (Meier *et al.*, 2001, Abstract). They propose that palliative care physicians—and others who care for seriously ill patients—become more self-aware, taking an active role in identifying, working with, and controlling the intense emotions that they experience.

Dosanhj *et al.* (2001) concur that physicians must take the time to process their own feelings when dealing with seriously ill patients—fears about delivering bad news to their patients prevented their full effectiveness in this context. Likewise, the lack of emotional support from other health care professionals and time constraints constituted significant barriers to physicians' efficacy in communicating with the seriously ill.

In a recent phenomenographic interview study conducted by Swedish medical caregivers, Friedrichsen and Milberg (2006) concluded that physicians who worked with the terminally ill suffered intense concerns about losing control when they were forced to communicate bad news to their dying patients. Breaking bad news to these patients involved a risk of losing control in several different ways, including emotions, oneself, confidence, professionalism, and patient trust. Though, as the authors attest, "nowhere in medicine is communication between the doctor and the patient more critical than in palliative care" (p. 674), apparently both doctors and patients frequently collude to avoid talking about difficult information (also see discussion of this phenomenon in Chapter 3 on the patient's perspective). Physicians acknowledge that patients with advanced or terminal disease want information about their prognoses and that such information is helpful to patients in decreasing their anxiety and giving them adequate preparation time for dying (Field and Copp, 1999), yet doctors also fear that discussing end-of-life issues will diminish or exterminate patients' hope (Curtis *et al.*, 2000).

In the interview study by Friedrichsen and Millberg (2006), physicians expressed fear of several types of loss of control when they had to deal with terminally ill patients. First, they believed that delivering messages that no one wants to hear went against the art of medicine and their entire medical socialization: "Having to exchange the role of healer for that of executor was difficult" (p. 676) and discussing death with a patient made them believe they had failed the patient and reminded them of their impotence in controlling their own death. Physicians experienced both fear and guilt in this role. As one expressed:

> I think that you feel inadequate. You want people to live and you have a strong desire to help them live. This is something that you have inside when you're a physician. But in this situation you feel like you've reached the end of the line with no way out. You're inadequate (p. 677).

In their analysis of the interview transcripts, Friedrichsen and Milberg (2006) further noted that many of the physicians' concerns were existential in nature:

> In palliative care, it is said that to be able to discuss existential matters a health care provider has to confront his/her own life and death concerns before being able to help others, because otherwise health care providers' own death anxiety will create fear and constitute an obstacle. However, the area of existentiality/ spirituality is not well studied in a medical context (p. 679).

The authors thus advocate that "theoretical education in existentiality/spirituality and clinical practice in a palliative context may help maintaining control" (p. 673).

It may be curious to communication researchers that both these groups of researchers (i.e., Friedrichsen and Milberg, 2006, and Meier *et al.*, 2001) are most concerned with physicians' experience of loss of control with their ill and dying patients. And yet medical socialization emphasizes "detached concern" (duPre, 2005) for patients such that physicians maintain professional distance from their patients. In the Friedrichsen and Milberg (2006) study, physicians stated that their maintaining control with their patients was essential to them; they feared the risk of losing objectivity and neutrality, showing one's own emotions, such as anger and sadness, losing trust in the patient's eyes when medical science could not cure, and losing the patient's perception of the doctor's medical competence, among others. Yet the Swedish doctors interviewed also feared loss of control of the trajectory of the conversation with dying patients who had to be informed that their curative treatments were being discontinued:

> You have to be 100% focused on this task … choice of words, eye contact … and create this environment so that when you deliver this message you know it will 'stick' and you have control … control over their reactions (p. 676).

> The problem, and what I think causes anxiety in these communications is that you don't know what will happen, what direction this dialogue will take (p. 676).

Once again, we are confronted with what Eggly *et al.* (2006) term the linearity of the scientific logic that has guided—and perhaps misguided—physicians in their desire to predict the pattern of doctor–patient discourse in the context of palliative care communication. Perhaps U.S. doctors are not as lock-step in this need as are their Swedish counterparts; nonetheless, the authors of this text suggest a theoretical perspective that goes beyond the concepts of linearity and causality that dominate science; if interactions between doctors and patients, particularly in the palliative care context, do not follow scripts, no party to the interaction logically can be said to "lose control." This does not mean, however, that doctors, given their socialization, don't face such fears in their interactions. It does mean, following the dictum of Eggly *et al.* (2006), that communication guidelines should encourage adaptive behavior on the part of palliative care physicians rather than prescribing particular behaviors that "cause" predictable responses in their patients.

How one physician practices palliative care communication: analysis of case studies

We thought it appropriate that this chapter should end with a discussion of how one of our authors, a palliative care board-certified academic physician, actually handles the difficult encounters with seriously ill and dying patients that she daily faces in her role as the director of the Palliative Care Program at the South Texas Veterans Health Care System. Accompanied by her interdisciplinary palliative care team, this physician evaluates very frail hospitalized patients on her daily rounds; frequently she is the physician who handles the tough mission of informing patients and families of their diagnosis and prognosis, advising them to talk candidly with their family members about their condition, and urging them to make the necessary medical decisions about advance directives, do-not-resuscitate (DNR) orders, and the like. In providing transcripts of her patient interactions (transcripts that were not literally transcribed but assembled through copious ethnographic field notes taken by one of the co-authors), we do not allege that such interactions with patients are typical in any respect. Never having seen transcripts from other palliative care physicians' patient encounters, we cannot make any claims of typicality with reliable accuracy. Rather, we present these excerpts to "test" the research findings presented in this chapter, to demonstrate how conversations with seriously ill and dying patients actually proceed and to present to the reader a prototypical ideal of how such interactions might best be handled. Though the communication strategies of our palliative care team in handling patient interactions have not been empirically linked to patient/family member satisfaction or other positive outcomes (such research has not yet been conducted at this hospital), we nonetheless believe that these interactions manifest one approach to palliative care interactions that is worthy of emulation. In fact, the transcripts that follow conform closely to a suggested example Christakis (2001) reports when he asks a colleague experienced in caring for the terminally ill to discuss how he thinks prognoses should be communicated ideally:

> Most patients with disease like yours live about three months, even with treatment, though I have seen exceptions. However, I can promise you that I will not abandon you. There is much that I can do for you, even if we are powerless to stop your disease. I am confident that we can respect your wishes as to how you want to live the rest of your life and that we can make sure that you do not have pain or other worrisome symptoms. Is there something more I can tell you about your condition?
>
> (Christakis, 2001, p. 199)

Our physician, unlike the physician in the above example, enlists and promises the expertise and competencies of her entire palliative care team (including nurses, psychologists, social workers, chaplains, and communication experts, among others) in her patient interactions, but more similarly to the physician cited above, her patient interactions reveal these promises to the patient (some more implicit than others):

- Your disease is advanced and incurable; you need to be making preparations for your death (including talking to your family, planning for end of life with advance directives, do not resuscitate (DNR) orders, etc.)
- Although we cannot cure your disease, we can treat your pain and other symptoms
- We can treat not only your physical pain but all your sources of pain (physical, spiritual, psychological, social)
- We can provide the kind of care that enables you to choose the way you wish to die (e.g., advance directive and DNR orders, dying at home vs. at the hospital)
- We will not abandon you as you confront your death.

One can note from the above listing, however, that along with employing a team approach, our physician's patient interactions deviate from the doctor's advice cited above in two additional ways: (1) She emphasizes that patients may be feeling other than physical pain—and that their possible depression, alienation from family, spiritual angst, and the like—can also be addressed by the specialists on the palliative care team, at the patient's request, and (2) she rarely accompanies her prognoses with statements that inform patients of exactly how much time they have remaining. The time line question, however, does come up, and this physician thinks it is fair to define intervals of time with indirection, stressing instead that patients and families should take full advantage of the time remaining, as in the following case:

MD: Your disease is very advanced, sir.

PATIENT: Can you give me a time line?

MD: I'm reluctant to, but probably weeks to months. This time is very valuable, it is a gift that you and your family are given. Tell everyone your wishes and use it to get your affairs in order. Please let us know if there is anything you need—anything. Would you like us to explain this to your son? Would that be helpful?

PATIENT: Yes, I've talked to him but I'd like a second person.

An inspection of several patient interactions reveals a pattern consistent with the features enumerated above. In the following interaction, our physician and her palliative care team enter a patient's room. He is a fifty-four-year-old man with diagnosed metastatic lung cancer and is undergoing palliative chemotherapy. His main symptom is shortness of breath. Our physician has explained to the palliative care team that his shortness of breath is one of his worst symptoms because it's not controllable; however, a room fan could stimulate his respiratory system, whereas oxygen has only a placebo effect in that it makes the mouth dry and can cause nose bleeding. She further tells the team that in the case of patients with shortness of breath, the family needs to be advised that their deaths are often accompanied by a loud death rattle—not uncomfortable for the patient but most distressing for the family if they haven't been told to anticipate it.

MD: How are you feeling today?

PATIENT: Okay, okay.

[Small talk ensues as the team enters the patient's room in protective gowns. He has an oxygen mask over his mouth and is sitting in a chair next to his bed. The doctor sits on his bed next to him with the team standing around him.]

MD: What have they told you about your chemo?

PATIENT: One doctor said stop everything—another said just one more round.

MD: You are willing to try chemo just to decrease the size of the cancer but not to cure the cancer.

PATIENT: Well, yes, I want to stay here.

[Talk continues about placement options; if he has more chemotherapy, he is guaranteed to stay at the VA Hospital; if not, it's possible he'll be moved to a veteran's center in a nearby town. The patient then asks how long he has to live.]

MD: I'm not sure how much time you have. But it's up to you about chemo.

[Patient then explains that he doesn't want to go to another town because it will be a burden on his family. The doctor tells him that his shortness of breath will get more pronounced.]

MD: Can your family bring in a fan? That will really help.

PATIENT: Yeah, yeah.

[The doctor then asks the patient if he is DNR and the patient explains that he never wants to be on a machine. The doctor tells him that the social worker will come see him in the afternoon to complete power of attorney paperwork.]

MD Okay, now we are going to talk about things that people don't like to talk about. The illness will take its course and you will die and pass away. It's time to think about unfinished business, see people you need to see and to say whatever you wish to say to your loved ones. We do not know for how long your mind will be clear, you know.

PATIENT: Yes. [pause] When I die will I be struggling for air? I won't want my wife to see me suffer. I want to die like my dad. [Patient tells story of watching his father die peacefully.]

MD: You will not struggle; you will be sedated at that point.

[During this discussion, some members of the palliative care team are fighting back tears.]

MD: There are five things I tell my patients to say to everyone in their last day of their lives. Please forgive me; I forgive you; I love you; I will miss you; Goodbye.

PATIENT: I'm not scared. I'm not scared. [begins to wipe at his tears]

MD: You have taught the team many things today, Mr. _____. The team is here to learn. What else would you like to teach them?

PATIENT: Live life. No, really, I'm not scared.

In the interaction above, the patient receives many explicit messages from our physician and implicit messages from the presence of her palliative care team: his chemotherapy is palliative, not curative; he can choose whether to remain on chemo or possibly be transferred to another VA facility; his shortness of breath will increase yet can be partially alleviated by a room fan and medications; he will not die struggling to breathe; yet he *will* die and thus needs to make provisions for DNR, power of attorney, and the like, in addition to saying goodbyes to his loved ones—and, perhaps, giving them the five messages. There are also numbers of meta-messages in the scene, messages that characterize all other communication and provide an all-encompassing psychological frame for the interaction which assists the patient in interpreting the meaning of the interaction (Goffman, 1974). For example, the mere presence of the palliative care team and the physician's promising the patient a visit from the social worker tells the patient that he is not being treated solely for physical pain and physiological symptoms; rather, his social and psychological pain are also being addressed. Further, the team provides tangible evidence that the patient will not be abandoned during his journey toward death. The interaction is also patient-centered in that the physician recognizes the man's right to be fully informed of his medical situation and asks the patient probing questions to ascertain the extent of his knowledge; this is obviously a physician who believes in full disclosure, yet note that she does not give the patient a projected time line for the course of his disease, even though he asks for this. Rather, she focuses on giving him hope for comfort, and in acknowledging the importance of these last moments, and in giving the patient a role that perhaps he or she never thought of—to be a teacher to families, other patients and, most important, medical teams.

Our physician also encourages patient disclosure by announcing, "Now we are going to talk about things that people don't like to talk about" and proceeding with advice about his impending death: "It's time to make amends ... to say your last goodbyes." Though such advice might sound paternalistic to some, the accompanying nonverbal behaviors are gentle and inviting, and the patient's response suggests that the physician's direct confrontation of his imminent death opens up another topic that needs airing for the patient: how he will die (with his stated preference for not having to struggle for air so that his wife will have to see him suffer, to which the doctor responds with a reassuring pledge that he will not). The patient also offers a narrative account of his father's peaceful death at this point in the interaction, this story perhaps also invited by the doctor's candid appraisal of his condition and her encouraging the patient to anticipate his death.

Typical of our physician's interaction style with her patients is her final question to the patient in which she further beckons him to be a full participant in this dramatic life–death discussion and the ensuing decisions surrounding his dying: she implicitly thanks him for teaching the palliative care team "many things today" and invites him to share anything else he would like to teach them. In this way, the patient is permitted to feel that his dying has meaning, not only for himself and his loved ones but for a team of professionals who are learning how best to treat the dying. Even though critically ill and imminently facing death, this patient's life and his lessons have value for others. Surely this is one of the most important gifts a palliative care team imparts to the dying.

Of course, some patient interactions challenge our palliative care team more than others. In the following case, the team is dealing with a seventy-three-year-old man who has had two brain tumors and a stroke (the reader should note that this is the same case presented in Chapter 3 to illustrate a critique of the SPIKES model from a patient's perspective). The patient currently refuses more chemotherapy though his brain tumors are incurable. The team meeting reveals that the patient is a good candidate for rehabilitation, with hospice care at home after approximately three weeks of rehabilitation. All members of the team realize that his cancer is terminal when they go to his hospital room to visit him. After introductions are made and a brief mental state examination is given to assess his cognitive capacity, this conversation ensues:

MD: So why are you in the hospital?

PATIENT: I have a brain tumor.

MD: What's going to happen?

PATIENT: Well, it sounds like to me a twice failed attempt to remove it [he briefly discusses two prior surgeries]. This distress is creating like headaches that I have because I'm thinking and I shouldn't be …

MD: What's gonna happen to you?

PATIENT: I believe I'm going to come out of this as well as normal because I believe this because I have never stayed …

MD: What did they tell you about the tumor?

PATIENT: Similar comments from the doctor. It seems I'm going to come out of this.

MD: But the tumor is not going to go away, and you don't want chemo.

PATIENT: But during the last operation they put a chemo disk in my brain to reduce the size of the tumor.

MD: Yes, but the tumor will not go away, sir. Your doctors asked me to come to see if you can do rehab … [at this point, the patient stirs in his bed and is mumbling]

MD: The tumor is not going to go away.

PATIENT: If you can monitor the tumor—

MD: Yes, but the tumor will not go away.

PATIENT: The treatment I am receiving now, whatever prognosis you can come up with, but I don't know one way or the other the best treatment.

MD: We can give you treatment but we cannot cure you, but we want to take care of your headaches.

In the case of this patient, he appears reluctant to believe that his tumor is incurable, despite the doctor's repeated, bold assertions that the "tumor will not go away." One might find these assertions blunt in their "broken record" redundancy, yet our physician obviously believes that one of her goals in delivering palliative care is to ensure that the patient has valid information about his prognosis. An interesting conversational strategy occurs at the point at which she asks the patient, "What did they [his doctors] tell you about the tumor?" She learns from the patient that her fellow doctors did not, in fact, disclose to this patient everything about his medical situation, yet she avoids impugning their professional credibility, opting instead to deliver the message that "the tumor is not going to go away" four more times in her next several utterances. And after a lengthy pause after her promise to "take care of your headaches," our physician then reconfirms the patient's understanding by asking, "Do you know what I'm saying, sir?" to which he responds with, "Yes, I know what you are saying."

Now that the patient has apparently understood that his tumors are incurable (and, presumably, that without additional chemotherapy, his death is near), our doctor can then broach the topic of hospice with him. During this exchange about what services hospice will provide for him and his wife at their home, the doctor responds to the fact that the patient's mouth is very dry by offering him some juice to drink. At this point in the interaction, the patient breaks down and sobs:

MD: How can we help you? [she reaches over and touches his shoulder when talking]

PATIENT: I have a headache.

MD: We are going to help you [she turns to an MD fellow and instructs him to "please go ask the team to get something right now."] I think your family loves you and they want to be with you. I think that's wonderful. What do you think?

PATIENT: [continues to cry]

MD: [begins to discuss advance directives and power of attorney with the patient]

Thus, in the course of this conversation, our physician and the team have influenced the transformation of the patient's belief from "I'm going to come out of this as well as normal" to a frank discussion of his wishes for the end of his life. Further, she has reassured the patient that, despite not being able to offer a cure for his tumors, she nonetheless can help ease the pain of his headaches. Later in the conversation, our physician offers help for the patient's potential emotional suffering in talking to his family about his end of life wishes (i.e., that he doesn't want to be kept alive on machines):

MD: Does your family know this?

PATIENT: I haven't told them. I think my wife understands.

MD: It would be a huge gift if you could tell her. She needs to know. Do you have any spiritual beliefs?

PATIENT: Well that's a hard thing for me to ... it's hard for me to transmit.

MD: Would you like to talk about that?

PATIENT: [continues to cry]

MD: Are you okay? What are you thinking?

PATIENT: I will talk to my wife. I know that I can because I know from ...

MD: You don't have to do it alone. Would you like someone here with you? We have a chaplain. Would you like her to be here with you when you talk to your wife?

PATIENT: Yes.

MD: You have a wonderful gift. You have time to make peace with everyone. Are you okay?

PATIENT: I'm almost to the point of release.

MD: Where?

PATIENT: My emotions.

MD: Is that a good thing?

PATIENT: I hope it is. I don't mean it to sound like a bad thing.

MD Would you like [names the chaplain] to stay with you?

PATIENT: [nods yes]

After the palliative care team leaves the hospital room, except for the chaplain who stays with the patient, the doctor explains to the team that patients can experience four types of pain: physical, psychological, social, and spiritual. During this patient visit and many others that we witnessed, the doctor addressed all four types, even proactively initiating the possibility that the patient was suffering from an as yet unnamed type of pain: "Does your family know this?" and "Do you have any spiritual beliefs?" Later, in a team discussion, our physician tells the team, "Pain is defined by whatever the patient is telling you. How is his pain?" She thus encourages her fellows and the palliative care team to believe a patient's assessment of his or her own pain.

A last word about the interactions among our physician, her palliative care team, and the patients to whom they regularly break bad news; transcripts of these interactions do manifest several of the complexities that Eggly *et al.* (2006) discuss in their recommendation for new communication guidelines for physicians who must give patients (potentially) less than desirable medical news. First of all, we note that it is difficult to ascertain from a patient's verbal responses (and perhaps even from his or her nonverbal reactions) whether the so-called bad news from the physician is actually perceived as bad news by the patient. Curiously, in fact, patients may display nonverbal indicators of having gotten bad news (e.g., crying) when the discussion turns to matters other than the medical prognosis itself, for example, when the doctor tells a patient the (relatively) good news that he will not struggle for breath when he dies but will be sedated. Without consulting the patient, it would be difficult to ascertain which particular chunks of information given by the physician are seen as bad news. Perhaps our physician's insistence that her patients become fully aware of the seriousness of their condition (e.g., "the tumor will not go away") could actually be perceived by some patients as news that removes uncertainty for them when their other physicians (oncologists and surgeons) have not confronted it and, as such, as news that permits them to face their futures realistically.

Moreover, these interactions suggest the validity of findings by Eggly *et al.* (2006) that many bits of information are exchanged in an alleged bad news visit; in the case of our palliative care team, the patient's medical situation is discussed as is her possible emotional, social (family), and spiritual suffering. Many agendas are concurrently at work in the hospital rounds. Also, many patient visits occur both with family members and other companions of the patient present and with several members of the palliative care team. Breaking bad news in this setting is hardly a private affair between doctor and patient; many of the traditional communication guidelines for maintaining patients' privacy during such a conversation appear outmoded. Thus, the ethnographic field notes and transcripts that form the data set for this book suggest that recommendations by Eggly *et al.* (2006) require additional scrutiny by oncologists and palliative care physicians who must often be the bearers of potentially bad medical news. We believe their dictum—that communication training should give physicians adaptive skills so that they can respond appropriately to all participants' needs during all stages of the interaction, rather than a set of communication do's and don'ts for breaking bad news—may be groundbreaking.

As we have discussed throughout this chapter, one of the forces that gravitates against physicians' actively choosing and implementing palliative medicine is their medical socialization —both in medical school and in their subsequent practice of medicine—that advocates so strenuously in favor of curing a patient and saving/prolonging his or her life.

Despite its introduction into medical education in the 1960s, palliative care has yet to be a required course in American medical education. As a result, courses in palliative and end-of-life care vary among medical schools, with students receiving anywhere from one or two lectures to fourteen hours of instruction; therefore, only few medical students receive palliative care training. A critical part of these curricula includes end-of-life communication skills. Recent studies have suggested that even if students have the opportunity of exposure to palliative care, they do not take end-of-life communication skills training seriously. However, end-of-life care curriculum interventions have resulted in an increase in empowering message strategies in important palliative care communication issues such as breaking bad news (Sanchez-Reilly *et al.*, 2007).

One of our doctor's goals is to train physicians in the philosophy and practice of palliative care. Training and fellowship programs have steadily grown over the last several years, producing palliative care specialists with expertise in dealing with symptoms, end-of-life communication difficulties, and interdisciplinary care for frail and dying patients and their families. Few interdisciplinary palliative care fellowship programs that exist in the United States train physicians and non-physicians to become palliative care experts. Fieldwork shared in this book manifests the results of one of these programs.

Palliative care is a sub-specialty in the field of medicine that transforms a physician's predilection toward curing a patient to one of comforting patient and family. As one of the palliative medicine fellows in a post-fellowship interview for this fellowship program explained when asked why he became involved in the palliative medicine fellowship:

> The most frustrating thing to me is to come to a patient when I don't have any type of solution … to come to a patient and say: "you know, I am unable to help you, there is nothing I can do." Because one of your roles is problem solving and the patient will really look after you to help them with the problem, that's why they come to you in the first place. So to me it's really frustrating when somebody comes and says, "'you know, doc, I have this problem" and I

say, "well, I'm sorry, there's nothing I can do, that's it." You know. It's kind of you saying, "I failed, I'm sorry."

From these interview data, it appears that the palliative medicine fellowship serves as a sort of antidote to this physician's dilemma of having no solution, no cure for many patient problems, particularly those involving serious advanced or terminal disease (or both). This same physician later states:

> When I started to get more interested in hospice and palliative care and started reading more about it, the whole idea is saying, "well this is not the end, this is still something I can offer." Then, then I found the answer that I was searching for. Which is, you know, I'm able to say, "well, it's no cure, but this is what I can offer."

This doctor also emphasizes the importance of communication skills that he honed during his palliative medicine fellowship, of taking the necessary time to really listen to patients in pain rather than quickly dispensing pain medication that might not address the problem.

He further notes that compassion is the attribute that is most needed for dealing with patients:

> I think if you have to just say one word, I would have to say compassion. If you do that, you would take care of, you would try to take care of every single aspect of patient care. And in medical school they teach you to be knowledgeable, but compassion you will have to develop and work at it.

When later asked by the researcher what advice this intern would give the next fellow in the palliative medicine fellowship program, he responded,

> First to make sure that this is what he wants. And second is to put his heart and his mind into it. Because you will walk home sad many days for what you see. But also you will have some days that you walk, you can walk home really with a chest full of, you know, gratitude for what you're doing. A beautiful death is probably as good as when you have a difficult case, somebody dying, and you take it to the OR and save that person's life.

5   The family/caregiver perspective

We just continue to move on with a positive attitude. We never really considered that Sam would die when he had Melanoma in eighty-one: that was never really part of the deal. Umm it was just he was gonna get better there was no question and I think that pretty much is our attitude this time too. Realistically not, but we just continue to function under the assumption that we'll keep going.

[Vera, on caring for Sam, stage 4 prostate cancer]

Both patients and their families are the unit of care in palliative medicine. This chapter describes the reciprocal connection between patient and family that is specific to terminal illness. Palliative medicine values the precious and painful experience of dying that is central to the unit of patient and family; this chapter seeks to identify areas of palliative care communication from the family/caregiver perspective that require awareness and improvement.

Bereaved family members are tapped as participants for studies that assess retrospective experiences of the patient concerning pain and anxiety before death. There is an entire body of literature that sets out to examine the validity of these studies by asking, "Can we trust the feelings and ideas of family members about their dying relative after death?" For our goals in this volume, we believe this point is unimportant. What is important is the inclusion of the family as central to palliative care and their ideas about the patient during the end-of-life experience. The fact that family shares in the journey of anxiety, depression, distress, fear, loss of social connections, loss of activities, loss of career—these are phenomena that require our consideration from a communication perspective. Family is now understood to be central to the research of palliative care. This chapter provides a portal into family interpretations of communication success and failure throughout the intense period near the end of life and the bereavement that follows. The pages ahead include stories of families varied across illness contexts and settings; we employ common participant profiles from Chapter 3.

Reception of a diagnosis/prognosis

> Hello Everyone, this is a very helpful and inspirational website [ACUPS (adenocarcinoma of unknown primary site) Listerv]! My mother was just diagnosed with Adenocarcinoma of Unknown Primary Site after finding an enlarged lymph node under her arm. Biopsy revealed a poorly differentiated adenocarcinoma and they have not found a tumor anywhere in her body except in other lymph nodes in her groin, the base of her neck and near her abdomen. She is only 62 and in perfect health (other than the cancer). The oncologist seems to want to take all hope from us, telling her he only gives her a 6 month average. Maybe I am in denial, but I feel like we caught this early, and that her health and youth should give us the best chance for the taxol/carboplatinum treatment to work. We are also trying to get her a second opinion from Fox Chase Cancer Center. Am I wrong in trying to keep her thinking positive? I am trying to remind her that all is not lost yet. I guess I need someone to tell me I am not completely out of touch with reality?
>
> Thanks, Marla.

Diagnosis response among family members is as varied as the dynamics in any family. Some family, or sometimes close friends, emerge as the primary caretakers and patient advocates. In the foregoing listerv posting, Marla, a daughter-in-law, is emerging as a primary caregiver in her family system, at least initially and through her publicly shared narrative. She is struggling to integrate the news of a deathly diagnosis in light of the life-filled presence of her mother-in-law. The family caregiver likely possesses knowledge of a patient that is unique. Family is often privy to a patient's motives and passions in the course of an illness. Other than the patient, family is most immediately affected by a terminal diagnosis: Their system is altered and will continue to radically evolve as the pressures of suffering bear down.

Marla is not alone in her need for caregiver information. The listserv she calls on has a small but active membership that busily rallies around any request for assistance. Many caregivers want direct diagnosis information about their loved one, time to process the information with their loved one, a reception of emotion by the physician, and inclusion in and integration of the decision making with the physician in the process of the illness (Ambuel and Mazzone, 2001).

Family communication in the physician office and in the home environment is infrequently studied but ripe for investigation, as we need to know how the family talks together and makes decisions about proceeding when faced with a life threatening illness. Wayne Beach (2002) shares his own family's story of assimilating bad cancer news; in his conversation analytic work of an inadvertently recorded telephone conversation, he notes that as family he and his father repeatedly present the polar "bright side" version of his mom's terrifying health situation (a malignant tumor). This bright side might be the salve needed so badly by a family in their moment of great collective terror. Marla also calls out for the bright side to be shared in her listerv posting.

Shaping decisions and collaborating about treatment

Hal has emerged as the primary caregiver for his brother Ted, with recently diagnosed ACUPS. Leaving his job and friends, Hal moves to another part of the country to care for his brother. In the following e-mail excerpt to coworkers and friends, he describes the process of finding medical treatment for Ted:

> The small town doctor and staff might show and demonstrate a greater care toward a patient, but lack the technique and specialty to deal with oddity. The giant comprehensive cancer machine is so compartmentalized that you are a number to the various departments (genitourinary, gastrointestinal, head and neck). They are harsh half the time. It is almost like the fact that everyone around there is suffering gravely makes them even more harsh—those stakes higher … but, their expertise can be found few other places in such force. So this is the exchange. The end result is that the family becomes the shepard [sic] to the patient—despite the path that is chosen.

Treatment and care often are collaborative decisions shared among patient, family, and medical staff. Often patients are not included in the decisions if their physical condition has deteriorated substantially. Social factors, treatment intrusiveness, family goals, finances, and patient beliefs all contribute to the choices a family makes concerning care when facing a serious illness.

For both patient and family, primary direction about treatment is provided by the physician—the interpreter of the disease—the purveyor of prognostication. For many families, pressing their loved one to pursue treatment is a way to work against the destruction of the disease and feel a sense of medical control.

Family is never more involved in the decisions about treatment care than when the patient is a child. Wolfe *et al.* (2000) researched parental understanding of their children's prognosis and the impact this had on treatment decisions. These authors note that children dying from cancer progression or treatment complication suffer fully inadequate palliation in the last month of life; they predicted that some barriers to palliative care include unrealistic physician and parental goals that lead to inappropriate treatment plans. There is an established trend for families with adult cancer patients to overestimate survival probabilities and opt for aggressive therapies (Weeks *et al.*, 1998); parental grief might even further suppress physician communication about a child's prognosis that would likely lead to aggressive treatment. Wolfe *et al.* (2000) found that at the time of diagnosis, 43 percent of physicians and 56 percent of parents believed a cure was likely for these children. The first recognition for parents that their child would not be cured was 150 days prior to death, and for physicians 330 days prior to death. An explicit documented communication for parents and family that there would be no cure lingered an extra three months plus behind the understanding of the physician (Wolfe *et al.*, 2000). These three months of time and resources spent treating a body with aggressive therapy could be redirected palliatively; the family and the physician could communicate and align palliative goals for the child to lessen suffering during these remaining months of life and live for quality rather than extension. In a related study of the same population, pain and fatigue were overwhelming symptoms that received little alleviation until death, according to the parents (Wolfe *et al.*, 2000). More than one-half of these children ultimately died in the hospital intensive care unit.

An additional pressure that might further pull families in the direction of aggressive therapy when it will not have a curative or even palliative effect is reimbursement. In 2001, chemotherapy was responsible for 50 percent of the profit in private practice. A very different medical service is the family meeting; this is a conference in which several health personnel and non-health personnel staff caring for a patient meet with a family to talk about the status of that person and the best course of treatment in light of the collective ideas of the group. The current Medicare and Medicaid actual reimbursement for the Family Conference, taking up to one hour, is zero dollars (Smith *et al.*, 2001). The monetary reward for medical facilities rests in administering something other than communication.

Communication with physician

Families report feeling disregarded and perplexed when their care preferences are not taken into account. Both patients and families value physician communication in palliative and end-of-life decisions and consider this a key component in a death that includes the best care and planning possible (Steinhauser *et al.*, 2000b).

Jo is married to Selie, survivor of MS and type I diabetes. Jo is a life-long member of the academy, a father, and a grandfather. Here he describes the communication dynamics he experiences in the examination room with Selie and the physician:

> I'm most welcome in the conference room when I keep my silence.
> Oh sometimes I speak directly to the doctor but frequently I speak to you [to Selie] reminding you of what of what you haven't said if we've talked about it on the way or in preparing for the meeting or reminding you of another example or instance that you're sharing about your health. There have been hard times when I've talked to Dr. Mobol. I get the feeling that-that when a doctor is meeting with a patient that they don't like third parties, spouses or whomever speaking up unless there's a really good reason and so most of the time I'm-I'm there. And I think my presence makes a difference in the way the doctor acts and they way you feel. But I-I don't say a lot in those sessions.

To serve as primary caretaker and feel welcome only in silence might create a high level of dissatisfaction for some family members. Medical professionals are the family's community of high contact in the end-stage of life. Caregiving and decision making will be further distressing and isolating if caregivers are ostracized by the physician providing medical advice and care for their loved one. The health community is central to a good illness and death journey. To improve the family's quality of life in this time of great difficulty, Hauser and Kramer (2004) suggest the following interventions.

> Rather than make assumptions, health care professionals need to listen to caregivers to determine what kinds of information would be most beneficial to them. Caregivers may need information related to (1) the illness and the needs of the care recipient (e.g., information to better understand symptoms of impending death, resources for the patient), (2) caregiver burden and practical strategies for support or respite, or (3) grief and loss associated with caregiving and support for the grief process (pp. 679–80).

Locating or reframing hope

From the ACUPS listserv, Clem posts a note of hope and time about his spouse-care receiver. Their hope is grounded firmly in the extension of life; living longer is a theme that is dominant in the literature investigating treatment selection on the part of patients and families:

> Deb appears today—two years [to the month] after her diagnosis—as vibrant and healthy as ever, giving some allowances of course to chemo fatigue, etc. Her strain of ACUP is "poorly differentiated"—not an especially good catch—and one which has complicated efforts (I am told) to nail down a primary because the cell tissues analyzed have dissipated "into mush," as one pathologist colorfully put it. In fact, they can't make heads or tails out of the tissue samples with respect to revealing an origin.
>
> But you know as long as we stay ahead of this—if we can—I don't really obsess over locating a primary as the darn thing (if it is still around) certainly seems to behave itself. Now, will it remain "indolent" forever? Probably not, and of course we still have to deal with at least one liver tumor. So that said, Deb and I will seize upon the outside window of "twenty years" and scramble for more.
>
> Anyone else got any thoughts on longevity, post-diagnosis? Odds sure seem better than they used to be … At least that's my strong sense … Clem.

Clem's narrative is rooted in what Groopman (2005) refers to as the paradox of uncertainty. There are no promises or strong evidences that there is a cure or good treatment to solve this illness; at the same time, there is a chance that this absence of assuredness provides a reason for hope—a chance that the outcome will be different and better. "Since the time of the ancient Greeks, hope has been considered vital to us as human beings. It is an elevating, energizing feeling that comes from seeing, in the mind's eye, a path to a better future" (Groopman, 2005, p. 3152). Quickly progressing and especially pernicious cancers can swiftly dim the future for a patient and family. Groopman (2005) believes that there is still hope when physical improvement is not a possibility, when clinical therapies should cease. Shifting focus from the body to the soul is a relocation of hope in the final phase of life for patient and family. Time near the end of life can be hopeful as relationships are repaired, family is cared for deeply, and collective unreconciled issues are addressed by family and patient. This is the hope that extends far beyond a "good death." Clem and many other ACUPS listerv members do not include ideas of hope that move beyond a focus on the physical.

Hope is a factor identified among caregivers that might account for those who are managing well with the crushing weight of chronic stress, severe fatigue, sleep deprivation, emotional distress, isolation, and unrelenting caregiving burdens (Herth, 1993). In mental health and health care literature, hope is described as a mitigator to stress. More recent studies exploring the notion of reciprocal stress and relief between caregivers and care receivers also inform a discussion of hope.

In a unique research piece exploring caregiver hope, Herth (1993) interviews caregivers at three collection points in the trajectory of their loved one's illness: (T1) within the first two weeks of admission to hospice, (T2) when the care recipient began to experience severe disability, and (T3) when death is projected to occur within two weeks. During the (T1) collection, family, friends, health care professionals, and God were identified as the primary sources of hope. By the (T3) collection, only health care professionals and God continued to be perceived as high levels of support offering hope. The three collection points reveal a chronology of hope for the caregiver who eventually comes to rely heavily on health professionals as a primary source of hope as their loved one approaches death.

Herth also identifies caregiver hope responses and groups them into the following categories: sustaining relationships, cognitive reframing, time refocusing, attainable expectations, spiritual beliefs, and uplifting energy (productive distractions). Hope-hindering categories include isolation, concurrent losses, and poorly controlled management of symptoms. These hindering categories have also been found as threats to hope in studies of terminal patients (Miller, 1989; Herth, 1990).

Clayton *et al.* (2005) find that family caregivers identify hope as (1) good care for their loved one and (2) pain and symptom control. A message from a caregiver on the ACUPS listerv resonates with this research. Jane describes how her husband's hope propelled her caregiving strength through their most difficult times of suffering. Jane's knowledge of his possession of hope enabled her to continue forward in the role of caregiver, despite her own suffering:

> My husband Jim died 15 months ago. What you describe is very similar to what we experienced; both the living and the dying. Jim's cancer went to his brain in the end too, but the radiation that destroyed the cancer in his brain was certain death as he had already had 22 treatments of radiation on a neck tumor 2½ years earlier. No one can live long or well with that much radiation.
>
> My husband never regretted the treatments and never lost hope, either. Everyday he would tell me, "life is good."

Looking back, I think that we were able to make almost everyday a good day because we had hope. His hope was stronger than mine at first, but my hope grew over time with his encouragement. He was a positive thinker.

I do believe that hope is what matters the most when you get bad news and you can't count on anything else. At times it was all I had.

Without hope and positive thinking, I would have checked out emotionally after Jim's initial diagnosis and poor prognosis. I learned about the value of hope from him during this challenging experience.

We must remember that some people have lived 20 years with ACUP, and life can and does continue for many years after a diagnosis of ACUP. Do not give up hope. Hope is a good thing ... Jane.

Reciprocal suffering: caregiver burden and anxiety

These are Jo's [of Jo and Selie] tape-recorded thoughts on the shared burden of caregiving and care receiving:

> I don't see caregiving and care receiving as a one way thing in this relationship at all. I don't see caregiving and receiving as directly related just to one or two illnesses; it's also how I feel about my day at the office or my relationship with this person or that person that I need to process with you [speaking to Selie] or an experience that you've had that you need to process with me. And so th-these roles switch back and forth.

Medical care and non–medical health professionals are embracing the idea that family caregivers are in essence "second-order" patients also requiring support and palliative care. Research performed in the last two decades recognizes the "intimate reciprocity of suffering by patients and families experiencing terminal illness" (Sherman, 1998, pp. 357–8). The caregiver and care receiver intertwine in a journey of pain, distress, loss, suffering, and intimacy like no other. For each party, there is the intrapersonal concern of coping with the suffering of self and the interpersonal concern of coping with the suffering of the other (Ferrell, 1996). Both the patient and the family caregiver share the odd duality of living with and dying of an illness; both wrangle with the desire to live as a functional member of the human race while also experiencing a desire to end the suffering of the illness.

The rewards of caring for a terminally ill relative can simultaneously produce profound psychological effects, increase anxiety and depression, cause deterioration in other relationships, and suppress professional roles and involvement in personally fulfilling and healthy activities (Higginson, 1998). Reducing caregiver mortality and morbidity is positively correlated with a reduction in the physical and emotional hardships consonant with caregiver burden (Hauser and Kramer, 2004).

As a patient's physical pain, suffering, and existential distress increase, so does the family's as they compensate to meet the formidable needs of their loved one. Hauser and Kramer (2004) find that the primary caregiver is most often a spouse

(70 percent), followed by a child (20 percent) or friends and more distant relatives (10 percent). More than 70 percent of caregivers are women, in most samples (Kramer *et al.*, 2006). Male caregivers report higher stress and more isolation than do women caregivers and as such are at higher risk for depression and other mental and physical distress.

Quality of life

Vera records her thoughts about caregiver quality of life in light of Sam's prostate cancer:

> I have come to understand now that I went into a grieving cycle with this because the initial prognosis that we found was eighteen to thirty-six months. And we anticipated the digression of quality of life very quickly, which virtually has not happened … but we wanted to do what we wanted to do now because you didn't know how long you had. But having this happen I was very angry, and as part of my process, grieving or adjustment or whatever to Sam's diagnosis, I carried a level of anger that actually impacted me at work. I-I became very abrupt and um very intolerant of stupidity. Which working for the Federal Government you're surrounded by stupidity and um it actually did affect my job performance.

McMillan and Mahon (1994) conceptualize quality of life to include four primary considerations: physical, psychological, social, and financial wellness. In their study of hospice family caregivers, they found a positive correlation between caregiver depression and difficulty with finances, family supportiveness, health problems, and lack of time in a daily schedule. "The terminal illness of an immediate family member often leads to the postponement or cancellation of educational plans, life events such as marriage, or career goals" (Sherman, 1998, p. 362).

Family caregivers can experience fear as their loved one changes profoundly in physical appearance and ability. The dominating needs of the terminally ill can be costly, causing social abandonment as friends and even family are unsure how to support the caregiver during acute days of palliative care. A loss in status at work or failure to keep a job also can contribute to the high cost of a changed life in the midst of offering palliative care to a loved one (Lederberg, 1998). These factors can contribute to a decrease in a family member's quality of life due to generalized psychological distress.

Stressors of caregiving

In Figure 5.1, Hauser and Kramer's (2004) stress process and end-stage caregiving model reveals diverse sources of stress and burden for family and friends in the provisionary efforts of illness support. The research range of Hauser and Kramer

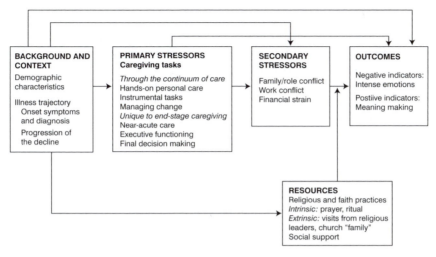

Figure 5.1 The stress process model and end-stage caregiving (Source: Hauser and Kramer, 2004, p. 671).

offers students of communication and medicine a useful conceptual network of consideration in light of the interaction complexities for family as they experience palliative and end-of-life suffering.

Caregivers supporting a loved one through the final months, weeks, and days of life encounter the physical exhaustion of sleep deprivation and near-constant vigilance of the care receiver but also the stressors of emotional care, reassurance, and support. Many caregivers describe all these tasks as precious and full of quality. The familial costs of these labors are worthy of note from a communication perspective.

The greater a patient's depression, anxiety, uncertainty, and pain, the greater the burden is for the caregiver. Studies that explore the effects of suffering and advancing cancer on the anxiety and distress of an affected couple (both the caregiver and care receiver) show that worry and anxiety are at least as high for the caregiver as they are for the terminally ill patient (Hoskins *et al.*, 1996; Kaye and Gracely, 1993).

A great deal of the burden for caregivers is produced from the shifting roles they must perform in a family structure as a result of a partner's, parent's, sibling's, or child's terminal illness. Basic family needs continue, and other members of the family often maintain many of their activities and involvements previous to diagnosis. The pressure of this increased juggling in addition to sometimes intense patient suffering can commingle to create feelings of high anxiety, frustration, confusion, anger, and loss.

Pain management

A 2002 study that ranked quality-of-life issues for family caregivers and their seriously ill care receivers found that pain management was unequivocally ranked as the number one priority in quality of life care by families and patients (Yurk *et al.*, 2002). There is evidence that dying patients might conceal their pain from their primary family caregiver to reduce the worry and burden on the caretaker (McPherson and Addington-Hall, 2004). A study of married couples dealing with profound cancer pain revealed that 60 percent of patients admitted to lying about the presence and intensity of their pain to protect their caretaking spouses (Dar *et al.*, 1992).

Poorly controlled physical symptoms of the terminally ill patient remain vivid in caregivers' minds. Herth (1993) finds that caregivers maintained stark recollections of the fear and loss of hope that accompanied the inability of the caregiver to relieve pain and provide comfort within a manageable period of time.

Mental and physical labor

Sam describes Vera's care in the form of researcher:

> Vera took a lot of the responsibility and so that caregiving really fell a lot on her shoulders. And I think it's partly something that she is attuned to anyways. We're a good team in that respect in that she is the type of ahh researcher and um the information that she was able to uncover regarding this type of prostate cancer is something that might have been too overwhelming for me and I might not have been able to deal with it or understand it, or remember all the information as well as she had. So in those terms I was really relying on her a lot. She took the initiative and became my mommy.

Depending on the stage of illness, family members are not only central in the decision-making and communicating processes for care but also heavily responsible for the day-to-day physical caretaking of the patient's body. In the later stages of illness, this task can dominate the activities and schedule of a household. In a survey by the National Family Caregivers Association (2000), more than one-half of the family caregivers provided help with activities of daily living, and 85 percent of the patients being cared for were fully reliant on their caregiver for this help. Family often provides for the activities of daily living, administering medications, changing dressings, and bathing and clothing a patient, but they also spend marked amounts of energy and time transporting the patient and keeping the household functioning (Hauser and Kramer, 2004). The physical caring demands upgrade to a high level of intensity that family carers are often unprepared for when patients enter end-stage living and require near-acute levels of care and time. Nausea, pain, confusion, distress, anxiety, incontinence, wound management, insomnia, and hygiene can become all-consuming for a caregiver's life. Previous research has shown a decrease in caregivers' psychological well-being and an increase in caregiver distress and burden, especially when dealing with agitated patients or patients with active symptoms (Markowitz *et al.*, 2003).

Caregiving at Life's End is a three-year project of The Hospice Institute of the Florida Suncoast funded by the Administration on Aging National Family Caregiver Support Program. The purpose of the project was to assess end-of-life caregiver needs to facilitate meaningful and supportive living for the family members and patients. Researchers found a positive influence in levels of comfort in the categories of caregiving, self-acceptance, meaning, and caregiver closure among families receiving relief from hospice caregivers supporting family or friends at the end of life or who were bereaved within the last six months to a year. There is no denying a caretaker's outstanding need for support and its proven supply of relief.

Financial concerns and burdens

Hauser and Kramer (2004) find the caregiving provided by family to be awesome in cost and labor. The economic value of the care provided might be $196 billion. "If the work performed by these caregivers was replaced by paid home care, it would cost $45 to $94 billion a year" (p. 673). Caregivers report spending an average of 20 hours per week providing direct care, and one-third of caregivers spend more than forty hours per week (Donelan *et al.*, 2002; Turner *et al.*, 1994).

Lederberg (1998) finds that 25 percent of caregivers cannot continue their work as a result of their at-home caregiver labors and requirements and that almost one-third of households lose a primary form of income or savings as a result of a terminal illness event. Vera describes the impact of caretaking on her status at work and the costs incurred at their oncologist's office where they are charged for thirty-minute units of time:

> The one experience that I am still, you know, somewhat paying a price for is the anger that I carried for a while without fully appreciating that it was there, which made me have a short fuse at work. And that has affected my um supervisor's view of my skills. So I'm st- I'm trying to repair some of that damage um but I'm also looking for work elsewhere so if the damage can't be repaired um, you know I'll move on.
>
> With Dr. Myers it's the cost. He's very thorough; he's very willing to talk to us as long as we want to talk to him, but he costs three hundred dollars every thirty minutes. If you go for thirty-three minutes that extra three minutes is an extra three hundred dollars. Initially we just said "we don't care, we will talk to him as long as we want" until we got the one visit that was nine hundred dollars when we had just barely gone over into the next thirty minutes. So we're a little um more cognizant of the time when talking to Dr. Myers.

Family conflict and palliative care

Death resulting from slow progressive illness is our collective reward for altering the more pernicious and swifter patterns of dying in previous decades. A longer period of dependence, weakness, and significant demands on family caregivers are products of the advances in modern medicine.

> Families are increasingly involved in elders' pain and symptom management, care coordination, and decision-making. They are fulfilling the roles of advocate, broker, liaison, case manager and hands-on care giver in helping elders access and utilize health and social services.
>
> (Kramer *et al.*, 2006, p. 791)

A family's response to the needs of their ailing relative combined with their own caregiving burdens commingle to impact the level of stress and conflict they experience in the course of caretaking. Familial conflict can become untenable as patients become too sick to communicate in the decision-making process for their care. Family conflict in the caretaking context erupts when one or more of five areas of disagreement emerge: (1) a perception unfolds that some family member or members are not supporting the caregiving effort with enough resource; (2) care coordination for the patient is not agreed on; (3) the patient's needs are not being met; (4) there is disagreement about the nature of the illness; and (5) historic conflicts from within the family are drawn out and magnified in light of the present conflict (Kramer *et al.*, 2006). It is readily imaginable that family conflict could detonate in light of these exigencies:

> Anger, denial, and other non-rational influences can lock family members into warring stances over whether to treat a devastating illness aggressively or discontinue life-sustaining measures. What is remarkable, given the intensity of the feelings at stake, is how rarely such conflicts make their way to court.
>
> (Bloche, 2005, p. 2371)

The effects of family conflict in the context of palliative care can be extremely taxing and potentially devastating. An easily recalled instance of enormous conflictual proportion is the Terri Schiavo case. The family conflict surrounding Ms. Schiavo's palliative care became so toxic that her right to medical privacy was abandoned, and her care coordination decision was paraded in front of and by politicians, the media, and politically motivated special interest groups. Though most family conflict in palliative care does not reach this fever pitch, the consequences can remain privately brutal for those involved in the process.

Caregiver burden can increase and health quality can decrease as a result of family conflict during this already very stressful period. High stress and depression for the caretakers increase as a result of family conflict (Semple, 1992). Researchers have considered the effects of conflict on primary caregivers. This singular focus on the effects of family conflict does not do justice to the complex ripple effect exemplified by the Terri Schiavo case. The interdisciplinary care teams, physicians, and broader context of health care communication are affected profoundly by the conflict engaged by families as their loved ones face terminal illness; it is the patients, though, who will pay the highest price for these end-of-life family conflicts.

Once a patient loses consciousness, there is a clear break in their participation with care. Delirium is an under-recognized process experienced by 40 to 80 percent of individuals at the end of life; this and a lack of consciousness present the same decision-making onus for the family (Boyle, 2006). The process of delirium is undertreated at the end of life, and patients suffer a great deal as a result. This frightening change in perception and cognition occurs with quick onset; families and care teams can be caught off guard and left to make major decisions for a patient who was lucid just moments earlier.

The most immediate and profound category of family-conflict consequence is the barrier of appropriate care for the patient. Health care workers have identified family conflict as the obstacle limiting the best care for the patient or serving as the primary interference in identifying preferences in end-of-life care for patients (i.e., life-sustaining treatments; Kayashima and Braun, 2001). In a 2006 examination by Kramer *et al.*, of 150 patient deaths, health care workers intimate with the process and families of each patient reported that family conflict was central in more than one-half of the deaths revisited in the study.

Family communication and meetings

The overwhelming advice offered by physicians to effect change in negative family conflict and the treatment plan of a patient is the investment of time. Kopelman (2006) recommends that the health care team take time to fully understand a family's reasons for asking for the life-sustaining efforts they desire in neonatal intensive care units. With this knowledge, he feels that a full assessment and conversation can be shared with the family about the realistic outcome of life for their premature baby. He also recommends several conversations as opposed to one visit. The onus is placed back onto the physicians with the support of the interdisciplinary team despite minimal availability of time and energy. Kopelman (2006) argues that the right choices and investments in family conversations will save immeasurable costs for all parties in the midst of and after the patient's death. "Meaningful communication with families is so crucial for making the right decisions … and to support the family, that adequate time for it must be found" (p. 585). Weissman (2001) also recognizes that family conflict in end-of-life choices is reduced through communication; "meaningful discussions about limiting life-sustaining treatments can only be conducted in the setting of trust" (p. 3).

Doukas and Hardwig (2003) propose a covenant among family, physician, and patient that will essentially replace the advance directive. This document is built previous to an acute health situation and also markedly decreases family conflict over what patients would have desired concerning their health. The faulty premises of advance directives rest in three primary areas: (1) the document can be created independent of a conversation with a patient's physician and medical information, (2) the patient's dying process is treated as an individual process in which loved ones have no interest, and (3) the values of the patient's family are immaterial (p. 1156). Proxies face the same difficulties within a family as well. The family covenant is a process-based approach in which the patient and physician first meet and discuss end-of-life care; then family members join the conferencing process. The covenant requires time and energy from all parties involved in an effort to stem the flow of conflict and "blood-letting" in the face of acute stress during palliative and end-of-life care communication.

When end-of-life decisions are made, direct input from an affected patient is obtained in fewer than 5 percent of cases, and information about patient preferences is usually unavailable. The many barriers to effective communication during end-of-life care are related to the patients, who are usually unable to communicate to family members. The family then must struggle with distressing emotions, a tendency toward denial, difficulty in understanding medical information, and a lack of preparedness for surrogate decision making (Lautrette *et al.*, 2006).

One advancement of palliative care is treating the family as a conduit to a patient and including them in each patient's plan of care through the construct of family meetings. Family meetings are usually interdisciplinary, and all members of the care team (see Chapter 6) are invited and encouraged to attend. Many times, the patient is unable to participate due to his or her clinical condition or the inability to communicate with others. Caregivers become their voice. The palliative care team's main goal is to "bring the patient into the room" to find out who this patient is as a loved one, as a person, as a whole human being, to help the caregiver think about what the patient wants based on his or her own values.

The death event

Hospice and palliative care recognize that family suffers in relation to an affected patient. Dying is about the patient experience but also what the family remembers of that collective event. The dying period extends far beyond the death of the patient into a season known as bereavement. Despite the proliferation of hospice as a movement, most people still die in hospitals; physician training in palliative medicine takes place in the hospital setting as well. The family's experience of the death event is of great interest as we consider palliative and end-of-life communication.

In a journal entry describing the death event of his brother Ted, Hal describes the family's need for direct medical communication:

> It seemed like a real possibility that Ted was dying. His breathing was so labored and rattley—pulling his entire head and neck around to the side as he heaved air in and out and in and out. It worsened over the two days he

had been unconscious with fever. But after each visit, the hospitalist would say, "let's see what those antibiotics can do, let's not give up. He could pull through this thing." At one point he even told my parents that Ted likely had six to twelve weeks to live. This seemed ludicrous in light of what the nurses were saying in an antiphonal response to the doctor. Twelve hours before he died, one nurse listened to his breathing and told us that he would die soon. Based on this communication, Ted's wife and I called in the family that was nearby and we camped out for the remainder of the night and next day.

Two hours before his death, the hospitalist was repeating his phrase: "He could pull through this." As he walked out of the room, I asked him, "How will we know Ted is dying in the moment?" We wanted to know what to watch for, how to be with him during this scary time of full body breathing. "Just watch the blood pressure monitor, it will get very high, and then bottom out to nothing." In supplying an answer he was acquiescing to the reality that Ted was dying, and the rigmarole about the antibiotics was just that—smoke and mirrors. So in the very end that is how we knew he was dying in the moment. A machine. I wish we could have done it differently—like not had any machines and a direct conversation with the doctor.

Satisfaction with care and communication with staff at death

Nearly one-fourth of patients who die in the hospital enter through the emergency room for their final stay. Billings and Kolton (1999) report that many family members with their loved one in the emergency room complained of long waits and poor pain management practices. As a patient's condition deteriorates, so increases the family's need for communication with physician and health care professionals (Hanson *et al.*, 1997). Thirty percent of the fifty respondents in Billings and Kolton's (1999) Massachusetts General Hospital survey reported extensive communication difficulties with their overseeing physician and medical staff at the end of life of their spouse. The data were gathered from caregivers five to twelve months after the death of a family member. Concerns and complaints covered many subjects, but the common theme was access to information:

- "When a family wants to talk to a doctor, they should be allowed to."
- "I wanted to know how he died."
- Another woman learned of her sister's death from a friend who worked at the hospital. No one had called her. "The hospital lied to me."
- Advance directives were ignored: "He was kept cold and white and gone and they still kept in the breathing tube ... why didn't they let him die in peace?"
- "It was just hard to find out what was going on."
- "It was like pulling information out of them."
- "They should have told me he was on his way out."

- "It would have been easier if someone had just told you what was going on" (p. 37).

Ted died in a small semi-rural hospital with no palliative care or hospice program. After Ted's death, his brother Hal writes a nurse who assisted them at that small rural hospital and also an interdisciplinary palliative care team at a comprehensive cancer center. His letters directly address communication issues from the family/caregiver perspective:

> I think you were just passing through the ER, but you saw us and saw that we were in bad trouble. And then you made a bunch of miracles take place. You found a room, vacant but used for sonograms? And it had a gurney. Ted could lie down. He was so sick, needed a catheter, and was incontinent. You just kept appearing with the things we needed, saying the right things that I was desperate to hear, and then I think it was you who got him a bed on the fourth floor to take fluids. You traveled up there with us; like all the other things you did, out of grace and care. You were our Good Samaritan.

Specific communication complaints are addressed to an entire palliative care team in the following excerpts of Hal's letters:

> Once Dr. H arrived on the scene she told us not to worry about taking notes, not to care about details—but that the new diagnostic possibility of leptomeningial carcinomatosis was fatal. When Ted asked how long he might have to live, Dr. H said "why do you want to know?" It seemed as though Dr. H. was considering this question a detail.
>
> The next day Dr. H and her nurse appeared once again. They joked about the "sexiness" of adult diapers in Ted's new encounter with loss of bladder and bowel control. They left, and then rushed back in, realizing they had forgotten to urge Ted to sign a living will with a DNR. Ted already had, several months earlier.
>
> Once we got home, we met with our local oncologist. As we walked in the familiar building with familiar faces, it was sort of like being at your own funeral. Staff quickly ushered us back to an examination room, and one by one the nurses, office staff, and finally doctor came back and embraced us. Apparently on the 26th, Dr. H. called our oncologist and said Ted had leptomeningial carcinomatosis, and that he was going onto hospice. In actuality, we left the cancer center with an inconclusive diagnosis, and no one had discussed hospice with us at all.

Bereavement and displacement

The death of a family member or significant loved one has been readily documented to have profound psychosomatic, somatic, and physical costs to the grieving.

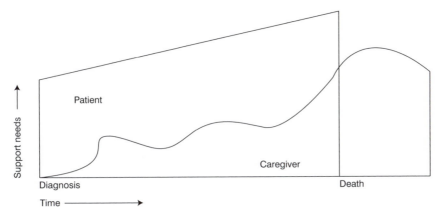

Figure 5.2 Diagram depicts support needs of patients (above curved line) and their caregivers (below curved line) during illness. Support and communication may be directed primarily to the patient at diagnosis when disability is minor. In later stages of illness, the support needs of patients remain, but support needs of caregivers increase dramatically (Source: Hauser and Kramer, 2004, p. 671).

Increased rates of mortality, alcohol consumption, cigarette smoking, depression, suicide, social anxiety, and use of medical services are attributed to grief and survival of a loved one (Billings and Kolton, 1999). Figure 5.2 includes Hauser and Kramer's (2004) image of time and support needs for the family caregiver, supporting the concept that family needs and suffering increase after the death of a care receiver.

In a Massachusetts General Hospital study, though one-half of the respondents reported a post-death contact with a hospital staff person, there was no repeated or sustained bereavement support offered by the hospital. One-fourth of those who did have contact were family-initiated or simply chance encounters. None of the families were talked to about bereavement counseling programs or services through their dying partner's physician (Billings and Kolton, 1999). This is consonant with earlier work that found physicians in an academic hospital had no contact with the bereaved spouse after the death of a partner unless initiated by the spouse (Tolle *et al.*, 1986).

Family members responding to the Billings and Kolton (1999) study reported feeling insulted if a physician who had worked with them and their family for an extended period of time had not acknowledged the death of their loved one. Some respondents also complained about not receiving information from the physician concerning questions about the illness or death.

The profound needs that accompany this massive chasm in any family's life call for routinized bereavement programming in hospitals. As long as people are dying with the support of the medical system and the medical world recognizes the family of the terminally ill as a second-order patient, it seems imperative to supply care for those enduring what might be their greatest loss. The demand of regular bereavement communication and care placed on physicians, nurses, social workers, and chaplains will not be possible without added standardized structures and resources.

Conclusion

> If we could do it all over again, I'd try and persuade him to not participate in the research. I'm not sure whether I'd succeed, though. Klaas agreed to everything.
>
> He didn't like to complain and be difficult. He thought it was terrible when I questioned what was going on. He'd say that we needed to trust them. He surrendered himself completely to the doctors...The most difficult thing is that we never discussed his death … If I could do things over then that's something I'd do differently. He knew that he was dying … He had already come to terms with it when the time came to die, whereas we still had to start. It would have been better for us if we had talked about it.
>
> Maybe the doctors should have been more clear about the fact that it was the end...I never heard them say that clearly. If they'd have done so it might have got through to us how serious the situation really was. But as it was, we kept on hoping. The X-rays were clear and we thought that things were going to be okay.
>
> Maybe we would have talked if it wasn't for the hope. Maybe if they'd been clearer we wouldn't have had so much hope … when someone says you're not going to get better, you don't immediately think you're going to die.
>
> (The, 2002, pp. 230–2)

The (2002) writes about her visit with Mrs. Wiersema three years after the death of Mr. Wiersema from non-small-cell lung cancer. Mrs. Wiersema also shares that she and her husband required more time with the physicians on diagnosis and throughout treatment. The Dekkers were another couple in The's non-small-cell lung cancer ethnography. On the death of Mr. Dekker, his wife "was determined to ask him [Dr. Liem] all the questions that were troubling her, but when it came to the crunch the questions dried up. Dr. Liem did not offer much information either" (p. 232). Mrs. Wiersema and Mrs. Dekker include their voices in the family caregiver struggle: treatment decisions, locating hope, caregiver burden, and bereavement. Three years after the death of their spouses, these issues remain vivid in their narratives.

The family perspective is central to palliative and end-of-life communication study. In many cases, caregivers travel with patients through each step of their disease process. We have tried to describe some of the hardships and journeys of the family and their communication in this volume; a qualitative-interpretive approach to this subject enforces the notion that all families' experiences defy orderly analysis. What is shared among all families enduring the journey of palliative and end-of-life illness is the experience of suffering. Hauerwas (1986) observes that this word has its "root sense" in the notion of humans being forced to endure "a set of circumstances" (p. 28). As such, we most often think of a patient in this way, as the sufferer. Our ideas and the ideas of palliative care research argue that the family is also suffering and, in fact, suffering further and with greater intensity in bereavement. The caregiver is the voice speaking at the end of a patient's life. This is an important voice with tremendous knowledge about how to care for the terminally sick and dying.

One of us picked up a magazine called *Cure* in a physician's lobby several months ago. The entire periodical is a lovely, shiny, colorful magazine of bright pages disclosing (advertising) new drugs, ways to treat cancer holistically, advice from a man (photographed with family) who weathered the storm of his wife's breast cancer, how to stave off esophageal cancer ... the people in the photos are surviving, not likely to succumb to or bereave their illness. This periodical might be the lens that most families look through when facing serious disease: pursue aggressive medical care (even beyond its utility). The pharmaceutical companies clearly paid for this gorgeous periodical that very enticingly extended the restoration narrative to the entire family.

Communication shared between people—patient, family, and health care providers—is the pathway to supporting caregivers as they suffer in the midst of palliative and end-of-life care. Families want contact with the patient's physician during and after care and need referrals for support during and after patient care as well.

Both physicians and families are inaccurate judges of a patient's preferences at the end of life, but family members are proven to be much more accurate (Tschann *et al.*, 2003). In a medical text about palliative care, an entire chapter is dedicated to the conflict between families and staff, with approaches offered to solve these conflicts. However, communication is never mentioned or suggested as a vehicle for resolution in this chapter by Jenkins and Bruera (1998). Areas of conflict are identified, but using communication as a tool to find some point of connection in those areas of conflict is not employed. It is in the more recent pieces of writing about conflict within families themselves that medical practitioners are seeing the efficacy and innovation of communication as a way to solve problems and save time by periodically meeting with families, learning about their connection to one another and to the patient, and hopefully circumventing the possibility of toxic conflict when the hard days of delirium and acute illness do arrive for a patient and family.

Coda

Two co-authors interviewed the physician (and fourth author) of our palliative care team to ascertain her experiences in dealing with family members in the delivery of palliative care. Families are the main client in palliative care, in addition to the patient, and one of the major responsibilities of the palliative care team is to meet with family members in an attempt to help them reach consensus in the plan of care for their loved one. These meetings, generally but not exclusively facilitated by the physician on the team, should occur early in the course of a family member's advanced or terminal illness, yet late referrals to palliative care, conflicting wishes of family members, and other problems can preclude this. At family meetings, the palliative care team must help to mediate any conflict that arises in response to a proposed care plan; it must also fully inform each family member of a patient's prognosis so that all members are making decisions with the same set of information. In fact, meetings are frequently held at the request of a family member who wishes to ensure that another member also hear what he or she has heard from medical staff or palliative care team members. Clarity of information is paramount to family members' successful decision making.

Whereas the goal of palliative care is always to elicit and fulfill the patient's wishes for end-of-life care, problems arise when a patient has not made her or his wishes known through a prior advance directive (and code directives) and becomes comatose or otherwise unable to communicate preferences. At this point, conflict is invited if family members disagree about how to proceed. Legally, even if a family member claims to know a patient's wishes from a past conversation about the end of life, these wishes cannot necessarily be implemented without an advance directive. Rather, the family's wishes would be honored in such a case, with a (legally married) spouse having first say, followed by the patient's children (each having equal voice regardless of birth order), and last, the patient's parents or other relatives. Many family members are painfully aware of the recent case of Terry Schiavo and thus wish to avoid the dreadful conflict that can ensue when spouses and other family members violently disagree about what course of action a patient would want were he or she able to speak for him or herself.

According to our palliative care physician, as many as 60 to 70 percent of her palliative care cases have involved family conflict. Frequently, family members experience conflict over such issues as how much pain medication their loved one should receive. Many family members find that the balance between medicating their loved one sufficiently so that she or he experiences minimal physical pain and yet maintaining lucidity so that final conversations and goodbyes can be expressed is a difficult one to achieve. The palliative care team can often intervene to help the family arrive at this difficult balance. Some family members' fear of opioid addiction is another problem that often must be faced. Again, the palliative care team can help to educate the family about the myth of drug addiction for patients who are in sore need of pain relief.

Other sources of family conflict involve the unmet needs of a patient or family; particularly when the family member either fears or actually encounters abandonment, conflict is experienced. However, the main source of conflict occurs owing to lack of information from health care professionals about the patient's prognosis. For example, a patient can be told by an oncologist that she or he merely needs another round of chemotherapy to put a tumor in remission; the next day, he or she might be advised by the palliative care team to enter hospice care. Oncologists, surgeons, and other medical specialists who are unwilling to confront a patient with a terminal prognosis (see Chapters 3 and 4 for extended discussions) often ask the palliative care team to deliver this message for them. As a result, patients can feel anger, even hostility, and certainly distrust of the entire medical staff, as can their families. An abrupt transition from the belief that one is being cured to the certainty that one is dying can lead to feelings of abandonment as well. In this instance, family meetings can communicate to all involved that neither the patient *nor* the family will be abandoned by the palliative care team.

It is critical in these meetings and in all their dealings with the patient and family members that palliative care team members withhold making judgments about the family; they must seek only to provide comfort to both, even to family members who abandon their dying loved ones. This undoubtedly is one of the most difficult tasks of the care team. Yet families respond positively to the honesty and candor that the palliative care team provides in giving them a prognosis that is as accurate as possible. Even bad news can be perceived as comforting in that it reduces uncertainty and enhances trust. The best palliative care comforts the family as well as the patient.

The physician on our palliative care team advocates what she terms "prophylactic palliative care," which involves conversations about the end of life and appropriate decisions (e.g., durable power of attorney, code orders, and the like) being made well in advance of a potentially terminal illness. Whereas physicians must become both knowledgeable about palliative care and aligned with its values (a goal that current medical school curricula are working to attain) so that they are more willing to refer patients to palliative and hospice care services, patients, too, must inform themselves about palliative care. Patient education needs to empower patients so that they believe that they, not their medical physicians, are the captains of their destinies. Patients also need to identify what constitutes an acceptable quality of life for them so that they then can make decisions about their end-of-life care and communicate these decisions both legally (i.e., advance directives and durable power of attorney) and to their families and loved ones. We are hopeful that the imminent aging of the baby-boomer generation—along with their advanced degrees, their affluence, their huge numbers, and their consumerist demands for excellence in all facets of their lives—will foster their increased education about palliative care and other aspects of end of life.

6 The health care team's perspective

He had, for all intents and purposes, made a promise to family that he would fight, and he came to a point when he asked me about euthanasia, when he was so tired. He sat there, he looked totally drained of energy, and he said, "I feel like crying." But he couldn't cry because he was so tired from fighting, he couldn't even cry. And he, he just wanted to rest, he wanted to stop fighting but he was struggling against that and the promise he'd made to fight.

—Palliative care psychologist

Palliative care is a unique care setting as it represents the liminality of life, the betwixt and between of living and dying where the struggle to live and fight is often a choice (Turner, 1982). The boundaries of death and dying are blurred by the struggle to find a cure and be cured, particularly because palliative care is offered simultaneously with other medical treatments. Patients and families are often left with conscious decisions that demarcate the limits of living and dying. Recognizing that family support systems are an instrumental and influential part in the decision-making and care process, palliative care practitioners provide an interdisciplinary approach to care with considerable attention given to the needs of both patients and families (Morrison and Meier, 2004).

The interdisciplinary care model is a process of care based on collaboration among health care providers with specialized knowledge from multiple disciplines (Geriatrics Interdisciplinary Advisory Group, 2006). These interdisciplinary teams (IDTs) are characterized by team members who work from different orientations while at the same time engaging in joint work. It has been suggested that an interdisciplinary care model improves health care processes, benefits the health care system and caregivers, and adequately prepares health care providers for better care of older adults (Geriatrics Interdisciplinary Advisory Group, 2006). Ideally, under this holistic approach patients are provided with care plans that have been assessed by experts in different disciplines (Dyeson, 2005).

The IDT approach is necessary to provide expert symptom management and holistic and continuous care for both patient and family. In palliative care, the role of the IDT is to offer assistance in helping patients and families to achieve their care goals, particularly end-of-life care. Each IDT member focuses on a patient's and family's needs and preferences rather than their own specific professional values (Connor *et al.*, 2002). In this manner, discipline-specific boundaries are blurred, and the entire interdisciplinary care team owns a shared holistic plan of care.

However, each discipline represented on an IDT approaches the holistic plan of care differently. Some members have a purely biomedical perspective whereas others approach the patient and family focusing on their psychosocial needs. Previous research has illustrated that not all disciplines collect information in the same manner, so sharing information with other disciplines can take on many different forms that may be confusing to other team members (Ellingson, 2003). A key aspect to effective interdisciplinary care is to be knowledgeable about one another's disciplines and to recognize and understand each discipline's perspective of the holistic care plan and goals.

Narrative accounts by IDT members reveal both the Voice of Medicine and the Voice of the Lifeworld (Mishler, 1984). The unique position of every IDT member allows them to hear the stories of dying patients and their families as they recount the experiences and emotions of dealing with impending death. These narratives have the potential to become a source of knowledge for other health care providers or to share with future patients and families (Geist-Martin *et al.*, 2003). By sharing the voices of palliative care team members, we hope to give voice to patients, families, and specific disciplines, to demonstrate the communication challenges embedded in the context of practicing palliative care, and to provide a patient-centered approach to these communication dilemmas. The communication challenges of palliative care will be explored in this chapter through the interdisciplinary voices of the palliative care team. Each team is unique in the number and kinds of disciplines represented, owing to the needs of the patients they serve, facilities, and resources available. As our team is composed of different disciplines, this chapter will focus on team members we have had the distinct honor to work with: the chaplain, the psychologist, the social worker, and the nurse.

Chaplaincy

The Association for Clinical Pastoral Education (ACPE) was formed in 1967 and initiated the development of clinical pastoral education (CPE). A unit of CPE requires at least 400 hours of clinical ministry along with theological reflections, case study, and group work. With time, the ACPE developed into the Commission on Accreditation of Pastoral Services and began working with the Joint Accreditation of Healthcare Organizations (JCAHO). In 1998, the JCAHO expanded the category of spiritual care. In 2000, the "White Paper" was produced by five of the largest professional pastoral care organizations. The document outlined for the first time the clinical scope of practice for health care chaplains. Today, the requirements for direct pastoral care to patients, families, and staff include educational requirements, triage, assessment, bereavement support, crisis support, and providing spiritual services as needed (Ford and Tartaglia, 2006).

As required by federal law under the Medicare hospice benefit, hospice IDTs must include chaplaincy. The law stipulates that all patients must be advised of the opportunity to have clergy visit patients and families. In addition to federal law requirements, the JCAHO requires hospice agencies to address all spiritual needs of patients, through either counseling or other spiritual support. Today, a hospice chaplain is one of the main members of the hospice IDT. Specifically, chaplains develop and implement spiritual plans of care; offer and provide pastoral care and counsel; function as a liaison between the patient and the community; and work closely with the IDT (Harris and Satterly, 1998). In palliative care, chaplains are viewed as a critical component to the medical approach to death. Their role involves helping patients to find encouragement, meaning, personal growth, and forgiveness. They provide bereavement counseling and support for staff and facilitate communication between patients, families, and staff (Ford and Tartaglia, 2006).

The end of life marks a reflective period for dying patients, characterized by the search for meaning; the chaplain's role is to provide hope and support, not answers (Harris and Satterly, 1998). The chaplain is there to listen; to assist with the reflective process; to find the sources of spiritual pain, such as guilt, fear, lack of forgiveness; and to allow individuals to discover their own meaning. The exploration of life issues in life stories through listening and reflection is an important aspect of the chaplain's role (Speck, 2003). Our palliative care chaplain explains:

> We're there really to walk with that person [patient]. We're there to help them explore their life story so that they can come to whatever end, whatever peace that is for them, and if I'm going to be honest with that person, we can't force it, and if you try to force it, then that's wrong. It is just wrong to do that.

The search for meaning is within, and the chaplain facilitates that journey as patients question the meaning of life and question their worthiness for God.

Exploring the boundaries of spiritual pain is a communicative challenge for the palliative care chaplain. Distinct from hospice, palliative care chaplaincy often emerges along with the terminal prognosis. As a result, many patients and families are in the early stages of accepting the prognosis, an important element that is needed before spiritual pain can be explored. Our palliative care chaplain summarizes it this way:

> And it's not my place, you haven't invited me to do that, or maybe the time hasn't been developed for you to trust me, or for whatever reason … You're angry, you're bitter, your life is up and you're leaving quickly and you haven't had time to sort those things out.

Some patients are ready to discuss/explore their spiritual pain, and others are not.

Palliative care chaplains are limited to the openness and willingness of patients to explore spiritual interpretations of the end of life and suffering. In the absence of a patient's spiritual beliefs, the tools of the chaplain are limited to quiet support and prayer. The powerlessness felt in these cases is described this way by our palliative care chaplain:

> Patients that seem to have no specific grip or ground that they can stand on for strength except who they were in life, except their education, the places they've been, jobs they've done, the careers they've built, what they've accomplished, their successes, their family, and not that those things aren't very important and certainly make us who we are, but there's this side of eternity. The saddest moments are to know that they [patients] have no security in what's next, and I have to stand quiet and let them pass.

In these contexts, the communicative support of a chaplain is articulated by his or her presence.

Particularly in Western culture, a chaplain is a symbolic representation of higher power and religious ritual. This is not accomplished through training but rather by the connotation of the title "chaplain" (Ford and Tartaglia, 2006). The chaplain represents a connection with a higher power and a closeness to the spiritual realm. In this regard, the palliative care chaplain is embraced by patients and families, and the following experience highlights the depth of this connection:

> He [patient] wanted to have strength and hang on to his faith and most patients do who have a strong faith. They don't want to lose that at the end, they're scared they're going to lose it at the end; that they won't be true to their faith at the end. It was just amazing to me how strong he really was until the end and how it, how he wanted to believe in the miracle, and had seen miracles that the Lord had brought. He invited me into that, that real sacred place of standing with him to have that strength in the end. It was precious…He allowed me to walk with him. And that's a real private thing to allow somebody to walk with you. I learned that no matter who we are, we have to walk that road alone, and we choose who we let walk side of us.

However, it is important to note that a chaplain's inherent connection with God or a superior being is not always perceived positively, especially given different cultural interpretations of disease and illness. For patients who believe that their illness comes from God, chaplains face complex communication challenges as their relationship with the spiritual realm creates a barrier to building a relationship with a patient.

Through a social constructionist approach to communication, these relationships and experiences illustrate the individualized acts on accepted spiritual beliefs, all of which transpire through language to create meaning. In these instances, discussions between dying patients and palliative care chaplains strengthen spiritual beliefs at the end of life and give specific and grounded meaning to spiritual interpretations about death and dying. In this manner, the dialectical tension between science and humanism dissipates as communication with a palliative care chaplain facilitates and gives voice and representation to a bigger picture of eternity.

This privileged position within culture/society creates a distinct communicative role for a palliative care chaplain. The association with a higher power affords the chaplain an assumed role of spiritual healer and confidant. For many patients and families, there is an accepted notion of confidentiality placed on chaplains that separates them from the rest of the health care team. Our palliative care chaplain explains:

> That's what I get paid for, is to actually sit there and listen, and to let them get angry or explore or talk bad about their doctor, whatever they want to do, because I'm the chaplain and I can't tell anybody. When they talk to a psychologist, the psychologist is going to analyze it, going to try to put it in a record somewhere. I'm a chaplain, what they tell me is confidential, they can truly have a safe place to get their fears out and I think if they get the stress and the fear and all of that stuff out of the way then the doctor can do the medicine.

This feeling of confidentiality emerges from a chaplain's position on the team, such that they are not seen as part of the team but rather as an added dimension to a patient's social support network. Embedded within this framework is the dialectical notion of science versus humanism, the "us-versus-them" ideology, with the chaplain on the patient's side. A palliative care chaplain is not considered similar to or even associated with the health care team, thus affording a unique role in the communication of palliative care, as described here:

> If there's conflict, the chaplain can come in and help (maybe) address the conflict, can solicit trust toward the medical team, toward the doctor… A lot of times we can clarify. There was one time I was talking to a patient and a doctor came in and gave him an explanation that they couldn't do any more chemo. The patient didn't hear it, just didn't hear it, so I was able to say, because I was the chaplain, I said pretty much the same thing as the doctor said, but I think because I was the chaplain, and I was just a normal person, he (patient) could hear me, and he didn't hear the doctor.

In this example, the physician represents the Voice of Medicine, and the palliative care chaplain represents the Voice of the Lifeworld. Given the symbolic representation that a chaplain fulfills for many patients, a palliative care chaplain is deemed trustworthy, perhaps more trustworthy than the physician. The dialectical nature of the Voice of Medicine and the Voice of the Lifeworld creates uncertainty for many patients and families. However, when these two voices merge and the same message is given, the certainty of the situation becomes clear. Palliative care chaplains are able to facilitate uncertainty management by virtue of their role, presence, and reiteration of information.

Though the role of a chaplain is clearly defined, the specific duties of the chaplain are less identifiable. Spirituality is interpreted in many different ways, and as such, individuals share and express spiritual beliefs in varying ways. Thus, a chaplain's specific duties and responsibilities are individualized to meet a patient's needs. The ambiguity of this role is due in part to society's ambiguity about spiritual matters. Thus, the goals of chaplaincy in palliative care are clear: to provide spiritual comfort and support; however, the implementation of those goals often varies between patients (Harris and Satterly, 1998).

The symbolic representation of the position also allows a palliative care chaplain a free voice within and among the palliative care team. Contrary to the biomedical model of health care teams wherein the physician is hierarchically placed at the top of the team, the interdisciplinary emphasis of palliative care places all team members as equal contributors with equal voices. Such structuring facilitates a unique team role for a palliative care chaplain. For example, the chaplain is able to share in team discussions about breaking bad news:

DOCTOR: Is he (patient) in denial?

PALLIATIVE CARE PHYSICIAN FELLOW: Yes.

DOCTOR: Does he know chemo is palliative?

PALLIATIVE CARE PHYSICIAN FELLOW: No.

DOCTOR: Does he need to know that he is dying?

PALLIATIVE CARE PHYSICIAN FELLOW: Yes

CHAPLAIN: Why didn't you do it [tell the patient he was dying]?

PALLIATIVE CARE PHYSICIAN FELLOW: Because I didn't feel it was my job.

DOCTOR: Actually, it's oncology's job, but they really don't. To tell you the truth, I would rather do it, because no one else will do it.

PALLIATIVE CARE PHYSICIAN FELLOW: Yes, I see it all the time in oncology. [Nurse agrees]

The doctor explains to the team that oncology is focused on cure. Many patients die receiving chemotherapy.

CHAPLAIN: Is this because they want to keep a good track relationship with their patient?

DOCTOR: No, they don't want to fail. Our goal with Mr. ___ is to tell him about his diagnosis. He's terminal: 6 months.

Thus, while patients and families view a palliative care chaplain as outside the team, it appears that the role of the chaplain is also viewed as being both inside and outside the team as well. This is clearly demonstrated in the palliative care chaplain's role in breaking bad news to patients. As a member of the palliative care team, the chaplain is there when the team delivers bad news. However, after these communicative transactions, the palliative care chaplain is left behind when the team leaves the patient's room. The palliative care chaplain thus facilitates the communication "clean-up" after the delivery of the bad news.

Psychology

Initially, the blending of psychology and health care originated with the treatment of mental health. The psychologist's role involved testing and evaluation of patients and has grown to include the holistic psychological assessment of patients (Kalus, 2003). Psychological care includes the provision of general emotional care and support. Extending beyond assessment, good psychological care includes skilled communication to enhance patient care, sensitive delivery of timely and relevant information, counseling, and specific psychological interventions (Payne and Haines, 2002).

Historically left to volunteers and self-help groups, health care psychology has recently embraced palliative care. In the United Kingdom, the National Council for Palliative Care specifically recommends that a psychologist be a member of hospital palliative care teams. However, psychology is a relatively new specialty service in the area of palliative and end-of-life care in the United States. After detailed studies on death and dying that emerged in the late 1990s, psychologists began to recognize a growing public health crisis in end-of-life care: the collective denial of death among the popular culture, the medical profession, and patients and families prompted psychologists to recognize palliative care as an area in need of their expertise (DeAngelis, 2002). Today, most psychologists working in palliative care are clinical psychologists.

Payne and Haines (2002) propose that psychologists can contribute to the field of palliative care in four areas: direct clinical services to patients and families, education and teaching, support at the organizational level, and research methods and approaches. Psychologists are "scientist-practitioners" or "applied scientists" because of their academic training and background and thus are able to provide both clinical service and clinical and organizational research (Kalus, 2003; Payne and Haines, 2002).

Moreover, palliative care psychologists are able to contribute to holistic plans of care by providing psychological assessments, team building, evaluating programs, facilitating communication between the team and patients and family members, and pain management techniques (DeAngelis, 2002). The aim of a psychologist is to reduce psychological distress and promote well-being. Especially within palliative care services, a palliative care psychologist can facilitate understanding of the cognitive, emotional, and behavioral aspects of responses to terminal illness (Payne and Haines, 2002). Psychological support also enables families to find their own well-being. Palliative care psychologists view affected patients as a part of the family system, which contributes to the overall continuity of care provided by the palliative care team (Alexander, 2004).

Palliative care psychologists are able to address clinical problems that arise in end-of-life contexts, such as abnormal grief reactions, adjustment disorders, psychological morbidity, and relationship and communication problems (Payne and Haines, 2002). Other psychologically oriented patient issues include self-perceived burden, which evokes feelings of guilt, distress, feelings of responsibility, and diminished sense of self (McPherson *et al.*, 2007).

According to the American Psychological Association (APA) (2006), palliative care psychologists provide assessment at the end of life, such as evaluation of mood and anxiety disorders, pain, family and caregiver interactions, psychological and cognitive functioning, and existential concerns. Additional responsibilities include counseling to facilitate emotional expression, effective listening, bereavement, and ethics committees. More important, clinical supervision of caregivers is needed to facilitate comprehensive palliative care (Payne and Haines, 2002).

Palliative care psychologists are also able to counsel patients and families about their fears of death and dying. Fears about dependency, loss of autonomy and control, and dignity are among the issues that dying patients are dealing with (APA, 2006). In conjunction with this, a palliative care psychologist also assists with the communicative needs of family members and communication between patients and caregivers. Their assistance in helping patients to deal with unfinished business has the potential to impact complicated grief and mourning for family members (APA, 2006). This is particularly important for family members who serve as a health care proxy and are responsible for making health care decisions, such as the removal of life-support systems.

Palliative care psychologists provide assistance in pain and symptom management. Pain interference and pain severity are associated with psychological distress (anxiety and pain), with "relations to other people" found to be associated with patient anxiety more than patient depression (Mystakidou *et al.*, 2006). Specifically, a palliative care psychologist can evaluate cognitive status and a patient's ability to make decisions. Particularly within palliative care, impaired cognitive functioning can be a temporary phenomenon for some patients due to pain, other symptoms, medications, or multiple factors. This syndrome of transient mental status change is defined as delirium, and an interdisciplinary intervention is needed to manage these types of patients. Patients with progressive advanced dementia are often evaluated by palliative care psychologists to improve behavior and educate caregivers. It has been suggested that palliative care psychologists are especially important for patients with dual diagnoses. Psychological and behavior management of patients with dementia, concern for families, and the complexity between dementia and pain experience are all areas that a palliative care psychologist can assist with (Alexander, 2004).

A study of psychologist referral rates in a hospice setting found that reasons for psychologist referral were depression, anxiety, pain, confusion, relative/family issues, anger/aggression, dementia, and disruptive behavior (Alexander, 2004). Interestingly, in this same study, medical and nursing staff also referred patients to the psychologist for assistance with pain control. The author concludes that this is representative of the team collaboration that occurs in a hospice and palliative setting, wherein the mind and body are treated as equal. Chronic and complex relationship problems also motivated staff to refer to a palliative care psychologist (Alexander, 2004). For instance, the issue of caregiver burden within the context of end-of-life care has received considerable attention, and initiatives such as pain support groups and bereavement interventions are often led by palliative care psychologists (McPherson *et al.*, 2007). In addition, palliative care psychologists are especially helpful in caring for patients with alcohol abuse issues.

Depression is the main reason for referral among palliative care and hospice patients, as this symptom is often linked to chronic diseases and active symptoms. Palliative care psychologists are currently pioneers in assessing and providing therapy to optimize quality of life among depressed terminally ill patients (Alexander, 2004). Our palliative care psychologist explains these communication challenges:

> I've had some patients who were simply diagnosed as "failure to thrive." It's a struggle to know when to push them to fight, when to do more extreme things, to intervene versus accepting their illness and that they are dying. It's a fine line because people who are physically healthy and suicidal, it's clear cut. You stop them. You admit them to a hospital for a time to stabilize them to prevent their suicide. You do anything to do that. Where as somebody who has a lot of medical problems, but that's not really what would kill them, they're just not trying to live, so therefore they're slowly dying. It's a slow kind of suicide, it's like passive suicide, and they do reach a point where you can't pull them back anymore because their health is so deteriorated. But it's hard to pin point that and hard to figure out sometimes when patients are in denial or just don't have the capacity to, to process feelings and to, to bring themselves back out of that.

Often, this results in patient desire-to-die statements and requests for euthanasia. A palliative care psychologist is then responsible for assessing the psychological, interpersonal, social, spiritual, economic, gender-related, and cultural reasons behind such requests (APA, 2006). Our palliative care psychologist explains:

> For example, when a patient asks about euthanasia, or says they want to kill themselves when they're terminally ill, they're really probably saying something else. So you need to ask further what that means, what they're saying. And with this patient, when, when he asked about euthanasia, what he was really saying is, "I'm so tired of fighting. I'm so tired." "Isn't, isn't there some way that I can rest? Isn't, wouldn't it be okay if I rest?"

In essence, one of the roles of palliative care psychologists is to take into account the totality of the situation. In this example, the psychologist's communicative role was to understand the whole situation, which relied heavily on the patient's concern for family impact.

Communication issues are also compounded by patient anxiety, loss of function, and impending death (Hudson *et al.*, 2006). Particularly in a palliative care context, it is difficult to determine whether a desire-to-die statement is a transient comment or a sincere request. Health professionals are able to "block" such statements by ignoring the statement, changing the topic, monopolizing the conversation, reverting to physical concerns, or offering premature or false reassurance (Hudson *et al.*, 2006). Discussions of euthanasia demonstrate the dialectical nature of end-of-life care and signify a transition. As a result of the ambiguity between life and death that is experienced by patients, a conversational change occurs wherein patients and families are no longer fighting death but rather begin to talk about death. Such communication signifies a conscious discussion about how to die rather than how to beat the disease and functions as a means to manage the uncertainty of the situation. Our palliative care psychologist explains it this way:

> The emotional reasoning will trump logic even though a person is aware of the whole logical argument for a decision, like putting in a feeding tube. They're fully aware that they're making an irrational, emotional decision that's really not consistent with what would be best, but they make it anyway just because of their pure emotional experience of the situation.

Primary communicative challenges emerge from a palliative care infrastructure that is grounded in the biomedical model of care. The biomedical approach has traditionally dominated the health care arena and psychologically oriented care, such as self-help groups, have been viewed as outside of service planning and development. As a result, palliative care psychologists experience the dialectical tension between the biomedical model and the psychological code of ethics (Kalus, 2003). The basic distinction between these two ideologies involves patient relationships. The biomedical model of care does not encourage patient relationships whereas psychological clinical standards necessitate relationships with a patient. Consequently, the dialectical nature of palliative care psychology has clinical implications. A palliative care psychologist explained,

> For example, I can't just drop my patients and move to another rotation. That's unethical according to my discipline's ethics code. I can't do that. Not that that means it's unethical for other disciplines to do that, they're different. They work differently.

Continuity of care is a very important concept to a palliative care psychologist, as compared to the other members of the team.

Psychologists must have a therapeutic relationship with their patients to conduct therapy and provide intervention services. A therapeutic relationship involves truly being with the person and developing an empathic understanding (Kalus, 2003). These relationships are established through collaboration with the health care team, patient, and family. Conversely, psychological therapy, characterized by a therapeutic relationship between therapist and patient, involves the behavioral level of changing the way in which difficulties brought on by treatment and disease/illness are managed (Kalus, 2003).

The margins between therapeutic relationships and therapy also exemplify the dialectical nature of IDT work. Palliative care psychologists are patient-centered, which can deviate from the overall palliative care team approach (Kalus, 2003). The nature of palliative care services, particularly in a hospital setting, necessitates the relatively quick transition of patients to appropriate care sites such that patients are typically seen by a palliative care team during their hospitalization and then transferred to a rehabilitation unit, inpatient hospice, or home hospice care setting. Consequently, palliative care psychologists struggle to maintain contact with patients after they have transferred out of palliative care as they continue to see new patients (see discussion under the heading "Relationship building with patients", p. 126).

Another communicative challenge that palliative care psychologists face is the label "clinical psychologist," which is often a deterrent in meeting patients and initiating therapeutic relationships. Contrary to the role and label of chaplain, the label of psychologist has socially embedded meaning within it. The connotation of the label could be a barrier in providing patient and family services. More important, the social meaning of the label triggers "rules" for communication between patients and their psychologist. These rules afford patients a known confidentiality on the basis of patient–client relationships and the psychologist's code of ethics. Furthermore, the rule management process establishes boundaries that are negotiated between patients and psychologists.

Despite much attention to the advantages of the involvement of a psychologist in palliative care, ambiguity over a psychologist's role has revealed mixed results over the field's emergence into the field of palliative care. In some instances, the palliative care team response has been "hostile" (Payne and Haines, 2002). Our palliative care psychologist summarizes it this way: "There's a struggle for my discipline as well, getting into that field because it's dominated by other disciplines. People prefer to pay a social worker instead of a psychologist." Palliative care psychologists are new to the field, so the team doesn't understand what their role is, what their function is on the team and to the patient and family, and they are seen as having little influence (Kalus, 2003). Our palliative care psychologist summarizes the state of the field: "A lot of people don't know what psychology can do in this area, and we are still trying to figure it out ourselves to some extent." In addition, she goes on to explain that training programs and infrastructure support are limited:

> You have to create your own structure. You have to go out there and just do things independently … It makes it harder to get mentoring because other post docs in the discipline have a direct person who works in that discipline, in that specialty area. There is no palliative care staff member in my discipline, so as other post docs have daily contact with their preceptors, I do not. That's a real challenge.

Social work

Social workers are trained to have a holistic approach to patient care, to deal with patients who have difficulty in communicating their emotions, and to work with families who are stressed, thus making them ideally prepared for a central role in the end-of-life care process (Rosen and O'Neill, 1998). Recent research has found that social workers facilitate decision making at the end of life by educating, initiating patient assessment, advocating for patient's rights, and serving as a liaison with the family and health care team (Black, 2006). Their goal is to understand and respond to the social dimensions of the experience of life-threatening illness (Napier, 2003).

Three basic aims of palliative care social work, according to Napier are to (1) address social concerns and problems, (2) create and strengthen social support environment, and (3) find ways of redressing social inequities. Social workers in palliative care provide personal assistance and empowerment and work with families, assisting and listening to reflection. Palliative care social workers assist with symptom management by teaching relaxation exercises, address psychological/ spiritual stressors by referring to counseling/psychology, problem-solve financial concerns and stressors, facilitate advance-care planning discussions and paperwork, and provide grief and bereavement support (Raymer, 2006).

One of the primary communicative challenges for social workers is to facilitate negotiation (Napier, 2003). For palliative care social workers, negotiation takes place within and among three different parties: (1) patients and families, (2) patients and families and themselves, and (3) patients and families and the palliative care team. When working with patients and families social workers must negotiate decision making. Typically, one of the responsibilities of palliative care social workers is to facilitate advance directive paperwork. A palliative care social worker must work to facilitate communication between patient and family. Our palliative care fellow in social work describes how her approach to working with patients and families changed throughout her fellowship:

> I have learned to reinforce [patients and families to] please to have these [end-of-life] conversations with people … with patients that are not comfortable talking with their family members: "I've tried to have this conversation, but my daughter doesn't want to hear it, or my wife doesn't want to hear it." [I've learned to be] a little more aggressive about encouraging them to let me facilitate that with them instead of just relying on them. Instead of just encouraging them to do it, take that extra step to really try to get them there to say, "Well now let's sit down and do this now."

She articulates how she had matured in her position as a facilitator of end-of-life communication. Over time, she learned that she needed to function as a moderator in the actual discussion between the patient and family.

Negotiating boundaries with patients and family members is also a communicative challenge. Our palliative care social worker explains:

> For example, when you're working with clients you have to be careful not to do too many things for them. As a social worker you're supposed to empower them and teach them how to do things for themselves, and at a palliative care hospice setting that's a difficult balance, because sometimes they can do things for themselves, and some situations you really need to get in there and do things for them. But what I really learned is in the earlier stages, when it's more of a palliative care issue and not so much hospice, when patients can do more for themselves, what I really learned is how detrimental it is to do too many things for them. Because when you're not there, they can't take care of themselves and it's just really, it doesn't make them feel in control, you're not doing them any good.

Finding the line between doing too much and doing just enough can be a challenge, particularly when working with palliative care patients who are in varying stages of the disease process.

Finally, social workers must negotiate communication between patients and families and the palliative care team. Landau (2000) conducted a survey of hospital social workers with regard to the factors influencing their contribution to the resolution of conflicts, such as ethical dilemmas in palliative care. The study found that social workers perceived their role primarily as advocates for patients and families before other hospital staff. Interestingly, Landau found that their impact on hospital wards depended on what key clinical staff viewed as the social worker's role. Social workers played a greater role if other team members viewed them as a source of valuable knowledge. Therefore, it is crucial for social workers to receive further training and expertise in palliative care, not only for the services afforded to patients and families but to increase the awareness of social workers' distinctive role on the IDT.

Nurse

Nurses have been the pioneers of palliative care as they provide direct patient care and family support at all times (Jocham *et al.*, 2006). Today, a nurse's role includes assessment, intervention, evaluation, and reevaluation of symptoms (Stanley and Zoloth-Dorfman, 2001). Within the scope of palliative care and end-of-life care services, a nurse works autonomously and is usually involved in advance care planning, prognoses, and "do-not-resuscitate" decisions (Stanley and Zoloth-Dorfman, 2001).

Though the priority for nurses is pain and symptom management, the role of nurses is not limited to this domain. In palliative care, one of the primary functions of a nurse is to provide supportive care by developing and maintaining relationships with patients and families (Stratford, 2003). By building relationships with patients and families, nurses uncover specific care goals and desires and are able to provide patient-centered care. Our palliative care nurse shares an experience in which her services went beyond pain and symptom management:

> One of the interesting cases was a patient that I felt had an extreme amount of pain and had a lot of aggressive therapies, and the family didn't like it either. So I thought it was interesting, the health care team didn't like it, the family didn't like it, yet the family was respecting the patient's wishes. And when he (patient) would have those moments of alertness, we'd double check, and he wanted everything done. So we served the patient's wishes. It was challenging, that one made me most reflective … I had to lean into my ethical model for practice on are we, are we doing the right thing? We served the patient and the family served the patient.

This palliative care nurse articulates the multiple communicative dimensions of a nurse's role. First, palliative care nurses facilitate problem solving by finding creative solutions and advocating for patient and family in decision making (Stratford, 2003). Above all, the patient's wishes were served, despite the nurse's personal values and beliefs about care. Second, the nurse demonstrated creative problem solving by helping the family to understand and find meaning (Stratford, 2003). In this case, the nurse was able to articulate to the family that the patient's wishes are most important in the palliative care process.

Nurses' multifaceted role emerges through the nature of their involvement with patients, families, and other members of the team. A clinical nurse specialist in palliative care embraces several roles: clinician, educator, researcher, resource, and change agent (Husband and Kennedy, 2006). Contrary to an acute care model, the individuality of a patient is the sole focus of palliative care. Specifically, the relationship among nurse, patient, and family is a necessary component in the healing process (Coyle, 2001). Coyle surmises that the role of palliative care nurses includes evaluating the distress of the physician, patient, and family; intervention; listening skills; comfort in talking about spirituality; and knowledge about pain and symptom management. Problematically, the theoretical role of palliative care nurses encompasses the many talents and expertise of the remaining members of a palliative care team.

As a result of their comprehensive role, palliative care nurses experience some of the following stressors: role overload (pressures of on-call duty, travel to patients, repeated crisis); role conflict (between team members, disagreement about care process/decisions, lack of control and power); and role strain (feeling inadequately prepared). Additional work environment stressors and patient and family stressors include the timeliness of referrals, team communication problems, continual involvement with dying patients, and stressful decision-making (Vachon, 2001).

These stressors are compounded by the problematic role of patient advocacy. Nurses are often called on to share diagnosis, prognosis, and treatment information with patients and families—primarily because nurses are more freely accessible, as compared to other members of the team (Stanley and Zoloth-Dorfman, 2001). However, patient advocacy should be shared among nurse, health professionals, patient, and family, and the role of primary informant among the three parties leaves the nurse with the burden of sharing communication and facilitating collaborative team communication (Wittenberg-Lyles and Parker Oliver, 2007; Vachon, 2001). The next section explores these dynamics and highlights the communication challenges that arise within the IDT.

Communication challenges

The importance of team communication has been well documented and emphasized in health care literature and research (Penson *et al.*, 2006). Effective interdisciplinary care teams reduce costs, improve patient outcomes, and enhance team members' individual job satisfaction and performance (Hall and Weaver, 2001). One of three types of team environments can emerge from interdisciplinary work. Opie (1997) proposes that team members and interdisciplinary collaboration impact the development of the team and thus dictate the type of environment that team members create. Thus, team types occur across a continuum. Initial team climates begin as multidisciplinary teams, characterized by varying team members who work parallel to one another to achieve coordination. IDTs are characterized by team members who work from different orientations while at the same time engaging in joint work. Last, IDTs develop into transdisciplinary teams that share a common language, free of professional jargon and terminology. Interpersonal collaboration is a primary contributor to the development of such high-level teams. This next section highlights the communicative challenges faced by the interdisciplinary palliative care team: structure, obstacles to teamwork, referrals, relationship building with patients, and maintaining self-care.

Structure

The responsibility for coordination of patient care falls to the primary physician who functions as the gate keeper to palliative care (Morrison and Meier, 2004). One of the more prominent obstacles in the delivery of palliative care is the different settings in which patients are cared for, such as surgery units. Surgery units are known for prescribing pain medication immediately after surgery and then failing to provide pain regimens for the following recovery period. Often, this leaves many patients in pain, either from surgery or withdrawal from a sudden drop in pain medication overnight. Though palliative care services can range from disease control to symptom control, many patients miss palliative care services that facilitate symptom control and go straight to hospice. A delay in referral to end-of-life care can be the result of the primary physician's problematic integration of the situation (see Chapter 4 for a lengthy discussion on the role of physicians in palliative care). This issue is further compounded by socioeconomic pressures that force care in the community where health care professionals are not geographically convenient or available (Hall and Weaver, 2001).

Generally, the primary care physician is largely concerned with probabilistic judgments in patient care; that is, determining the likeliness of a patient's death. Given that physicians are trained in the biomedical model of care, they are more likely to experience a divergent form of problematic integration, wherein there is a discrepancy between the desired outcome (healing-cure) and what is likely (death). Communication challenges emerge between physicians, patients, and families, creating an uncomfortable communication environment. For many physicians who struggle with the uncertainty of the situation, a referral to a palliative care team is the answer. This referral to the palliative care team enables them to manage this uncertainty by ridding them of the entire communicative situation.

As a result, the structured referral process has turned palliative care teams into a "dumping ground" for many hospital physicians and other services. It is not uncommon for palliative care teams to receive referrals to patients who have never been told that they are terminally ill. Palliative care teams are then faced with the challenge of breaking bad news and initiating end-of-life care plans within a short timeframe.

Overall, there are three physicians who must work together: the primary care physician, an internal or family medicine specialist, or geriatrician, and the palliative medicine physician with an interdisciplinary care team. The palliative care team is concerned with the evaluative judgments of patient care decisions, an emphasis on quality of life in making care decisions. Differences in probabilistic orientations between the palliative care team and the primary physician can result in mixed messages to patients and families. A formal system of communication is needed between the primary physician and the end-of-life care team to enable agreement on probabilistic orientations (Morrison and Meier, 2004).

Though the palliative care team provides an orchestration of a better death, there is a lack of control in attempting to reach this goal. First, there is a lack of control over referrals and the timing of the referral to their services. Second, there is a lack of control that comes from having to work with so many physicians. Third, there is a lack of control that emerges from IDT work. It is imperative that IDTs collaborate to deliver efficient palliative care services.

Obstacles to teamwork

A crucial part of infrastructure support for palliative care is daily and weekly meeting and rounds schedules to facilitate interdisciplinary collaboration/holistic plans of care (Meier and Beresford, 2005). The IDT meeting was developed as a means to producing an interdisciplinary plan of care for each patient. During the IDT meeting, teams form a single service plan wherein team members share responsibilities and implement their part of the plan (Sabur, 2003b). Previous research has illustrated that under this approach, patients receive more comprehensive care, thereby reducing overall health care costs (Dyeson, 2005).

It has also been demonstrated that there is a connection between higher levels of team functioning and reduced medical services, fewer doctor visits, and increased client satisfaction (Reese and Raymer, 2004).

The IDT meetings allow for open communication so that all team members are cognizant of a patient's status, including patient transfers, deaths, on-call nurse communication, new admissions, and any problems that need immediate attention (Williams, 1997). Research on hospice IDTs reveals that highly functioning teams have clearly understood goals and a positive interpersonal climate that allows for trust and providing technical and emotional support. Exploratory research has also illustrated that highly functioning teams are able to learn from their mistakes (Connor *et al.*, 2002). More important, job satisfaction has been found to be significantly correlated with team functioning. Team members who reported fewer instances of conflicting roles and an increased sense of team functioning also reported high job satisfaction (DeLoach, 2003).

However, not all interdisciplinary care teams are able to achieve high functioning collaboration among their IDT members (Connor *et al.*, 2002). Common problems in IDT meetings include interpersonal conflicts and "turfdom" wherein team members become protective of their discipline and their contributions based on their expertise (Larson, 2003). Preliminary research on information sharing practices in IDT meetings revealed that tensions between team members result from a primary emphasis on biomedical information sharing. Consequently, psychosocial information sharing about a patient is considered secondary information, thereby distorting the interdisciplinary goal of hospice care (Wittenberg-Lyles, 2005). Overall, an ineffective IDT meeting can leave team members feeling incompetent, less important when compared to other team members, and in a degrading role within the IDT care process (Sabur, 2003a).

Preliminary research on attitudes toward working in interdisciplinary health care revealed that interprofessional differences exist. Specifically, there was disagreement over the physician's role, with 73 percent of medical residents, as compared to 44 to 47 percent of social work and nursing students, believing that the team's primary purpose was to assist the physician (Leipzig *et al.*, 2002). In the same study, medical residents were least likely to view IDT work positively. Perceptual differences of IDT work are due in part to specific disciplinary backgrounds, which cause a disciplinary split, defined as the attitudinal and cultural traditions of the different health professions (Reuben *et al.*, 2004). For example, health care disciplines such as social work and nursing necessitate collaboration with other team members, predominantly physicians, to be able to carry out discipline-specific responsibilities. Conversely, there is a historical context for disciplinary independence in the field of medicine (Reuben *et al.*, 2004). Other factors contributing to disciplinary splits include regulatory requirements, level of training, and hierarchy within the healthcare system (Reuben *et al.*, 2004).

Given increasing patient needs that necessitate an interdisciplinary care model, it would seem likely that health care training would focus on the development of team communication skills and interdisciplinary training. However, many medical students are never exposed to interdisciplinary training unless they are in a special interdisciplinary program, such as geriatrics or palliative care (de Haes and Teunissen, 2005; Howe and Sherman, 2006). Current pedagogical approaches to interdisciplinary training within such programs are facilitated through didactic and clinical educational structures (Howe and Sherman, 2006). For example, in team-based geriatrics and palliative care, fellows are expected to learn what other team members do through seminars and by attending teamwork sessions (de Haes and Teunissen, 2005). Overall, there is a consensus in the health care literature that interdisciplinary care models are encouraged and the appropriate curriculum is necessary to see that this happens. Such curriculum should address team-building skills, role blurring, group communication, conflict resolution skills, and education about the different disciplines represented on the IDT (Hall and Weaver, 2001).

Referrals made within the team

The experience of living with a terminal illness is not static. As a result, communication is fluid and flexible, and given the dialectics of living and dying that patients and families face, palliative care teams must be flexible to meet the changing needs of both patient and family. All palliative care team members have the responsibility of being an advocate for both patient and family to the other disciplines on the team. The interdisciplinary care model provides a framework for team member flexibility, allowing team members to assume roles outside of their expertise when necessary. Such role blurring occurs, for example, when a nurse engages in spiritual care or a chaplain has conversations with patients about the desire to die.

Role blurring is particularly obvious in family meetings conducted to enable open communication and end-of-life-care decision making among patients, families, and a palliative care team. During these meetings, it is not uncommon for team members to engage in multiple roles. Our palliative care nurse describes it this way:

> Your overall goal is to journey with the family and the patient for the patient's best outcome, respecting the family. And our role went from basically bringing knowledge and options to comforting the family, and saying, "That's okay, you did the best you could." And letting them know that being human is okay … When we went in at the beginning it was, "Okay, here are the options, how can we help you with it," then all of a sudden it switched into caring for the family, which it typically does. I think in the family meetings you're caring for the family, but your focus changes.

This nurse describes the fluidity of her role—from information giver to comforter. Though it is outside their scope of expertise, team members have the flexibility to engage in these conversations.

Despite the perceived benefits of this holistic care approach, the blurring of discipline-specific roles undermines the required expertise to engage in such conversations and contributes to role strain, particularly for nurses who take on multiple roles in palliative care. For example, one of the unique challenges of the IDT is determining who is responsible for determining the patient's faith. Ford and Tartaglia (2006) surmise that a patient's spiritual assessment also involves determining if the patient's spirituality requires further intervention. Particularly in busy hospitals, palliative care physicians will conduct a spiritual assessment of a patient and then ask the chaplain to see that patient. In this sense, the physician is a gatekeeper for spiritual care—and he or she has no formal training in spiritual assessment. Thus, spiritual assessments are twofold: determining a patient's faith and screening the patient's spirituality for further intervention. Likewise, the boundaries between psychological support and psychological interventions are left to the physician who determines when a referral to the palliative care psychologist is appropriate (Payne and Haines, 2002). Thus, team conflict can occur over evaluation of and intervention with patients.

Relationship building with patients

Relationship building is essential for a palliative care team as they are one of three health care providers to approach a patient, especially during a clinical stay. The ability to quickly develop relationships with patients becomes a communicative challenge for the palliative care team as they compete with primary care physicians and specialists, all of whom have enjoyed a somewhat longer history with a patient up until this point. Ironically, the team is often faced with the challenge of earning the patient's trust while in the context of delivering bad news and discussing advance directives.

Moreover, each interdisciplinary-specific service, and if necessary evaluation and intervention, requires time to build relationships with patients to effectively deliver proper care. Building a relationship with a patient is a necessary component to the delivery of each team member's specific discipline. For example, a chaplain cannot gain access to spiritual pain without first developing and initiating a relationship with a patient, the psychologist must initiate therapeutic relationships for proper intervention, and social workers and nurses must get to know the patient and family to provide patient-centered care.

Learning to balance information with patients is a necessary communicative skill in the relationship-building process. Team members struggle "not to force" relationships, not to force discussions of advance directives, death and dying, and exploration of the dimensions of spiritual, psychological, and emotional pain. Our palliative care psychologist summarized this complex communication dynamic in this way:

> Although a lot of issues can come up for people that they want to process and deal with, other patients don't. They've never looked at that in their life and

they don't want to do it now…. they have enough to deal with, and with their energy levels that would just drain them all the more to, to try to open things up and, and work through those. So balancing how much to, to try to engage people as opposed to just letting them choose what they, how they want to deal with things.

Sustaining relationships with patients and families enables a palliative care team to truly reach patient-centered care. Our palliative care nurse recalls a moment when trust was established with a family:

NURSE: There was one case with a patient in ICU where he had just everything, and, um, the fa-, we met with the family and the family said y-, as they were talking about what the patient wanted, they had the awareness of what they'd done, and [interrupted]

INTERVIEWER: Which was prolonging life?

NURSE: Yeah, and it was all the things he hadn't wanted, but they had done them well intended. But to see their awareness of what they had done and how it wasn't what he wanted, and you know how you have those "ah ha's"? The family had their "ah ha."

INTERVIEWER: In the family meeting?

NURSE: In the family meeting. And then it was, and then your role [snaps her fingers] sw-, you know, the, the, your role switches in that moment.

INTERVIEWER: How so?

NURSE: Um, to se-, you know, like you're imparting, your overall goal is to, is to journey with the family and the patient for the patient's best outcome, respecting the family … And, and our role went from basically bringing knowledge and options to comforting the family, you know, and saying, "That's okay," you know, "you did the best you could." Um, and, and uh, letting, letting them know that being human is okay. Where, the, when we went in at the beginning it was, "Okay, here are the options, how can we help you with it," then all of a sudden it switched into, um, caring for the fam-, which it, which it typically does. I think in the family meetings you're caring for the family, but your focus changes.

The team's ability to care for the family rested on the fact that the family trusted them, that a relationship had been established between the patient's family and the team, such that the family was open to hearing what they had to say about their loved one's care and their actions.

Family meetings are just one way that the palliative care team works to initiate relationship building with patients and families. The palliative care team also employs other strategies to expedite relationship building. First, team members go together on initial patient consultations. In this manner, all members of the IDT are introduced to patient and family at once. This enables the patient and family to meet members of the team and, more important, this can make initial visits by specific team members much easier, as patients and family members already know who they are and that they have knowledge of the patient's case. Given that many health care providers approach patients and families during their clinical stay, this is particularly valuable as team members are now in a position where they have entrance and do not have to explain their role or ask questions about a patient's case on their return visit. This is especially important when patient visits include communicating bad news.

Second, the team employs the services of family members and caregivers to gain access to a patient. For example, the chaplain might ask a patient's spouse if it would be okay to stop by and say a prayer for the patient. By initiating a relationship with a family member/caregiver, IDT members are often able to gain access to a patient. Third, by sharing psychosocial information about a patient, team members are able to articulate knowledge of that patient and find common ground for communicating. Observations of our palliative care team revealed that the sharing of personal information about a patient, obtained either from discussions with family members or from their medical chart, impressed patients and provided an opening for relationship building.

Maintaining self-care

One of the unique communication challenges that a palliative care team faces is maintaining self-care. Our palliative care social worker describes the difficulty of working in end-of-life care:

> Just learning to get accustomed to the cascade of tragedy, all these horrible things all day long. That was one of the hardest parts, getting used to that, and trying to incorporate that into, you know, my world, and being able to go home where everything's fine … that was difficult.

The inclination to work long hours is inherent to the nature of the job. Additionally, team members become actors in the health crisis that unfolds with many patients and families. Our social worker continues:

> It's so hard when you don't know what the patient wants, and that's the part that really is hard for me. When you see the family members struggling: "I don't know, I don't know. I know, I know what I would want, but I don't want what he would want." And so, that's what's hard.

Consequently, many team members struggle to find where their participation begins and ends. Our social worker explains this struggle:

> It's hard to just leave. It's hard to just leave. For me, at the end of the day, when there's something that's not done, and, and no-, this may not wait till tomorrow, this patient may be dead tomorrow. And that's the hardest, is to

realize that you do have to protect your personal life, but when you know this patient is actively dying, and they might not be there tomorrow, and there's something you wanted to say or something like that, it's, it's hard…to leave if you really need to go.

There are two unique aspects of a palliative care environment that aid team members in self-care. First, the promotion of self-care begins with the realization that dying patients have much to contribute about living. Palliative care thus becomes technical at one point as team members must learn how to receive from patients. Our palliative care social worker describes this as an elastic process: "You go to a bad place to be able to go to a good place and appreciate your job."

Intrinsically, team members face challenges of overwhelming feelings about caring for the most complicated patients and family situations in the hospital or other settings. It is important that team members are allowed to share painful experiences with other members and to discuss ways of coping with stress. Self-care sessions must be implemented to facilitate the team's own health and well-being. One of the key members of the team, the chaplain, is often looked to for assistance with the team's own self-care.

Second, unlike other hospital health care team members who must suffer in isolation, the palliative care team serves both one another and patients and families. Team members are able to get energy from each team member, creating a synergy among the group. Team meetings that provide for debriefing provide a context for venting emotions and strengthen interpersonal collaboration (Wittenberg-Lyles and Parker Oliver, 2007). Additionally, both the chaplain and psychologist assist team members with self-care and coping.

In summary, each member of the interdisciplinary palliative care team needs time—time with patients to develop relationships necessary to provide solid care services. Unfortunately, all patients do not get time with (or get served by) *each* IDT member. Time is lost due to gate keeping at the referral level and to disease progression. Time is lost due to socially constructed barriers of the team member's role, which keep patients from embracing their services. Fortunately, despite communication challenges, the interdisciplinary nature of a palliative care team ensures that *each* patient is served, each patient has an advocate, and each patient's pain is attended to on all four levels (physical, spiritual, emotional, psychological) by at least one member of the team.

7 The authors' voices

We have relied heavily on a social constructionist, narrative approach to palliative care communication throughout this book, primarily because we believe that patients, whose voices must be privileged above all others, are "active interpreters, managers, and creators of the meaning of their health and illness" (Vanderford *et al.*, 1997, p. 14). Yet, we also have found the voices of all those involved in the offering and implementation of palliative care—physicians, family members, and the interdisciplinary palliative care team—to be paramount to an understanding of the complexities and challenges of palliative care communication. Thus, we have structured this volume in an attempt to represent the multitude of perspectives inherent to the delivery of palliative care.

Rather than conclude our book with the conventional "summary of findings" and "suggestions for further research" (or for "best practices"), we decided it wisest to end with the authors' voices, with our own narratives—to permit the reader an interior glance at the motivations and passions of the four of us who are unwaveringly dedicated to advancing the teaching and the practice of palliative care. Our common experience with the deaths of patients and loved ones, along with the writing of this book, constitute a reflexive process, one that has helped to shape our anguish about the way many of us die in the United States and our hope for an antidote in palliative care. The authors' stories that follow are deeply personal ones, yet we wanted to allow the reader to witness our auto ethnographic journeys.

Sandra Ragan

I think the first time I heard the phrase "palliative care" was early in 2001; it was spoken by Dr. Diane Meier in a videotaped documentary hosted by journalist Bill Moyers called "On our own terms: Moyers on Dying." This PBS televised series of four programs on death and dying impressed me profoundly, in part because I was teaching health communication at both the undergraduate and graduate levels and believed I could share excerpts from the series that would be meaningful to my students; almost none of our research or textbooks in communication addressed this area in much detail. However, I also was particularly attuned at that time to any discussion about how to die a "good death." I had recently experienced the protracted illnesses and deaths of two people whom I loved: Robert Hopper, my Ph.D. advisor, mentor, and friend at the University of Texas, who had died of colon cancer in December, 1998, and my father, Alex Ragan, who died of prostate cancer the next year in October, 1999. Even more salient to me at that time was my sister's deteriorating health as a result of advanced, metastatic breast cancer. Sherry had been given her diagnosis in April, 1995, the same month that I also was given a diagnosis of non-Hodgkins' lymphoma. However, unlike my own, Sherry's cancer never stayed in remission for more than a year at a time; and even though she frequently complained that she didn't like wearing the label "brave," she courageously managed its hold on her life for almost six years.

In the spring of 2001, I saw the Bill Moyers documentary and incorporated those parts of it that dealt with a "new kind of care"—palliative care—in my undergraduate health communication course. Ironically, as it turned out, I taught a section on death and dying the week before our March spring break. I then spent the week of spring break with my sister in Bethesda, Maryland. The cancer had spread to her brain, and she was no longer able to drive, so my mission during that week was to help her locate and hire a driver. Though she'd recently retired as a Senior Executive Vice President at MCI, she was consulting for several start-up telecommunications firms, and she did not want to give up her consulting or her mobility. I stayed with Sherry until the last Sunday of my spring vacation and then returned home to Oklahoma. She went into a coma the following Wednesday and died that Saturday, March 31, 2001.

My first writing about palliative care was inspired by a need to deal with the deaths of my loved ones, particularly my sister's. An academic conference on communication and gerontology, coordinated by Dr. Lisa Sparks, then at George Mason University, and a subsequent special issue of *Health Communication* guest-edited by Dr. Sparks, were the impetus for me to critique the medical literature in palliative medicine (along with two University of Oklahoma graduate students, Elaine Wittenberg and Tom Hall). I was struck by the oddity that palliative medicine seemed the best place for the practice of the biopsychosocial approach to medicine (which is what everyone in health communication was advocating), yet much of the literature I was reading in palliative medicine continued to address only the medical, physiological aspects of patient care: pain management and symptom control dominated the research.

Subsequent explorations of the literature of palliative care in chapters written for health communication anthologies convinced me (1) that research in health communication had not dealt adequately with death and dying and (2) that, though communication was inherently central to the practice of palliative or comfort care, it posed many challenges for all involved: medical providers, patients, and their family members and other loved ones. The writing of a chapter with Joy Goldsmith, one of my interdisciplinary OU doctoral students who also had directed the play "Wit," finally convinced me that a book had to be written that addressed the medical literature in palliative care from a communication perspective. In the meantime, my former doctoral student, Elaine Wittenberg, who had written a dissertation about communication in hospice care, was now involved in research with an MD certified in geriatrics and palliative care, Dr. Sandra Sanchez-Reilly. I was thrilled to learn that Dr. Sanchez-Reilly had been a fellow in Dr. Diane Meier's palliative care program at Mt. Sinai Hospital and was further thrilled when she accepted our invitation to join Elaine, Joy, and me in writing this book.

I lament that neither my father nor my sister experienced the gifts of a palliative care team as described throughout this book. Both of them were in semi-comatose states before I recall anyone's actually verbalizing the fact that they were actively dying. In my dad's case, he was in a hospital at Emory University in Atlanta, being treated for prostate cancer that had metastasized to his bones. Several weeks before his death, he endured surgery that his surgeon and his oncologist must have known to be exclusively palliative in nature, but family members were not informed of this. Nor was he, to my knowledge. Instead, Dad thought that he'd get well enough to go back home to Puerto Rico. Many of our conversations revolved around his wanting to cook for himself so that he would find his meals more appetizing than the gargantuan portions his wife had been serving him. Dad did not receive the services of a chaplain, psychologist, or social worker in his expensive hospital suite where he literally was attended by an on-staff chef (though it comforts me that he did share several televised Atlanta Braves games with a hired caregiver and fellow baseball fan).

My sister, who in the fall of 1999 must have been painfully aware that she likely would die of her own cancer, was the only one of us, medical or otherwise, who tried at the end to engage Dad in any conversation about his dying. Our family was in conflict about how much pain medication Dad should be given and whether insulin and other drugs should be stopped, as his doctor advised would be most merciful; his three children concurred that Dad should get as much morphine as he needed for his pain and that other life-prolonging medications should cease, but his wife disagreed. As Dad struggled for lucidity under the influence of morphine, my sister queried, "Haven't you had an interesting life? Haven't you done most of what you wanted to do?" Dad responded by quizzically raising one eyebrow in an expression we all knew well in him. That is the only exchange I remember in which any acknowledgement was made about his dying.

I wrote these words about my sister's death in 2003 (Ragan *et al.*, p. 220):

> My sister, Sherry, a brilliant, senior vice president at MCI, had never heard the term palliative care (PC), to my knowledge. She was receiving chemotherapy, both allegedly curative and palliative, until the end of her life; simultaneously she was taking medications that controlled her pain, anxiety, and depression. When the cancer that had 7 months earlier been irradiated from her brain returned to that organ and could not be treated again by radiation, she vehemently told her partner that she did not want to die in a hospital. Nor would she permit the brain surgery that the emergency room

doctors recommended to relieve the swelling and bleeding in her brain. She would not be kept alive by feeding tubes, hydration, and the like. Sherry died peacefully in her own home with no medical intervention other than oxygen, a catheter, and the blessing of morphine and ativan. Her family and loved ones surrounded her, and throughout her last night, she was cradled by her daughter and her beloved cocker spaniel. Two African hospice nurses provided expert care and comfort to both Sherry and to her friends and family in her dying. Yet I continue to lament that we did not provide all the PC my sister may have wished …

My lament in 2003 has now turned to a profounder grief that I did not try to engage Sherry or my dad or their many physicians in any discussions about their impending deaths (my sister's oncologist had only a week before her death referred to Sherry in her office as "my comeback kid" in recognition of the months and years Sherry had beaten the odds in responding —temporarily as it were—to further rounds of chemo. When I telephoned her oncologist on the morning that Sherry died, I believe that this excellent doctor was shocked and grief-stricken, but she said almost nothing to me). Nor did I try to insist to anyone that hospice be contacted when I was pretty certain that my dad and sister were actively dying. Sherry had the benefits of hospice nurses only after she was comatose; my dad never knew them. I think that both my dad's and my sister's physical pain was contained at their deaths, but no one bothered to help them explore possible emotional, social, or spiritual pain.

Witnessing the ministry of palliative care of Dr. Sanchez-Reilly and her team—and I do consider it a ministry—I now believe that it is incumbent on me, as family member or close friend, to also invite "comfort communication" with a dying loved one—to give that person emotional space and grace to explore with me their thoughts and feelings about leaving. It's my hope that this book will provoke medical caregiver, communication expert, and layperson alike to reexamine their own feelings and beliefs about how best to walk beside the dying.

Sandra Sanchez-Reilly

One of many cases

His tears just come out suddenly as we are having THE conversation. I am no longer able to see his eyes, they are so blurred; I hear silence. Silence is so very noisy!! The members of the team can barely breathe, some of them cannot avoid crying, and others are ashamed of crying. One of our learners cannot take the silence and tries to comfort Mr. Saenz. Mr. Saenz is no longer listening. The worlds "terminal cancer" burn inside like plain fire … It is so bad that he even forgot about his unbearable back pain for a moment.

Mr. Saenz was 49 two weeks ago; now he feels like 108, he said. He was a very active man, loving husband and a responsible father and grandfather. When he was younger, Mr. Saenz had tried intravenous drugs and heavy alcohol intake. After some time, Mr. Saenz went to rehabilitation, fell in love with his wife and his life improved. Mr. Saenz became a construction worker, building a dream house for his bride. They enjoyed dancing, they did some traveling, they had pets. Kids were born, and life just went on.

However, Mr. Saenz was given a diagnosis of hepatitis B and C during a screening visit to his physician not so long ago. The Saenz family was devastated by the news at the time, but loving and forgiving as they were, they all supported Mr. Saenz into seeking treatment to control this chronic disease. But Mr. Saenz kept losing weight, his skin color changed to a jaundiced tone, his appetite was almost gone, and he experienced increasing lower back pain. More doctors' visits followed, and then, the news: CANCER, the C word! What can I do? I can tell them the truth in a way they can understand, I can give them hope for comfort and a better quality of life, I can give them our team's support, I can secretly pray for them, I can educate their health care providers to make things easier, I can relieve suffering. It sounds very nice and productive, but unfortunately, I cannot change their prognosis, and that is exactly what my patients want. It is what it is: palliative care, the art of relieving suffering and comforting patients and families.

How did I get here?

Well, I was always interested in caring for older adults. My maternal grandmother was the biggest influence in my life when I was growing up. She was a strong woman who suffered a great deal when she raised her family. She shared all her wisdom, prayers, and tenderness with me. My grandmother died in my arms, her eyes opened, when I was eleven, and since then, I wanted to "cure everybody." I thought that medical school would teach me how to save people from dying, but soon after, I realized how erroneous my thought process was at the time. I learned that I could make a difference in learning to improve chronic diseases, particularly in the elderly. Throughout my internal medicine residency, I was able to learn to "control" illnesses. This brought some closure to my desire of helping older folks; however, I felt that what I was doing was not enough.

One night, as I was doing my "night float" rotation, I saw an older gentleman hugging his wife as she lay on her ICU bed with a ventilator connected to her throat. He would sing to her in Russian, he would tell her about their home and old memories. As I was visiting other patients of the ward, this gentleman would continue to provide this tender care toward his wife. As I came the next night, and the next one until I completed my nocturnal rotation thirty days later, this gentleman was there every night, doing the same thing. I complained to my husband every day about my lack of sleep owing to this rotation, but this older adult just stayed there, comforting his wife. How lovely, I thought, wishing that some day I could do something for that gentleman and hoping that his wife would get better. Weeks later, as I was admitting patients in the emergency room, this older gentleman showed up. Mr. R was 85, and was admitted for chest pain. Mr. R had no family, and his wife had died recently. I talked with him; you could tell he did not want to live anymore, not without her. I tried to alleviate his physical pain, cardiac tests showed coronary blockage, and surgery was needed. He did not care. He just lay there, hoping that his wife would come and comfort him. Mr. R slowly recovered, but I was unable to alleviate his pain. At the time, I thought that medication would make a difference; not now—I never addressed his total pain. He needed a team; I did not know what a team was. Mr. R ultimately passed away after a long code. We could not figure it out. He was in pain, and that was painful to me.

One day, my father-in-law taped a TV series for me, saying, "It is about dying, in case you are interested." This TV show, which happened to be the Bill Moyers series called "On our own terms: Moyers on Dying," changed my life and what I wanted to become. The show was developed at Mount Sinai Hospital, in New York City, and it was about the "proper way" of caring for dying patients. Doctors and other health care professionals would get intimately involved in these private and precious moments of a person's last moments in life. Relieving suffering was the focus of the "team." A team, I thought: what an interesting concept. A team for what? Now, I smile when I think about my own naïveté. Years passed, and I was successfully accepted to one of the most prestigious geriatric fellowship programs in the United States. I did not really care about prestige at the time, but it was all about that TV show. Happily, I entered my geriatric and palliative care fellowship at Mount Sinai School of Medicine. My mentors taught me more than I ever expected I would learn in caring for frail older adults and terminally ill patients. During my training, I developed leadership skills, team-building skills, and mostly, clinical expertise. My mentors and patients taught me to become a teacher. I realized that I could not be complete without teaching this precious gift given to me. That gift is the art of comforting.

Research and academia were inculcated into my set of values, and I decided I needed to be a leader in the field and a teacher. Years later, I realize that every day I learn more than I could ever teach. My patients and their families are my mentors now, and they constantly remind me of the need of advocating for them and the need to truly relieve their suffering. Sometimes, even with knowledge and experience, this is not possible, and it is most frustrating.

A case of the famous palliative care team …

Mr. K was a sixty-seven-year-old patient who came to our VA hospital transferred from a rural setting on a Friday late afternoon. The intern who admitted the patient called our palliative care team as soon as he heard this patient's story. We were pleased at the prompt referral and rushed to Mr. K's room, happily identifying ourselves at the hospice team. Mr. K, infuriated, yelled at us and kicked us out of his room. We just had a bad start …

Mr. K was a very healthy man until about two months prior to this admission. Mr. K was a truck driver and enjoyed very much traveling. Mr. K lived on a ranch, had several pets and some cattle. Mr. K personally attended to his ranch. Mr. K had no close family but a neighbor who was very close to him. One day, Mr. K woke up with excruciating back pain. It was so bad that he could not move, and his neighbor rushed him to the local emergency room, thirty miles from their home, located in a rural area of Texas. Mr. K was sweating, pale, and agitated owing to the pain. After pain medications were administered and multiple tests run, the doctor determined this is a "heart thing." Mr. K was then admitted to the hospital, and a cardiologist was called to see him. Mr. K's pain was controlled, so he went home, but from now on he would visit doctors' offices on a daily basis. Cardiac catheterization was performed, followed by pulmonary tests and multiple imaging studies. Nothing was wrong with Mr. K, and doctors decided this was related to stress and let him go. Mr. K was never happy with this determination, and frequently he looked for a second opinion in the rural community he lived in. Unfortunately, opinions were not very different.

Mr. K went on with his life, unable to work owing to his now-constant back pain and the need for medications. One day, Mr. K not only had back pain but he also did not feel his legs anymore and was unable to walk. Mr. K was very upset with the medical system but had to go back to be rechecked. At this point, he was hospitalized for a longer period of time, and suddenly, he was given a diagnosis of pancreatic cancer with metastases to his spine. Mr. K was devastated, and very angry. Mr. K sought the opinion of an oncologist, and this physician told him that his malignancy was curable, that surgery was a possibility, and that he needed to be immediately transferred to a tertiary facility, where he would receive curative treatment. Or at least, this is what Mr. K heard.

We knew that Mr. K did not have a possibility of being cured at this point on the basis of the type and staging of his malignancy. The incidence of pancreatic cancer increases with age and becomes an important disease in the elderly, with approximately 85 percent of patients with disseminated or locally advanced disease. Mr. K did not want to wait another minute, and on he went to the closest largest city—San Antonio—and, as a veteran, he ended up in our hospital, and this is where we came along.

Mr. K arrived at our institution after a six-hour ride in an ambulance, livid with pain and anxiety, demanding to see an oncologist to start treatment right away. Of course, he was polite with us, we were the "death doctors" and "the hospice team." We tried to come back that day, but he would not see us. We tried to relieve his pain, but he refused to take any medication until he saw an oncologist. One of our oncologists came along and accurately explained to Mr. K the gravity of his prognosis. Mr. K was infuriated and asked for a second opinion. After the second opinion was similar, he asked to be left alone. He refused to eat for days and insisted that the oncologist provide him with some sort of treatment. Ultimately, palliative radiation was provided.

Finally, Mr. K did see us, and we were able to control his physical pain, and team members worked really hard in trying to alleviate his spiritual, psychological, and social pain. Mr. K would not accept his diagnosis. He would not hear of planning for the future or being comfortable as his main goal or contacting his family. For weeks, Mr. K's whole pain deeply affected us, and we, the palliative care experts, were unable to help. Or maybe we did; up until this day, I do not know.

Mr. K became very ill, and he called me to tell me that he did want his neighbor to make decisions for him. I asked him what his preferences were; he said, "I am not ready to die, my preference is to change this, can you help?" I could not, but I could listen, and I did. Mr. K became comatose and, on the basis of his wishes, his neighbor focused everyone's efforts on comfort care. Mr. K died peacefully in our hospice unit, with all of us by his bedside. He told me and the rest of the team that we knew nothing about relieving pain, that we needed to listen, that we needed to "feel their pain" to be able to understand. Mr. K told me that we too have limitations, and most of all, that our patients are our best teachers.

The team

Looking back, I wonder … how could medicine survive without an interdisciplinary team? We physicians think that we know it all. My team has taught me otherwise. From interdisciplinary meetings to daily rounds to hall encounters, each team member does bring a unique expertise that makes our team and the service provided much better. It is crucial that teams get together, that teams have self-care activities, and that everyone on the team is equal.

Mr. M is an eighty-seven-year-old patient who has been admitted ten times over the last three months. He was recently started on hemo dialysis as his kidneys do not work anymore. He has leg ulcers and received a leg amputation a few months ago owing to vascular disease. He is almost blind from his diabetes and in constant pain owing to peripheral neuropathy. Mr. M has a lovely wife who is wheelchair-bound and has many illnesses. He has two daughters who live out of town. A family meeting has been called to better help the family with decisions regarding his plan of care, specifically comfort care and code status. The meeting, however, was not planned by physicians; it was our chaplain's idea. The meeting was conducted by our nurse, who marvelously was able to listen to the family's concerns. The meeting was successful because all members were there. Medical questions were answered by the physician, information about placement possibilities and benefits was given by our social worker, and prayer was offered by our chaplain. The family was comforted by the team. I saw the family smiling, I saw them happy, they had answers and they had a plan. We, the team, complemented one another. We accomplished a mission as a team.

The other side of your life: home

So, you are ready to go home. It is late in the afternoon, you are tired and "talked out." Conferences, meetings, rounds, notes, and finally, you get to go home. Home? I remember, yes, home. Where I have a nice house and a loving husband and beautiful kids waiting for me, at the other side of my life. How can I go home when I have so much to do? How can I leave my patients and my team? But the answer is: You must. You belong to your family first; you are who you are because you are part of your family. They need to see me, and support me, and listen to the marvelous stories I have to tell them about my patients.

It is such an honor to care for terminally ill patients and their families! They share with us some of the most important moments of their existence: their transition out of this world, their suffering, and their conflicts. And we must give our patients everything we have to help them. Part of that is who we are, and part of who we are is our family. I have to go home to help my patients "go home." So then I go, and my child's laugh takes me back to appreciate how beautiful life is, and my husband's questions remind me of the living memories of my patients, and I start again: "Honey, let me tell you a story …"

Joy Goldsmith

NAME: Goldsmith, Janet C

\# 098-29-8493

███████████, M.D.

DATE: 02/21/2002

ROOM#: 9MAI095003

OPERATIVE REPORT

PREOPERATIVE DIAGNOSIS: Abdominal mass, rule out neoplasm.

POSTOPERATIVE DIAGNOSIS: Metastatic adenosquamous carcinoma to inguinal nodes, rectus muscle and pulmonary nodules.

OPERATION: Excision of right inguinal lymph node; incisional biopsy right rectus mass.

ANESTHESIA: General.

INDICATIONS: Janet Goldsmith is a 33-year-old white female, Presbyterian minister from Milledgeville, Georgia who was seen and worked up over their [sic] by her gynecologist for fertility studies and has seen Dr. ███████████ for diabetes studies, she has got a huge right rectus mass, inguinal nodes, CT scan showing positive bilateral pulmonary nodules and patient needs to have tissue diagnosis, we need a piece of this to go from there. Detailed this to her and her husband at length, see the detailed history and physical.

PROCEDURE: The patient was brought to the operating room with her and her husband's full consent, full understanding, placed on the operating room table, anesthesia included, the abdomen is examined under anesthesia, it is rock hard in the entire right rectus, there is a multinodular mass in the rectus. There is also some prominent inguinal adenopathy. The right inguinal adenopathy is most prominent and the left is scanty shotty nodes. We prepped the abdomen, right rectus and groin area, draped it off in a sterile fashion.

First, a transverse incision is made over the large right inguinal node. I dissected down and took out a 2 cm diameter pale tan-gray node entirely intact. I sent it down to Dr. █████████, she did a frozen section and called back and her first comment was that this was compatible with metastatic adenosquamous carcinoma of endocervix, and we then did a rectus muscle biopsy; we just simply opened the skin over one of these bulging nodules in the mid rectus and this thing was hard as a piece of balsa wood. We carved a shaving off of it and it was compatible with metastatic adenocarcinoma. I conversed at length with Dr. ████████ and gave her several extra pieces of tissue for cytology, etc.

That makes this lady have a positive tumor diagnosis, we have got to obviously wait for cell studies, cytologic assays, etc., but we have now got pulmonary, abdominal wall and inguinal masses. This is not good.

We closed the wounds and 2-0 Chromic and skin with staples and a pressure dressing applied. Patient was sent to the recovery room.

At this point I went out and very diplomatically got father ██████, the hospital chaplain, to come meet with me and her husband and her sister in Ms. ████████'s office, with █████████████████ from the recovery room. I explained to Mr. Goldsmith precisely what we had found, got him encouraged to be upbeat with her. I explained to him how bad a diagnosis this is and how it became a nonsurgical problem and it is now clearly an adjuvant therapy problem. He understood this very well.

It was pretty emotional for him but it was handled well.

After we got finished with this, I asked him some more of the history and it turns out that the history is more intriguing than before.

In September 2001, she went to the gynecologist in █████████, Illinois for fertility workup, had an endocervical punch biopsy that was sent to the local pathologist and read it as positive for adenocarcinoma. They sent out for a second opinion because of her age, Indianapolis pathologist reported no cancer was present. Even further now with the two diagnoses, they went to the ███████ Clinic, it was sent there and they came back from the ████████ Clinic and said there was no carcinoma. They pursued the fertility workup.

Subsequently, she had to have laparoscopic removal of an ovary and then laparoscopic removal of a cyst and she was told with some swelling in the rectus muscle at █████████, that this was a hematoma of the rectus muscle, so she came down to Milledgeville three weeks ago, finally decided that this mass was growing and came to see me.

Therefore we have already have been in consulatation with Dr. , the pathologist here, got her department seeking as much information from █████████, Il, Indianapolis as possible.

We will get Dr. ████████████ to help with this patient.

This lady has now got a terrible diagnosis and a prognosis is very very dismal. The husband was very understanding. We then went in and had a very long talk with her in the recovery room with several people listening. She was very appreciative for the straightforward honesty.

███████████, M. D.
D: 02/21/2002 T: 02/22/2002 8:57 P

In the operation report for my sister, Dr. E effectively and at times warmly describes the marked change in life that was upon us that day. Jan and I would revisit this report and read it with a longing for that warmth in the physicians we were subsequently surrounded by. Dr. E. had a way about him that let us know he hated this news and he wanted things to be different than the way they had turned out.

I remember my reaction when he told us in the room with the chaplain. I knew things were strange because we were herded to a room far away from where we had been waiting, and a man in a green blazer was there; he seemed to be doing "pastoral" things on our entry. Dr. E told us he had the "worst possible news he could have": that my big sister had metastatic adenocarcinoma. I remember calling my parents and telling them how sorry I was; before I told them, I called their pastor and made sure he was on his way to their house. I remember sobbing on the floor of the public waiting area; the TV was blaring and an unknown woman came and sat with my husband and me; he explained what was wrong, and the woman prayed for Jan. When we were with Jan in the recovery area, Dr. E told her the same way he told us: "this is the worst news I could have for you." She was groggy, but seemed to get it. She saw our eyes and his and said "This is so disappointing."

She fully awoke on the oncology floor of the same hospital. There were brochures for buying/fitting wigs and dealing with chemo and radiation side effects next to her hospital bed. Dr. E was not an oncologist but rather a surgeon who specializes in excising infectious spider and snake bites. We had been sent on to the world of oncology without him. We did not see an oncologist until late the next afternoon. Twenty-four hours was a lifetime to spend without any more information. We did not have this operation report, or even know we had the right to go find it. Finally at 5:00 PM on that Friday afternoon, Dr. D, an oncologist, came to see us. He was sick with stomach flu and nearly vomited in her room. He was there for less than one minute. We were hurling questions at him, desperate to learn about her diagnosis and what we should/could do to care for her. He looked terrible and was backing out of her room sweaty and pale. Dr. D. indicated that we should come and see him on Tuesday—four days later. He left. I called his practice and left a message with his partner asking some questions, like "what is adenocarcinoma," "what is metastatic disease," "what should we do"? The physician did return the call but would not speak with me about the case as this was her partner's patient and case. We quizzed the nurses who came to supply postsurgical care about the few words we retained from Dr. E and Dr. D, but they were reticent to speak of even basic definitions.

Though Dr. E's operative report indicates Jan's husband "understood …very well" that she would benefit only from adjuvant care, I can tell you for certain that we as family had no idea what was truly going on with her life other than she had cancer all over her body. We did not know; she did not know; we were desperate for a conversation with an oncologist, and it was five days after diagnosis before we were able to experience this. As a family, we have speculated about which was the more bizarre occurrence—her diagnosis or the communication we experienced in those days after her biopsy surgery.

We Goldsmiths fall into the category of the inquisitive. I moved to be with my sister and take care of her. All of my family wanted information, unpacked language, explanations, physician communication, and most of all whatever Jan wanted. From a retrospective view, especially now as a health communication researcher, our path was full of frantic steps. I was tenacious and fierce as her caretaker; these are not always great qualities when negotiating health care. That Tuesday with Dr. D, at last recovered from his flu, was a dark day. The visit was very short—less than fifteen minutes in my recollection. There were many of us together in his office: my dad, Jan, me, her husband, and her best friend. Dr. D stood for the appointment. He shared that this was likely metastatic cancer with no known source and Jan would have less than a year of life. We all were weepy, asked him what would keep us from pursuing help at a comprehensive cancer center, and he indicated that nothing would. This ends part one of our diagnosis. We knew she had cancer all over. We did not know enough; what was it, where did it start, why did she have it, what could we do? There was a world of trouble that we were consumed by, and there was no conversation to be had about our local oncology experience. There was also no discussion about palliative care.

My other sister Kath called our cousin-in-law, Karen, a radiation oncologist in St. Louis. This was the first we had heard of something called unknown primary. Adenocarcinoma of unknown primary site (ACUPS) is a diagnosis given to metastatic cancer patients with an unclear cell pathology; there is no indication via tissue cytology as to the beginning point of the cancer—thus no clear way to treat the disease. In essence, we received from a distant relative clarification about Jan's diagnosis a week after her biopsy.

Our next move was a questionable one, in hindsight. We worked mightily to gain entry into a comprehensive cancer center in Texas for further diagnostics and treatment. Several more weeks of tests and biopsies did make ACUPS the official diagnosis. We opted for an aggressive treatment regimen of chemotherapy and radiation. This marked a shift from the simple prognosis of "one year or less of life" to "the next treatment." Her treatment plan mushroomed; she almost immediately gained a harem of doctors that trailed from Texas to Georgia treating various segments of her illness involving her eyes, skin, skeletal system, diabetes, nerves, muscles, pain, physical digression, inguinal and rectus tumor growth, and blood quality. Throughout our nine-month journey, there were twenty plus physician-cooks in the kitchen: surgeon, gynecologists (two), oncological gynecologists (two), endocrinologist, oncologists (five), radiation oncologists (two), radiation ophthalmologist, ophthalmologists (two), dermatologist, pain and palliative care physicians (three), vascular physician, and a hospitalist. We could not see the forest for the trees. Her care dominated. In pursuing cancer treatment, we were pursuing aggressive therapies—many of which had no impact on the course of the disease and a costly effect on her quality of life.

Metastatic cancer of unknown primary site ACUPS is a common occurrence, accounting for between 2 and 15 percent of all cancer diagnoses (Hainsworth & Greco, 2000; Shahab & Perry, 2005). A more pernicious subset of unknown primary site is ACUPS, poorly differentiated; Jan was in this subset. Only 5 percent of all unknown primary diagnoses are poorly differentiated. Despite the frequency of the disease, minimal attention and treatment progress have been made; this syndrome lags behind many other less common cancers. Hainsworth and Greco (2000) believe that the extremely poor prognosis and therapy effects for patients have been the primary reason for the lack of effort in this area.

The overall prognosis of ACUPS is poor. The median survival for these patients as a whole is three to five months, and less than 25 percent are alive after one year. People with multiple sites of involvement, including lung, brain, and liver, have a life expectancy measured in weeks (Hoskin & Makin, 2003, p. 256). Kagan and Steckel (2000) note that ACUPS is incurable, as it is unidentifiable until it is overwhelmingly metastatic, and in most cases there is still no effective oncological palliative treatment available. Any gain from chemotherapy is likely to be minimal and unclear. Around 30 percent of patients show a short-term response that can mitigate symptoms and depression (according to some physician authors) but is unlikely to increase the life of the cancer patient; median survival rates for patients receiving chemotherapy are still only four to five months (Hoskin and Makin, 2003).

No one knew this better than the oncologists we came to know. Though bizarre and inadequate, Dr. D with the flu was the most straightforward about my sister's prognosis, though we were fully doubtful of his knowledge and care for her by the time we were able to meet with him five days after her biopsy operation. We did not trust him. A very unclear explanation of her deathly illness combined with our own desperate need for a restoration narrative led us down the path of exhaustive chemotherapeutic and radiologic treatments. Some of these were palliative in nature, but many were not.

Early on in our forest-for-the-trees treadmill of travel, treatment, and side effect illness, Jan and I would ask her oncologists, "What if this does not work?" as if neither of us could remember the initial diagnosis. Trained with the same protocols, they all redirected our thinking onto the next task or hurdle and kept us from seeing the longer road ahead. Ironically, she died with no will in place and a bookshelf of knowledge in her pastor's study about "helping your family grieve a loved one." Though we possessed some awareness that she was declining and losing and she talked about her death, we did not know it was happening or live in a way that would celebrate the quality of life outside of biomedical success. There were not conversations about the illness and its groundswell, even as she became incontinent and suddenly discovered masses on her arm and skull. Dying was not communicated as part of the illness process by the physicians who took care of her.

Training programs in oncology continue to be dominated by research into the development and application of chemotherapeutic agents. Weissman (2003) notes that "95 percent of the questions on the Oncology Board Examination focus on cancer diseases, their diagnosis and chemotherapeutic and radiologic management" (p. 860). This emphasis on treatment leaves little room for discussions of end-of-life care and palliation.

Palliative care must become part of the conversation between physicians and their patients—whatever the ailment. Discussions early on in any disease process and visited throughout the disease process will give patients and family an opportunity to digest information and plan. Waiting and denying difficult conversations might decrease stress in the moment but create an enormous impact for patient and family near the end of life. Integrating palliative care means a change in medical education, communication training, and patient care: a paradigm shift of enormous proportion.

Palliative care education is receiving increasing attention and time in medical school. This trend will continue as palliative care was just approved by the Medical Board as an area of specialization. Palliative care fellowships are increasing in number, and more physicians are receiving exposure to specific training in this area of medicine. At present, this special kind of doctoring is fairly compartmentalized; palliative care teams are the clean-up crew for the larger medical system. Without integrating palliative thought into medicine as a whole, compartmentalized palliative care enables other kinds of physicians not to discuss end-of-life care and dying with patients. This process can and should be altered with a heavier presence of palliative care pedagogy in all programs of health care education.

In our patients' perspectives chapter, patients near the end of their lives shared that they wanted more information and time with their physician. This is what Jan and I longed for as well —information and time. As palliative care education takes hold in medical schools, the patients' perspective should be valued heavily in the curriculum. SPIKES protocol is the primary vehicle for teaching palliative care physicians about sharing difficult news with patients. Research that asks patients about their experience with SPIKES reveals that the protocol is of secondary concern to the amount of time that physicians spent with their patients. Time is the most precious resource that any person has. As with many models and protocols, I believe that the SPIKES protocol includes space for improvement. It will be worthwhile to discover a better route to the patient's perception of their illness. In many instances, the SPIKES protocol reveals that patients are wrong about the curative status they have hopefully described to the doctor. What patients have the right to know, if they wish, is the knowledge about their prognosis. SPIKES requires a patient first be put through a testing period of questions to decrease the stress on the physician.

The physician is short of time because of the enormous demands of a job with elastic boundaries; dying patients have even further reduced time and need information—or simply the presence of the relationship with their physician. Time spent with a patient is time in the realm of thirty minutes, as opposed to fifteen minutes or less. Changes must be made so that this can be the priority for care. Mistakes made about disease perception and painful memories of communication incompetence are high costs for patient and family and for physician. Time and information are two ingredients that are proven mitigating factors in sharing difficult news and the process of dying.

Elaine Wittenberg-Lyles

Not long after I began my first graduate course in health communication, my father-in-law, a one-year lung cancer survivor, made an announcement at the dinner table one night: "They say it's in my head now." Five months later, he died peacefully in bed one early evening. However, the events that transpired in the last five months of his life were hardly ideal. The last day of his life was spent at the hospital, waiting for and receiving a flu shot and, though he was enrolled in hospice care, their services were provided for approximately six hours. I remember seeing him return from the hospital around 4 PM the day he died. He could barely walk, and I can vividly remember hearing him struggle to breathe, a concept I now more familiarly know as a death rattle. Within the next two hours, he became incontinent, but his family somehow managed to dress him and put him to bed. His last words were to my husband as he tucked him in bed: "I'm tired. I just want to rest."

Though my father-in-law's death could be described as a 'good' death by many standards (he died in bed, seemingly asleep, and most of his immediate family were home), his journey reveals some of the many atrocities occurring in our health care practices and system, many of which illustrate the overwhelming need for palliative care. His journey was lonely—he drove himself to his own radiation appointments; the family knew very little about what was going on; and his wife struggled to manage his care by herself. Those last five months went by quickly and it's unclear whether or not he knew he was terminal. Though I suspect that this is the way he wanted it, preferring not to be a burden to his family, I can't help but think how different his journey would have been with palliative care services: his physician would have talked to him about advance care planning and his disease progression, the family would have become more involved (it's likely he was by himself if given the bad news), and support services could have been provided for his wife and later bereavement support for his family. More important, his final day of life would have been spent at home and not at the hospital.

This experience, coupled with my graduate education in health communication, emerged as a pivotal point in defining my life's passion of promoting and educating others about the many benefits of end-of-life care. My doctoral dissertation focused on hospice volunteers, and I spent countless hours collecting stories from volunteers, attending volunteer meetings and workshops, and undergoing volunteer training. Without much personal experience with death or as a hospice caregiver, I felt a need to get more involved to really understand the complex communicative dynamics that surface in end-of-life care. A year later, I again witnessed a journey without palliative care and very little hospice care—the journey of my uncle—and I began to realize the important features of early palliative care.

My uncle was given a diagnosis of lung cancer in the fall and, by Christmas, he had been in and out of the hospital numerous times. On hearing about the diagnosis, I wanted to send information about palliative care. I was discouraged by friends and other family members and never did. I struggled with the appropriateness of sending literature on a service that included end-of-life care when the diagnosis was so new. I realized that even friends and families have communication challenges when a loved one or friend is terminally ill. Negotiating the fine line between hope and quality of life is difficult, even for outsiders not caught up in the crisis. Often friends and family are aware of the terminality of the disease but never suggest such care services.

Before his death in March, I saw my uncle twice. Each time, he adamantly reassured me that he would beat his disease. Two weeks before he died, our family convened in his hospital room for a visit. No one talked about hospice, death, or dying, and my uncle continued to talk about new treatment options and his health. In a vivid moment that I will never forget, he publicly declared his love for my aunt and shared with everyone how much she meant to him and how well she had cared for him in the last months. I am thankful that I experienced that moment, that he shared his thoughts so openly with others, and it stands out as a crucial turning point that has shaped my own ideas and beliefs about palliative care.

His journey was without palliative care, and he fought long and hard to triumph over his disease. The desire to fight is an inherent quality of the culture's ideas and beliefs about medicine, and the transition from a hope for a cure to a hope for the best quality of life is difficult, particularly when friends and family subscribe to the same ideologies. Fears about acknowledging the end of one's life and losing hope are seen as pessimistic view points in light of the modern miracles of medicine and science. I now know that a palliative care team helps families and patients to make this transition and, without palliative care, patients and families continually strive to fight the disease-illness, and patients undergo unnecessary treatments, losing quality time that could be spent sharing final thoughts with loved ones. The palliative care team helps patients and families to manage uncertainty about the health crisis by opening up communication about death, dying, and unfinished business. Though my uncle's journey was without palliative care, that moment in his hospital room captured the meaning of palliative care and provided me with a glimpse of the richness of palliative care services.

Shortly after my uncle's death, I contacted a local hospice and invested more time with patients, families, and hospice interdisciplinary teams. I felt a need to get closer, more involved in hospice care services to understand end-of-life care and contexts; and I believed that this was my duty and responsibility as a researcher in this area. How could I study death and dying if I had never really experienced the health crisis that many patients and families go through? How could I study hospice care if I didn't understand staff responsibilities and daily experiences and the health care system in which it operates? How could I study death and dying without talking to dying patients and capturing a glimpse of their journey? At the same time, I realized that I needed to face my own fears about death and dying and fears about talking to terminally ill patients and families. Thus, my decision to engage in in-depth field research was for both personal and professional reasons.

A local hospice welcomed me into their organization, and I became a regular attendee at interdisciplinary team meetings. More important, I was afforded the opportunity to shadow case managers and hospice admission representatives on their initial patient visits. I interviewed staff about their experiences, their hardships, and the perceived benefits of their job and began to experience the incredible world of hospice care. During my time with several different hospices, I continued to witness the struggle to broach topics, such as death, dying, and hospice, and observed the hardships involved in making such care decisions. One patient stands out very vividly from my time spent with hospice.

On one occasion, I accompanied a nurse case manager on a follow-up visit with a woman who was having a hard time deciding whether to enroll in hospice care. It was one of my first hospital visits, and as I entered the room, I quickly noticed the woman's husband standing at her bedside. The patient was crying, telling the hospice nurse that she was afraid of hospice. She was afraid of what would happen to her, where she would go from the hospital, and of the pain she was experiencing. I watched as the nurse and the patient discussed hospice care and services; the patient continued to re-focus the conversation around her physical pain, and the husband would intermittingly tell her that this is why she needed hospice. Suddenly, the husband broke down and began to cry. He took his wife's hand and said to her, "I've been married to you for almost twenty-five years. I have never cheated on you. I have never lied to you. I'm not lying to you now. You need hospice. I need hospice. We need hospice." He leaned into her, and the two of them began to sob. The hospice nurse and I quietly excused ourselves and gave them some time alone. I was so touched by his statement, by his approach to his wife, and by how much this apparently meant to her. Looking back on this and other experiences, I have realized that there is no such thing as vulnerability when a person is terminally ill; fear of being vulnerable is forgotten, and end-of-life care can create this loss of vulnerability that can facilitate important dialogue, important conversations between terminally ill patients and family members.

Ultimately, however, I felt I could not fully understand patient and family experiences primarily from hospice research. For example, I couldn't understand why so many patients did not want hospice services. Why was this woman so afraid of hospice? Why were so many patients and families like her not willing to elect hospice care? More important, I was shocked to find out that many patients we visited had never heard of hospice, didn't understand what hospice care services included, and that *many* patients *did not know* that they were hospice-appropriate. One hospice nurse told me that she never says "hospice" when she initially calls a patient to set up an initial visit. She had made the mistake of doing this early on in her career and found out that her visit is *often* the first time the patient and family hear about hospice.

Reflecting on my experiences in hospice, I realized that I met many hospice patients and their families who had never been exposed to palliative care services. Many of the patients had been in and out of hospitals and had been seen by several specialists who each provided a different scenario, none of which included discussions of terminal illness or hospice care. I knew that I needed to learn more about what happens to patients and families prior to the arrival and introduction of hospice care. I knew that I had to go to where the entire process began, I had to learn more about the health care system, physicians, and palliative care in action. I had to go to the hospital.

Again, with no personal experience in a clinical setting, I embarked on a journey to the unknown. For six months, I followed a geriatric palliative care team at a local veteran's hospital. I attended interdisciplinary team meetings, participated in research with fellows, went on patient consultations, and interviewed fellows. After one of my early days at the hospital, one of my reflective writings in my journal highlighted my initial fears and feelings:

> End of the first two weeks at the hospital and patient rounds. I'm still nervous about being there. I consciously do not put on perfume the days that I go to the hospital—I'm not sure why. I guess I think it will interfere with the patients. I'm very conscious about what I wear. I've been wearing the white jacket during rounds. I don't put it on until I get to the room where I meet the rest of the team. I feel like a fake doctor wearing it. I want to tell patients and families that I am not really with them. I'm just a researcher.

Initially, I was afraid of the patients—I was afraid of hurting them. I was afraid I would say something wrong. I was afraid they would ask me something. I was afraid someone would mistake me for a doctor because of the jacket and expect me to save their life. Later, my journal writings reflect how much I wanted to be part of the team. I wanted so much to contribute to the care they provided patients, and I found myself spending more and more time at the hospital. Each time I would leave the hospital, I would call my mother, my best friend, or my husband. I would profess love to them, I would recall the day's experiences and remind them of how thankful we should be for everything in our lives. I would cry. I would drive to my office crying for patients, for families, for the suffering that I witnessed, for the love that I was able to feel between patients and family members, and for the gratefulness that I have for my health. I called friends and family members and let my wishes be known—and said what had been unsaid in many important relationships.

The patients, families, and palliative care team members created unbelievable experiences. Overall, it took time with a palliative care team and their patients to begin to understand the complexity of and communication challenges embedded in the provision of palliative care. The nuances of end-of-life communication have become increasingly transparent, and I continue to learn from these experiences, both professionally and personally. After more than a year of in-depth field research, I recognize that many of the patients and families that I have had the privilege of observing are living through some of their first hospital experiences with a palliative care team.

We share our personal backgrounds as a means of tracing our own experiences in palliative care and offer some final thoughts. First, palliative care must begin at diagnosis if we are to properly provide effective and sufficient end-of-life care for *all* patients. Particularly as an aspect of end-of-life care, palliative care is an intervention that empowers patients and families and gives them choices. I have learned from my uncle and others that each patient has different care goals. Each patient has a different journey; some patients wish to fight to the end, whereas others wish to take a more pragmatic approach. Either way, palliative care increases the likelihood that communication about death and dying takes place through *awareness* that certain illnesses are life-threatening and that suffering can be ameliorated.

Second, early palliative care practices ensure that patients receive the full benefits and expertise of the entire palliative care team. Namely, more time is needed with patients to develop relationships between patient, family, and team. Third, barriers to palliative care exist because of preconceived ideas about death and dying. There is a lack of education about palliative care, hospice care, and the goals of end-of-life care in general in the United States. As a result palliative care team members approach patients and families "under cover" or "incognito." But whom do we educate? Do we educate patients to ask for palliative care? Do we need to educate more physicians about end-of-life care? We would respond with an unequivocal *yes* to the need to educate both patients and physicians about palliative care. Finally, caregivers and family members are an important part of palliative care. Often, palliative care and palliative care team members work through caregivers to provide services to patients. Caregivers and family members are a valuable resource in the provision of palliative care and warrant more attention.

Japp *et al.* (2005) explain that personal narratives are the core of public knowledge. In this volume, we have championed the personal narrative for its insight and grit and what it can teach all players in the journey of advanced and terminal illness and end-of-life care. These soulful, detailed stories unpack problems, build rhetorical positions, reveal feelings, inform, convince, judge, and provide a "face" for the particular issue of suffering at the end of life. The many personal stories of the participants and authors bring meaning to the larger public narrative concerning communication and palliative care.

Bibliography

Abraham, A., Kutner, J., and Beaty, B. (2006) Suffering at the end of life in the setting of low physical symptom distress. *Journal of Palliative Medicine*, 9(3), 658–65.

Accreditation Council for Graduate Medical Education (2006) ACGME Board adds hospice and palliative care as new subspecialty. Retrieved August 1, 2006 from www.acgme.org/acWebsite/newsReleases/newsRel_07_20_06.asp.

Alexander, P. (2004) An investigation of inpatient referrals to a clinical psychologist in a hospice. *European Journal of Cancer Care*, 13(1), 36–44.

Alexander, S.C., Keitz, S.A., Sloane, R., and Tulsky, J.A. (2006) A controlled trial of a short course to improve residents' communication with patients at end of life. *Academic Medicine*, 81(11), 1008–12.

Ambuel, B., and Mazzone, M. (2001) Breaking bad news and discussing death. *Primary Care*, 28(2), 249–67.

American Academy on Communication in Healthcare (2004) Upcoming courses and meetings. www.aachonline.org.

American Psychological Association (APA) (2006). End-of-life issues and care: the role of psychology in end-of-life decisions and quality of care issues. Retrieved January 4, 2007 from www.apa.org/pi/eol/role.html.

Amitabha Hospice Service (2007) A brief history of hospice care. Retrieved February 1, 2007 from www.amitabhahospice.org/hospice/general_history.php.

Arnold, S.J., and Koczwara, B. (2006) Breaking bad news: learning through experience. *Journal of Clinical Oncology*, 24(31), 5098–100.

Babrow, A.S. (1992) Communication and problematic integration: understanding diverging probability and value, ambiguity, ambivalence, and impossibility. *Communication Theory*, 2(2), 95–130.

Babrow, A.S. (2001) Uncertainty, value, communication, and problematic integration. *Journal of Communication*, 51(3), 553–74.

Babrow, A.S., and Mattson, M. (2003) Theorizing about health communication. In T. Thompson, A. Dorsey, K. Miller, and R.A. Parrot (eds), *Handbook of Health Communication*. Mahwah, NJ: Lawrence Erlbaum.

Back, A.L., Arnold, R.M., Tulsky, J.A., Baile, W. F., and Fryer-Edwards, K.A. (2003) Teaching communication skills to medical oncology fellows. *Journal of Clinical Oncology*, 21(12), 2433–6.

Baile, W., Buckman, R., Lenzi, R., Blober, G., Beale, E., and Kudelka, A. (2000) SPIKES—a six step protocol for delivering bad news: application to the patient with cancer. *Oncologist*, 5(4), 302–11.

Bakhtin, M.M. (1981) *The Dialogic Imagination: Four Essays by M. M. Bakhtin* (M. Holquist, ed.; C. Emerson and M. Holquist, trans.) Austin, TX: University of Texas Press.

Bakhtin, M.M. (1984) *Problems of Dostoevsky's Poetics* (C. Emerson, ed. and trans.) Minneapolis, MN: University of Minnesota Press.

Bakhtin, M.M. (1986) *Speech Genres and Other Late Essays* (C. Emerson and M. Holquist, eds, V. McGee, trans.) Austin, TX: University of Texas Press.

Balmer, C. (2005) The information requirements of people with cancer: where to go after the "patient leaflet"? *Cancer Nursing*, 28(1), 36–44.

Barnard, D., Towers, A.M., Boston, P., and Lambrinidou, Y. (2000) *Crossing Over: Narratives of Palliative Care*. New York: Oxford University Press.

Bateson, G. (1972) *Steps to an Ecology of Mind*. New York: Ballantine Books.

Baxter, L. (1988) A dialectical perspective on communication strategies in relationship development. In S. Duck (ed.), *Handbook of Personal Relationships: Theory, Research and Interventions*. New York: John Wiley and Sons.

Baxter, L. (1992) Interpersonal communication as dialogue: a response to the "social approaches" forum. *Communication Theory*, 2(4), 330–7.

Baxter, L. (1994) A dialogic approach to relationship maintenance. In D.J. Canary and L. Stafford (eds), *Communication and Relational Maintenance*. New York: Academic Press.

Beach, W. (2002) Between dad and son: initiating, delivering and assimilating bad cancer news. *Health Communication*, 14(3), 271–98.

Berger, P.L., and Luckmann, T. (1966) *The Social Construction of Reality: A Treatise in the Sociology of Knowledge*. Garden City, NY: Doubleday.

Bern-Klug, M., and Chapin, R. (1999) The changing demography of death in the United States: implications for human service workers. In B. de Vries (ed.), *End of Life Issues: Interdisciplinary and Multidimensional Perspectives*. New York: Springer.

Billings, J.A., and Block, S. (1997) Palliative care in undergraduate medical education: status report and future directions. *Journal of the American Medical Association*, 278(9), 733–8.

Billings, J., and Kolton, E. (1999) Family satisfaction and bereavement care following death in the hospital. *Journal of Palliative Medicine*, 2(1), 33–49.

Black, K. (2006) Advance directive communication: nurses' and social workers' perceptions of roles. *American Journal of Hospice and Palliative Medicine*, 23(3), 175–84.

Bloche, M. (2005) Managing conflict at the end of life. *New England Journal of Medicine*, 352(23), 2371–3.

Bloom, S.W. (1988) Structure and ideology in medical education: an analysis of resistance to change. *Journal of Health and Social Behavior*, 29(4), 294–306.

Boyle, D. (2006) Delirium in older adults with cancer: implications for practice and research. *Oncology Nursing Forum*, 33(1), 61–78.

Brashers, D.E., Neidig, J.L., and Goldsmith, D.J. (2004) Social support and the management of uncertainty for people living with HIV or AIDS. *Health Communication*, 16(3), 305–31.

Brooks, P. (1984) *Reading for Plot: Design and Intention in Narrative*. New York: Vintage Books.

Brown, B.B., Altman, I., and Werner, C.M. (1992) Close relationships in the physical and social world: dialectical and transactional analyses. In S.A. Deetz (ed.), *Communication Yearbook* 15. Thousand Oaks, CA: Sage Publications.

Buckman, R. (1998) Communication in palliative care: a practical guide. In D. Doyle, G.W.C. Hanks, and N. MacDonald (eds), *Oxford Textbook of Palliative Medicine* (2nd edn) New York: Oxford University Press.

Buckman, R. (2005) Breaking bad news: the S-P-I-K-E-S strategy. *Community Oncology*, 2(2), 138–42.

Burke, K. (1945) *A Grammar of Motives*. Berkeley, CA: University of California Press.

Burke, K. (1957) *Philosophy of Literary Form*. New York: Vintage Books.

Callahan, D. (2000) *The Troubled Dream of Life: In Search of a Peaceful Death*. Washington, DC: Georgetown University Press.

Campbell, M.L., and Guzman, J.A. (2003) Impact of a proactive approach to improve end-of-life care in a medical ICU. *CHEST*, 123(1), 266–71.

Carson, R. (2002) The hyphenated space: liminality in the doctor–patient relationship. In R. Charon and M. Montello (eds), *Stories Matter: The Role of Narrative in Medical Ethics*. New York: Routledge.

Cassell, E.J. (2004) *The Nature of Suffering and the Goals of Medicine* (2nd edn) New York: Oxford University Press.

Center for Medicare and Medicaid Services (2002) Program information on Medicare, Medicaid, SCHIP, and other programs of the Center for Medicare and Medicaid Services. Retrieved February 1, 2007 from http://www.cms.hhs.gov/TheChartSeries/02_CMS_Facts_Figures.asp#TopOfPage.

Center to Advance Palliative Care (2007) Organizational website. Retrieved January 25, 2007 from http://www.capc.org/.

Charon, R., and Bruner, J. (2002) Narratives of human plight: a conversation with Jermone Bruner. In R. Charon and M. Montello (eds), *Stories Matter: The Role of Narrative in Medical Ethics*. Routledge: NewYork.

Cherny, N., and Catane, R. (2003) Attitudes of medical oncologists toward palliative care for patients with advanced and incurable cancer. Report on a Survey by the European Society of Medical Oncology Taskforce on Palliative and Supportive Care. *Cancer*, 98(11), 2502–10.

Christakis, N.A. (2001) *Death Foretold: Prophecy and Prognosis in Medical Care*. Chicago, IL: University of Chicago Press.

Clayton, M., Butow, P., Arlond, R., and Tattersall, M. (2005) Fostering coping and nurturing hope when discussing the future with terminally ill cancer patients and their caregivers. *Cancer*, 103(9), 1965–75.

Connor, S.R., Egan, K.A., Kwilosz, D.M., Larson, D.G., and Reese, D.J. (2002) Interdisciplinary approaches to assisting with end-of-life care and decision-making. *American Behavioral Scientist*, 46(3), 340–56.

Costain Schou, K. (1993) Awareness contexts and the construction of dying in the cancer treatment setting: "micro" and "macro" levels in narrative analysis. In L. Clark (ed.), *The Sociology of Death*. Oxford: Blackwell.

Costain Schou, K., and Hewison, J. (1999) *Experiencing Cancer: Quality of Life in Treatment*. Buckingham: Open University Press.

Cowan, C., Catlin, A., and Smith, C. (2004) National health expenditures, 2002. *Health Care Financing Review*, 25(Summer), 143–66.

Coyle, N. (2001) Introduction to palliative nursing care. In B.R. Ferrell and N. Coyle (eds), *Textbook of Palliative Nursing*. Oxford: Oxford University Press.

Craig, R.T. (1999) Communication theory as a field. *Communication Theory*, 9(2), 119–61.

Curtis, J., Patrick, D., Caldwell, E., and Collier, A. (2000) Why don't patients and physicians talk about end-of-life care? Barriers to communication for patients with acquired immunodeficiency syndrome and their primary care clinicians. *Archives of Internal Medicine*, 160(11), 1690–6.

Dar, R., Beach, C., Barden, P., and Cleeland, C. (1992) Cancer pain in the marital system: a study of patients and their spouses. *Journal of Pain and Symptom Management*, 7(2), 87–93.

Dartmouth Atlas of Health Care (1999) Organizational website. Accessed at www.dartmouthatlas.org.

Dartmouth Atlas of Health Care (2006) New study shows need for a major overhaul of how United States manages chronic illness. Retrieved February 17, 2007 from www.dartmouthatlas.org/press/2006_atlas_press_release.shtm.

Daughtery, C.K. (2005) Personal communication, October 18.

Davies, E, Clarke, C., and Hopkins, A. (1996) Malignant cerebral glioma: Part II. Perspectives of patients and relatives on the value of radiotherapy. *British Medical Journal*, 331(3071), 1512–16.

Davis, H. (1991) Breaking bad news. *Practitioner*, 235(1503), 522–6.

Davison, K.P. and Pennebaker, J.W. (1997) Virtual narratives: illness representation in online support groups. In K.J. Petrie and J.A. Weinman (eds), *Perceptions of Health and Illness: Current Research and Applications*. London: Harwood.

DeAngelis, T. (2002) More psychologists needed in end-of-life care. *Monitor on Psychology* 33. Retrieved January 8, 2007 from www.apa.org/monitor/mar02/endlife.html.

de Haes, H., and Teunissen, S. (2005) Communication in palliative care: a review of recent literature. *Current Opinion in Oncology*, 17(4), 345–50.

DeLoach, R. (2003) Job satisfaction among hospice interdisciplinary team members. *American Journal of Hospice and Palliative Care*, 20(6), 434–40.

de Montigny, J. (1993) Distress, stress and solidarity in palliative care. *Omega*, 27(1), 5–15.

de Swaan, A. (1985) *Het Medisch Regiem*. Amsterdam: Meulenhoff.

Dickerson, S., Boehmke M., Ogle C., and Brown, J. (2006) Seeking and managing hope: patients' experiences using the internet. *Oncology Nursing Forum*, 33(1), 8–17.

Dillard, J.P. and Carson, C.L. (2005) Uncertainty management following a positive newborn screening for cystic fibrosis. *Journal of Health Communication*, 10(1), 57–76.

Diver, F., Molassiotis, A., and Weeks, L. (2003) The palliative care needs of ethnic minority patients: Staff perspectives. *International Journal of Palliative Nursing*, 9(9), 348–351.

Donelan, K., Hill, C., Hoffman, C., Scoles, K., Hollander, F., and Levine, C (2002) Challenge to care: informal caregivers in a changing health system. *Health Affairs*, 22(4), 222–31.

Dosanjh, S., Barnes, J., and Bhandari, M. (2001) Barriers to breaking bad news among medical and surgical residents. *Medical Education*, 35(12), 197–205.

Doukas, D., and Hardwig, J. (2003) Using the family covenant in planning end of life care: obligations and promises of patients, families, and physicians. *Journal of the American Gerontology Society*, 51(8), 1155–8.

Dowsett, S.M., Saul, J.L., Butow, P.N., Dunn, S.M., Boyer, M.J., Findlow, R., and Dunsmore, J. (2000) Communication styles in the cancer consultation: preferences for a patient-centered approach. *Psychooncology*, 9(2), 147–56.

Doyle, D., Hanks, G.W.C., and MacDonald, N. (1998) Introduction. In D. Doyle, G.W.C. Hanks, and N. MacDonald (eds), *Oxford Textbook of Palliative Medicine* (2nd edn). New York: Oxford University Press.

DuPre, A. (2005) *Communicating About Health: Current Issues and Perspectives* (2nd edn). New York: McGraw Hill.

Dyeson, T.B. (2005) The home health care team: what can we learn from the hospice experience? *Home Health Care Management and Practice*, 17(2), 125–7.

Earle, C., Neville, B., Landrum, M., Ayanian, J, Block, S., and Weeks, J. (2004) Trends in the aggressiveness of cancer care near the end of life. *Journal of Clinical Oncology*, 22(2), 315–21.

Egbert, N., and Parrott, R. (2003) Empathy and social support for the terminally ill: implications for recruiting and retaining hospice and hospital volunteers. *Communication Studies*, 54(1), 18–34.

Eggly, S., Penner, L., Albrecht, T.L., Cline, R.J.W., Foster, T., Naughton, M., Peterson, A., and Ruckdeschel, J.C. (2006) Discussing bad news in the outpatient oncology clinic: rethinking current communication guidelines. *Journal of Clinical Oncology*, 24(4), 716–19.

Ellingson, L. (2003) Interdisciplinary health care teamwork in the clinic backstage. *Journal of Applied Communication Research*, 31(2), 93–117.

Emanuel, E.J., Fairclough, D. L., Slutsman, J., Alpert, H., Baldwin, D., and Emanuel, L.L. (1999) Assistance from family members, friends, paid caregivers, and volunteers in the care of terminally ill patients. *New England Journal of Medicine*, 341(13), 956–63.

Emanuel, E.J., Young-Xu, U., Levinsky, N., Gazelle, G., Saynina, O., and Ash, A. (2003) Chemotherapy use among Medicare beneficiaries at the end of life. *Annals of Internal Medicine*, 138(8), 639–43.

Engel, G.L. (1977) The need for a new medical model: a challenge for biomedicine. *Science*, 196(4286), 129–36.

Faden, R., and German, P.S. (1994) Quality of life: considerations in geriatrics. *Clinical Geriatric Medicine*, 10(3), 541–51.

Fallowfield, L. and Jenkins, V. (2004) Communicating sad, bad, and difficult news in medicine. *Lancet*, 363(9405), 312–19.

Ferrell, B. (1996) *Suffering*. Sudbury, MA: Jones and Bartlett.

Field, D., and Copp, G. (1999) Communication and awareness about dying in the 1990s. *Palliative Medicine*, 13(6), 459–68.

Field, M.J., and Cassel, C.K. (eds), (1997) *Approaching Death: Improving Care at the End of Life*. Washington, DC: National Academy Press.

Finlay, I.G., Higginson, I.J., Goodwin, D.M., Cook, A.M., Edwards, A.G.K., Hood, K., Douglas, H.R., and Norman, C.E. (2002) Palliative care in hospital, hospice, at home: results from a systematic review. *Annals of Oncology: Journal of the European Society for Medical Oncology*, 13(4), 257–63.

Fisher, E.S., Wennberg, D.E. Stukel, T.A., Gottlieb, D.J., Lucas, F.L., and Pinder, E.I. (2003) The implications of regional variations in Medicare spending: health outcomes and satisfaction with care. *Annals of Internal Medicine*, 138(4), 288–98.

Fisher, W. (1987) *Human Communication as Narration: Toward a Philosophy of Reason, Value, and Action*. Columbia, SC: University of South Carolina Press.

Fisher, W. (1989) Clarifying the narrative paradigm. *Communication Monographs*, 56(1), 55–8.

Forbes.com (2007) Hospitals embrace the hospice model. Retrieved January 7, 2007 from www.forbes.com/health/feeds/hscout/2007/01/07/hscout600766.html/.

Ford, T., and Tartaglia, A. (2006) The development, status, and future of healthcare chaplaincy. *Southern Medical Journal*, 99(6), 675–9.

Foster, E. (2006) *Communicating at the End of Life: Finding Magic in the Mundane*. Mahwah, NJ: Lawrence Erlbaum.

Frank, A.W. (1995) *The Wounded Storyteller: Body, Illness and Ethics*. Chicago, IL: University of Chicago Press.

Frank, A.W. (2005) Stories by and about us. In L. Harter, P. Japp, and C. Beck (eds), *Narratives, Health, and Healing: Communication Theory, Research, and Practice*. Mahwah, NJ: Lawrence Erlbaum.

Friedrichsen, M., and Milberg, A. (2006) Concerns about losing control when breaking bad news to terminally ill patients with cancer: physicians' perspective. *Journal of Palliative Medicine*, 9(3), 673–82.

Gage, B., Miller, S.C., Mor, V., Jackson, B., and Harvell, J. (2000a) *Synthesis and Analysis of Medicare's Hospice Benefit: Executive Summary and Recommendations* (DALTCP No. 100-97-0010). Washington, DC: U.S. Department of Health and Human Services.

Gage, B., Miller, S.C., Coppola, K., Harvell, J., Laliberte, L., Mor, V., and Teno, J. (2000b) *Important Questions for Hospice in the Next Century* (DALTCP No. 100-97-0010). Washington, DC: U.S. Department of Health and Human Services.

Geist, P., and Gates, L. (1996) The poetics and politics of re-covering identities in health communication. *Communication Studies*, 47(3), 218–28.

Geist-Martin, P., Ray, E.B., and Sharf, B.F. (2003) *Communicating Health: Personal, Cultural, and Political Complexities*. Belmont, CA: Thomson-Wadsworth.

Geriatrics Interdisciplinary Advisory Group (2006) Interdisciplinary care for older adults with complex needs: American Geriatrics Society position statement. *Journal of the American Geriatric Society*, 54(5), 849–52.

Gillotti, C.M. (2003) Medical disclosure and decision-making: excavating the complexities of physician–patient information exchange. In T.L. Thompson, A.M. Dorsey, K.I. Miller, and R. Parrott (eds), *Handbook of Health Communication*. Mahwah, NJ: Lawrence Erlbaum.

Girgis, A., and Sanson-Fisher, R.W. (1995) Breaking bad news: consensus guidelines for medical practitioners. *Journal of Clinical Oncology*, 13(9), 2449–56.

Glaser, B., and Strauss, A. (1965) *Awareness of Dying*. Chicago, IL: Aldine Publishing Company.

Goffman, E. (1959) *The Presentation of Self in Everyday Life*. New York: Anchor Doubleday Books.

Goffman, E. (1974) Keys and keyings. In *Frame Analysis: An Essay on the Organization of Experience*. New York: Harper and Row.

Goffman, E. (1976) Replies and responses. *Language and Society*, 5(3), 257–313.

Goffman, E. (1981) *Forms of Talk*. Philadelphia, PA: University of Pennsylvania Press.

Goldman, A.H. (1980) *The Moral Foundations of Professional Ethics*. Totowa, NJ: Rowman and Littlefield.

Golubow, M. (2002) *For the Living: Coping, Caring and Communicating with the Terminally Ill*. Amityville, NY: Baywood Publishing.

Groopman, J. (2004) *The Anatomy of Hope: How People Prevail in the Face of Illness*. New York: Random House.

Groopman, J. (2005) A strategy for hope: a commentary on necessary collusion. *Journal of Clinical Oncology*, 23(13), 3151–2.

Hagerty, R., Butow, P., Ellis, P., Lobb, E., Pendelbury, S., Leigh, N., McLeod, C. and Tattersall, M. (2005) Communicating with realism and hope: incurable cancer patients' views on the disclosure of prognosis. *Journal of Clinical Oncology*, 23(6), 1278–88.

Hainsworth, J., and Greco, A. (2000) Neoplasms of unknown primary site. In R. Bast, D. Kufe, R. Pollock, R. Weichselbaum, J. Holland, and E. Frei (eds), *Cancer Medicine* (5th edn) London: BC Decker.

Hall, P., and Weaver, L. (2001) Interdisciplinary education and teamwork: a long and winding road. *Medical Education*, 35(9), 867–75.

Han, P., and Arnold, R. (2005) Palliative care services, patient abandonment, and the scope of physicians' responsibilities in end-of-life care. *Journal of Palliative Medicine*, 8(6), 1238–45.

Hanson, L., Danis, M., and Garrett, J. (1997) What is wrong with end of life care? Opinions of bereaved family members. *Journal of American Geriatric Society*, 45(11), 1334–9.

Harris, M.D., and Satterly, L.R. (1998) The chaplain as a member of the hospice team. *Home Healthcare Nurse*, 16(9), 591–3.

Hauerwas, S. (1986) *Suffering Presence: Theological Reflections on Medicine, the Mentally Handicapped, and the Church*. Notre Dame, IN: University of Notre Dame Press.

Hauerwas, S. (2005) *Naming the Silences: God, Medicine, and the Problem of Suffering*. New York: T and T Clark.

Hauser, J., and Kramer, B. (2004) Family caregivers in palliative care. *Clinics in Geriatric Medicine*, 20(4), 671–88.

Herth, K. (1990) Fostering hope in the terminally ill. *Journal of Advanced Nursing*, 15(11) 1250–9.

Herth, K. (1993) Hope in the family caregiver of terminally ill people. *Journal of Advanced Nursing*, 18(4) 538–48.

Higginson, I. (1998) Defining the unit of care: who are we supporting and how? In E. Bruera and R. Portenoy (eds), *Topics in Palliative Care*, Vol. 2. New York: Oxford University Press.

Hines, S.C., Babrow, A.S., Badzek, L., and Moss, A. (2001) From coping with life to coping with death: problematic integration for the seriously ill elderly. *Health Communication*, 13(3), 327–42.

Hoffman, M., Morrow, G., Roscoe, J., Hickok, J., Mustian, K., Moore, D., Wade, J., and Fitch, T. (2004) Cancer patients' expectations of experiencing treatment related side-effects: a University of Rochester Cancer Center—Community Clinical Oncology Program study of 938 patients from community practices. *Cancer*, 101(4), 851–7.

Hoskin, P., and Makin, W. (2003) *Oncology for Palliative Medicine* (2nd edn). New York: Oxford University Press.

Hoskins, C., Baker, S., Budin, W., Ekstrom, D., Maislin, G., Sherman, D., Steelman-Bohlander, J., Bookbinder, M., and Knauer, C. (1996) Adjustment among husbands of women with breast cancer. *Journal of Psychosocial Oncology*, 14(1), 41–69.

Howe, J.L., and Sherman, D.W. (2006) Interdisciplinary educational approaches to promote team-based geriatrics and palliative care. *Gerontology and Geriatrics Education*, 26(3), 1–16.

Hudson, P. L., Schofield, P., Kelly, B., Hudson, R., Street, A., O'Connor, M., Kristjanson, L.J., Ashby, M., and Aranda, S. (2006) Responding to desire to die statements from patients with advanced disease: recommendations for health professionals. *Palliative Medicine*, 20(7), 703–10.

Husband, J., and Kennedy, C. (2006) Exploring the role of community palliative care nurse specialists as educators. *International Journal of Palliative Nursing*, 12(6), 277–84.

Japp, P.M., Harter, L.M., and Beck, C.S. (2005) Overview of narrative and health communication theorizing. In L.M. Harter, P.M. Japp, and C.S. Beck (eds), *Narratives,*

Health, and Healing: Communication Theory, Research, and Practice. Mahwah, NJ: Lawrence Erlbaum.

Jenkins, C., and Bruera, E. (1998) Conflict between families and staff: an approach. In E. Bruera and R. Portenoy (eds), *Topics in Palliative Care*, Vol. 2. New York: Oxford University Press.

Jocham, H.R., Dassen, T., Widdershoven, G., and Halfens, H. (2006) Quality of life in palliative care cancer patients: a literature review. *Journal of Clinical Nursing*, 15(9), 1188–95.

Johnson, A.J., Wittenberg, E., Villagran, M.M., Mazur, M., and Villagran, P. (2003) Relational progression as a dialectic: examining turning points in communication among friends. *Communication Monographs*, 70(3) 230–49.

Kagan, A.R., and Steckel, R. (2000) Imagine cancers of unknown primary site. In R. Bast, D. Kufe, R. Pollock, R. Weichselbaum, J. Holland, and E. Frei (eds), *Cancer Medicine* (5th edn). London: BC Decker.

Kalus, C. (2003) Palliative care and psychology. In B. Monroe and D. Oliviere (eds), *Patient Participation in Palliative Care: A Voice for the Voiceless.* New York: Oxford University Press.

Kaur, J. S. (2000) Palliative care and hospice programs. *Mayo Clinic Proceedings*, 75(2), 181–3.

Kayashima, R., and Braun, K. (2001) Barriers to good end-of-life care: a physician survey. *Hawaii Medical Journal*, 60(2), 40–7.

Kaye, J., and Gracely, E. (1993) Psychological distress in cancer patients and their spouses. *Journal of Cancer Education*, 8(1), 47–52.

Kearl, M.C. (1996) Dying well: the unspoken dimension of aging well. *American Behavioral Scientist*, 39(3), 336–60.

Keeley, M.P. (2004a) Final conversations: survivors' memorable messages concerning religious faith and spirituality. *Health Communication*, 16(1), 87–104.

Keeley, M.P. (2004b) Final conversations: messages of love. *Qualitative Research Reports*, 5(1), 34–40.

King, C., Haberman, M., Berry, D., Bush, N., Butle, L., Dow, K., Terrel, B., Growt, M., Gue, D., Hinds, P., Kreuer, J., Padilla, G., and Underwood, S. (1997) Quality of life and the cancer experience: the state of knowledge. *Oncology Nursing Forum*, 24(1), 27–41.

Klitzman, R. (2006) Improving education on doctor–patient relationships and communication: lessons from doctors who become patients. *Academic Medicine*, 81(5), 447–53.

Kopelman, A. (2006) Understanding, avoiding, and resolving end-of-life conflict in the NICU. *The Mount Sinai Journal of Medicine*, 73(3) 580–6.

Kramer, B., Boelk, A., and Auer, C. (2006) Family conflict at the end of life: Lessons learned in a model program for vulnerable older adults. *Journal of Palliative Care*, 9(3) 791–801.

Kübler-Ross, E. (1969) *On Death and Dying: What the Dying Have to Teach Doctors, Nurses, Clergy, and Their Own Families.* New York: Routledge.

Lamont, E.B., and Christakis, N. (2001) Prognostic disclosure to patients with cancer near the end of life. *Annals of Internal Medicine*, 134(12), 1096–105.

Landau, R. (2000) Ethical dilemmas in general hospitals: social workers' contributions to ethical decision-making. *Social Work Health Care*, 32(2), 75–92.

LaPuma, J., and Lawlor, E.F. (1990) Quality-adjusted life-years. *Journal of the American Medical Association*, 263(21), 2917–21.

Larson, D. (2003) Exploring the nature of the interdisciplinary team: An excerpt from *The Helper's Journey*. *Hospice Palliative Insights*, 4(2), 6–8.

Lautrette, A., Ciroldi, M., Ksibi, H., and Azoulay, E (2006) End-of-life family conferences: rooted in the evidence. *Critical Care Medicine*, 34(Suppl. 11), 364–72.

Lawton, J. (2000) *The Dying Process: Patients' Experiences of Palliative Care*. London: Routledge.

Lederberg, M. (1998) The family of the cancer patient. In J. Holland (ed.), *Psychooncology*. New York: Oxford.

Leipzig, R.M., Hyer, K., Ek, K., Wallenstein, S., Vezina, M.L., Fairchild, S., Cassel, C.K., and Howe, J.L. (2002) Attitudes toward working on interdisciplinary healthcare teams: a comparison by discipline. *Journal of the American Geriatrics Society*, 50(6), 1141–8.

Leleszi, J., and Lewandowski, J. (2005) Pain management in the end-of-life care. *Journal of the American Osteopathic Association*, 105(3) S6–S11.

Littlewood, J. (1993) The denial of death and rites of passage in contemporary societies. In D. Clark (ed.), *The Sociology of Death: Theory, Culture, Practice*. Cambridge, MA: Blackwell.

Loscalzo, M., and Zabora, J. (1998) Care of the cancer patient: response of family and staff. In E. Bruera and R. Portenoy (eds), *Topics in Palliative Care*, Vol. 2. New York: Oxford University Press.

Maguire, P., and Faulkner, A. (1988a) Communication with cancer patients: 1. Handling bad news and difficult questions. *British Medical Journal*, 297(6653), 907–9.

Maguire, P., and Faulkner, A. (1988b) Communication with cancer patients: 2. Handling uncertainty, collusion, and denial. *British Medical Journal*, 297(6654), 972–4.

Markowitz, J., Gutterman, E., Sadik, K., and Papadopoulos, G. (2003) Health-related quality of life for caregivers of patients with Alzheimer disease. *Alzheimer Disease and Associated Disorders*, 17(4) 209–14.

Matsuyama, R., Reddy, S., and Smith, T. (2006) Why do patients choose chemotherapy near the end of life? A review of the perspective of those facing death from cancer. *Journal of Clinical Oncology*, 24(21) 3490–6.

McCluskey, L., Casarett, D., and Siderowf, A. (2004) Breaking the news: a survey of ALS patients and their caregivers. *Taylor and Francis Health Sciences*, 5(3), 131–5.

McCormick, T., and Conley, B. (1995) Patients' perspectives on dying and on the care of dying patients. *Western Journal of Medicine*, 163(3), 236–43.

McMillan, S., and Mahon, M. (1994) The impact of hospice services on the quality of life of primary caregivers. *Oncology Nursing Forum*, 21(7), 1189–95.

McPherson, C., and Addington-Hall, J. (2004) Evaluating palliative care: bereaved family members' evaluations of patients' pain, anxiety, depression. *Journal of Pain and Symptom Management*, 28(2), 104–14.

McPherson, C.J., Wilson, K.G., and Murray, M. (2007) Feeling like a burden: exploring the perspectives of patients at the end of life. *Social Science Medicine*, 64(2), 417–27.

Meador, K., and Henson, S. (2000) Growing old in a therapeutic culture. *Theology Today*, 57(2) 185–202.

Meier, D. (2000) Kinder caring. *Hospitals and Health Networks*, 74(12), 84.

Meier, D., and Beresford, L. (2005) Infrastructure supports what is most important in palliative care. *Journal of Palliative Medicine*, 8(6), 1092–5.

Meier, D.E., Back, A.L., and Morrison, R.S. (2001) The inner life of physicians and care of the seriously ill. *Journal of the American Medical Association*, 286(23), 3007–14.

Meier, D., Morrison, R.S., and Cassel, C.K. (1997) Improving palliative care. *Annals of Internal Medicine*, 127(3), 225–30.

Miller, J. (1989) Hope inspiring strategies of the critically ill. *Applied Nursing Research*, 2(1) 23–9.

Mishler, E.G. (1981) *Social Contexts of Health, Illness, and Patient Care*. New York: Cambridge University Press.

Mishler, E.G. (1984) *The Discourse f Medicine: Dialectics of Medical Interviews*. Norwood, NJ: Ablex Publishing.

Montgomery, B.M. (1993) Relationship maintenance versus relationship change: a dialectical dilemma. *Journal of Social and Personal Relationships*, 10(2), 205–23.

Mooney, K. (2003) Understanding our place: the importance of professional boundaries. *Hospice and Palliative Care Insights*, 3(2), 15–18.

Morrison, R.S., and Meier, D.E. (2004) Palliative care. *The New England Journal of Medicine*, 350(25), 2582–90.

Moyers, B. (2000) *On Our Own Terms: Moyers on Dying*. Films for the Humanities and Sciences. Public Affairs Television, Inc. New York.

Mystakidou, K., Tsilika, E., Parpa, E., Katsouda, E., Galanos, A., and Vlahos, L. (2006) Psychological distress of patients with advanced cancer: Influence and contribution of pain severity and pain interference. *Cancer Nursing*, 29(5), 400–5.

Napier, L. (2003) Palliative care social work. In B. Monroe and D. Oliviere (eds), *Patient Participation in Palliative Care: A Voice for the Voiceless*. New York: Oxford University Press.

National Center for Health Statistics (1998) New study of patterns of death in the United States. Retrieved February 1, 2007 from www.cdc.gov/nchs/pressroom/98facts/93nmfs.htm.

National Council for Palliative Care, www.ncpc.org.uk.

National Family Caregivers Association (2000) Caregiver survey. Retrieved November 2, 2006, from http://www.thefamilycaregiver.org/who_are_family_caregivers/2000_survey.cfm.

National Hospice and Palliative Care Organization (2007) Organizational Website. Accessed at www.nhpco.org.

Nietzsche, F.W., Kaufmann, W.A., and Hollingdale, R.J. (1967) *The Will to Power*. New York: Random House.

Novack, D.H., Plumer, R., and Smith, R.L. (1979) Changes in physicians' attitude: telling the cancer patient. *Journal of the American Medical Association*, 241(9), 897–900.

Nuland, S.B. (1993) *How We Die: Reflections on Life's Final Chapter*. New York: Random House.

O'Neill, B., and Fallon, M. (1997) ABC of palliative care: principles of palliative care and pain control. *British Medical Journal*, 315(7111), 801–4.

Opie, A. (1997) Thinking teams, thinking clients: issues of discourse and representation in the work of healthcare teams. *Sociology of Health and Illness*, 19(3), 259–80.

Palacas, A.L. (1992) Forms of speech: linguistic worlds and Goffman's embedded footings. In Shin Ja J. Hwang and William R. Merrifield (eds), *Language in Context: Essays for Robert E. Longacre*, Summer Institute of Linguistics and the University of Texas at Arlington Publications in Linguistics, 107. Dallas, TX: Summer Institute of Linguistics and the University of Texas at Arlington.

Parrott, R., Silk, K., Weiner, J., Condit, C., Harris, T., and Bernhardt, J. (2004) Deriving lay models of uncertainty about genes' role in illness causation to guide communication about human genetics. *Journal of Communication*, 54(1), 105–22.

Payne, S., and Haines, R. (2002) The contribution of psychologists to specialist palliative care. *International Journal of Palliative Nursing*, 8(8), 401–6.

Penson, R.T., Kyriakou, H., Zuckerman, D., Chabner, B.A., and Lynch, T.J. (2006) Teams: communication in multidisciplinary care. *The Oncologist*, 11(5), 520–6.

Petronio, S. (2002) *Boundaries of Privacy: Dialectics of Disclosure.* Albany, NY: State University of New York Press.

Ptacek, J.T., and Eberhardt, T.L. (1996) Breaking bad news: a review of the literature. *Journal of the American Medical Association*, 276(6), 496–502.

Quill, T.E. (2000) Perspectives on care at the close of life: initiating end-of-life discussions with seriously ill patients – addressing the "elephant in the room." *Journal of the American Medical Association*, 284(19) 2502–7.

Quill, T.E. (2001) *Caring for Patients at the End Of Life: Facing an Uncertain Future Together.* Oxford: Oxford University Press.

Rabow, M.W., and McPhee, S.J. (1999) Beyond breaking bad news: how to help patients who suffer. *Western Journal of Medicine*, 171(4), 260–3.

Ragan, S.L., Mindt, T., and Wittenberg-Lyles, E. (2005) Narrative medicine and education in palliative care. In L.M. Harter, P. Japp, and C.S. Beck (eds), *Narratives, Health, and Healing: Communication Theory, Research, and Practice.* Mahwah, NJ: Lawrence Erlbaum.

Ragan, S.L., Wittenberg, E., and Hall, H.T. (2003) The communication of palliative care for the elderly cancer patient. *Health Communication*, 15(2), 219–26.

Ragsdale, D., Kotarba, J., and Morrow, J. (1992) Quality of life of hospitalized persons with AIDS. *Journal of Nursing Scholarship*, 24(4), 259–65.

Raymer, M. (2006) Death and dying—how social workers help—the role of social work in hospice and palliative care. Retrieved January 24, 2007 from http://www.helpstartshere. org/health_and_wellness/death_and_dying/how_social_workers_help/how_social_workers_help.html.

Reese, D.J., and Raymer, M. (2004) Relationships between social work involvement and hospice outcomes: Results of the National Hospice Social Work Survey. *Social Work*, 49(3), 415–22.

Reuben, D.B., Levy-Storms, L., Yee, M.N., Lee, M., Cole, K., Waite, M., Nichols, L., and Frank, J.C. (2004) Disciplinary split: a threat to geriatrics interdisciplinary team training. *Journal of the American Geriatrics Society*, 52(6), 1000–6.

Richards, M., Ramirez, A., Degner. L., Fallowfield, L., Maher, L., and Neuberger, J. (1995) Offering choice of treatment to patients with cancer. A review based upon a symposium held at the 10th annual conference of the British Psychosocial Oncology group, *European Journal of Cancer*, 31A(1), 112–16.

Rosen, A., and O'Neill, J. (1998) Social work roles and opportunities in advance directives and health care decision-making. Retrieved October 17, 2005 from the National Association of Social Workers website, www.socialworkers.org/practice/aging/advdirct.asp.

Rosenbaum, M.E., Ferguson, K.J., and Lobas, J.G. (2004) Teaching medical students and residents skills for delivering bad news: a review of strategies. *Academic Medicine*, 79(2), 107–17.

Roth, P. (2006) *Everyman.* New York: Houghton Mifflin.

Ryndes, T., and von Gunten, C.F. (2006) The development of palliative medicine in the USA. In E. Bruera, I.J. Higginson, C. Ripamnoti and C.F. von Gunten (eds) *Textbook of Palliative Medicine.* London: Hodder Arnold.

Sabur, S. (2003a) Creating an optimal culture and structure for the IDT. *Hospice Palliative Insights*, 4(4), 22–3.

Sabur, S. (2003b) Measuring the success of the interdisciplinary team. *Hospice Palliative Insights*, 4(4), 47–9.

Sanchez-Reilly, S., Wittenberg-Lyles, E.M., and Villagran, M. (2007) Using a pilot curriculum in geriatric palliative care to improve communication skills among medical students. *American Journal of Hospice and Palliative Medicine*, 24(2), 131–6.

Saunders, C. (1967) *The Management of Terminal Illness*. London: Hospital Medicine Publications.

Saunders, C. (2003) A voice for the voiceless. In B. Monroe and D. Oliviere (eds), *Patient Participation in Palliative Care: A Voice for the Voiceless*. Oxford: Oxford University Press.

Schechner, R. (2002) *Performance Studies: An Introduction*. New York: Routledge.

Schneiderman, L.J., Gilmer, T., Teetzel, H.D., Dugan, D.O., Blustein, J., Cranford, R., Briggs, K.B., Komatsu, G.I., Goodman-Crews, P., Cohn, F., and Young, E.W.D. (2003) Effects of ethics consultations on nonbeneficial life-sustaining treatments in the intensive care setting: a randomized control trial. *Journal of the American Medical Association*, 290(9), 1166–72.

Sell, L., Devlin, B., Bourke, S.J., Munro, N.C., Corris, P.S., and Gibson, G.J. (1993) Communicating the diagnosis of lung cancer. *Respiratory Medicine*, 87(1), 61–3.

Semple, S. (1992) Conflict in Alzheimer caregiving families: Its dimensions and consequences. *Gerontologist*, 32(5), 645–55.

Servaty, H.L., and Hayslip, B. (1997) Death education and communication apprehension regarding dying persons. *Omega*, 34(2), 139–48.

Servaty, H.L., and Hayslip, B. Jr. (1999) The communication apprehension regarding the dying scale: a factor analytic study. In B. de Vries (ed.), *End of Life Issues: Interdisciplinary and Multidimensional Perspectives*. New York: Springer.

Servaty, H.L., Krejci, M.J., and Hayslip, B. (1996) Relationships among death anxiety, communication apprehension with the dying, and empathy in those seeking occupations as nurses and physicians. *Death Studies*, 20(2), 149–61.

Shahab, N., and Perry, M. (2005) Metastatic cancer, unknown primary site. *Medicine*. Retrieved April 4, 2006, from http://www.emedicine.com/med/topic1463.htm.

Sharf, B.F., and Vanderford, M.L. (2003) Illness narratives and the social construction of health. In T.L. Thompson, A.M. Dorsey, K.I. Miller, and R. Parrott (eds), *Handbook of Health Communication*. Mahwah, NJ: Lawrence Erlbaum.

Shaw, B., Hawkins R., Arora N., McTavish, F., Pingree, S., and Gustafson, D. (2005) An exploratory study of predictors of participation in a computer support group for women with breast cancer. *Computers, Infomatics, Nursing*, 24(1), 18–27.

Sheldon, F. (1997) *Psychosocial Palliative Care: Good Practice in the Care of the Dying and Bereaved*. Cheltenham: Stanley Thornes.

Sherman, D. (1998) Reciprocal suffering: the need to improve family caregivers' quality of life through palliative care. *Journal of Palliative Medicine*, 1(4), 357–66.

Singer, P.A., Martin, D.K., and Kelner, M. (1999) Quality of end-of-life care: patients' perspectives. *Journal of the American Medical Association*, 281(2), 163–8.

Smith, T., Girman, J., and Riggins, J. (2001) Why academic divisions of hematology/oncology are in trouble and some suggestions for resolution. *Journal of Clinical Oncology*, 19(1), 260–4.

Smith, T.J., Coyne, P., Cassel, B., Penberthy, L., Hopson, A., and Hager, M.A. (2003) A high-volume specialist palliative care unit and team may reduce in-hospital end-of-life care costs. *Journal of Palliative Medicine*, 6(5), 699–705.

Speck, P. (2003) Palliative care and chaplaincy. In B. Monroe and D. Oliviere (eds), *Patient Participation in Palliative Care: A Voice for the Voiceless*. New York: Oxford University Press.

Stanley, K.J., and Zoloth-Dorfman, L. (2001) Ethical considerations. In B.R. Ferrell and N. Coyle (eds), *Textbook of Palliative Nursing*. Oxford: Oxford University Press.

Steinhauser, K.E., Christakis, N.A., Clipp, E.C., McNeilly, M., McIntyre, L., and Tulsky, J.A. (2000a) Factors considered important at the end of life by patients, family, physicians, and other care providers. *Journal of the American Medical Association*, 284(19), 2476–82.

Steinhauser, K., Clipp, E., McNeilly, M., Christakis, N., McIntyre, L., and Tulsky, J. (2000b) In search of a good death: observations of patients, families, and providers. *Annals of Internal Medicine*, 132(10), 825–32.

Stratford, M. (2003) Palliative nursing. In B. Monroe and D. Oliviere (eds) *Patient Participation in Palliative Care: A Voice for the Voiceless*. New York: Oxford University Press.

Striff, E. (2003) Introduction: locating performance studies. In E. Striff (ed.) *Performance Studies*. New York: Palgrave Macmillan.

SUPPORT Investigators (1995) A controlled trial to improve care for seriously ill, hospitalized patients: The Study to Understand Prognoses and Preferences for Outcomes and Treatments (SUPPORT). *Journal of the American Medical Association*, 274(20), 1591–8.

Tamburini, M., Buccheri, G., and Brunelli, C. (2000) The difficult choice of chemotherapy in patients with unrespectable non-small cell lung cancer. *Support Care Cancer*, 8(3), 223–8.

Teno, J.M., Clarridge, B.R., Casey, V., Welch, L.C., Wetle, T., Shield, R., and Mor, V. (2004) Family perspectives on end-of-life care at the last place of care. *Journal of the American Medical Association*, 291(1), 88–93.

The, A. (2002) *Palliative Care and Communication: Experiences in the Clinic*. Philadelphia, PA: Open University Press.

Tolle, S., Bascom, P., Hickam, D., and Benson, J. (1986) Communication between physicians and surviving spouses following patient deaths. *Journal of General Internal Medicine*, 1(5), 309–14.

Tolle, S.W., Tilden, V.P., Rosenfeld, A., and Hickman, S.E. (1999) The Oregon report card: Improving care of the dying. Retrieved February 1, 2007 from www.ohsu.edu/ethics/docs/barriers2.pdf.

Tolstoy, L.N. (2004) *The Death of Ivan Illych and Other Stories*. New York: Spark Publishing.

Thomasma, D.C. (1994) Telling the truth to patients: a clinical ethics exploration. *Cambridge Quarterly of Healthcare Ethics*, 3(3), 375–82.

Tschann, J., Kaufman, S., and Mico, G. (2003) Family involvement in end of life hospital care. *Journal of the American Geriatric Society*, 51(6), 835–40.

Tulsky, J.A. (2003) Doctor–patient communication. In R.S. Morrison, and D.E. Meier (eds), *Geriatric Palliative Care*. New York: Oxford University Press.

Turner, H., Catania, J., and Gagnon, J. (1994) The prevalence of informal caregiving to persons with AIDS in the United States: caregiver characteristics and their implications. *Social Science Medicine*, 38(11), 1543–52.

Turner, V. (1982) *From Ritual to Theatre: The Human Seriousness of Play*. New York: Performance Arts Journal Publications.

Ufema, J. (2004) Insights on death and dying. *Nursing*, 34(7), 66.

Vachon, M.L.S. (2001) The nurse's role: the world of palliative care nursing. In B.R. Ferrell and N. Coyle (eds), *Textbook of Palliative Nursing*. Oxford: Oxford University Press.

Vanderford, M.L., Jenks, E.G., and Sharf, B. (1997) Exploring patients' experiences as a primary source of meaning. *Health Communication*, 9(1), 13–16.

von Gunten, C.F. (2002) Secondary and tertiary palliative care in U.S. hospitals. *Journal of the American Medical Association*, 287(7), 875–81.

von Gunten, C.F., and Romer, A.L. (2000) Designing and sustaining a palliative care and home hospice program. *Journal of Palliative Medicine*, 3(1), 115–22.

von Gunten, C.F., Ferris, F.D., and Emanuel, L.L. (2000) The patient–physician relationship-ensuring competency in end-of-life care: communication and relational skills. *Journal of the American Medical Association*, 284(23), 3051–7.

Waitzkin, H. (1985) Information giving in medical care. *Journal of Health and Social Behavior*, 26(2), 81–101.

Weeks, J., Cook, E., O'Day, S., Peterson, L., Wenger, N., Reding, D., Harrell, F., Kussin, P., Dawson, N., Connors, A., Lynn, J., and Phillips, R. (1998) Relationship between cancer patients' predictions of prognosis and their treatment preferences. *Journal of the American Medical Association*, 279(21) 1709–14.

Weissman, D. (2001) Medical oncology and palliative care: the intersection of end-of-life care. *Journal of Palliative Medicine* 6(6) 859–61.

Williams, S. (1997) Early morning staff meetings in home hospice. *Home Healthcare Nurse*, 15(1), 242.

Wittenberg-Lyles, E.M. (2005) Information sharing in interdisciplinary team meetings: an evaluation of hospice goals. *Qualitative Health Research*, 15(10), 1377–91.

Wittenberg-Lyles, E.M. (2007) Narratives of hospice volunteers: perspectives on death and dying. *Qualitative Research Reports*, 7(1), 1–6.

Wittenberg-Lyles, E.M., and Parker Oliver, D. (2007) The power of interdisciplinary collaboration in hospice. *Progress in Palliative Care*, 15(1), 6–12.

Wolfe, J., Klar, N., Grier, H., Duncan, R., Salem-Schatz, S., Emanuel, E., and Weeks, J. (2000) Understanding of prognosis among parents of children who died of cancer: impact on treatment goals and integration of palliative care. *Journal of the American Medical Association*, 284(19), 2469–75.

Yabroff, R., Davis, W., Lamont, E., Fahey, A., Topor, M., Brown, M., and Warren, J. (2007) Patient time costs associated with cancer care. *Journal of the National Cancer Institute*, 99(1), 14–23.

Yurk, R., Morgan, D., Franey, S., Stebner, J., and Lansky, D. (2002) Understanding the continuum of palliative care for patients and their caregivers. *Journal of Pain and Symptom Management*, 24(5), 459–70.

Zachariae, R., Pedersen, C.G., Jensen, A.B., Ehrnrooth, E., Rossen, P. B., and Maase, H. (2003) Association of perceived physician communication style with patient satisfaction, cancer-related self-efficacy, and perceived control over the disease. *British Journal of Cancer*, 88(5), 658–65.

Index